# The Good Retirement Guide 2016

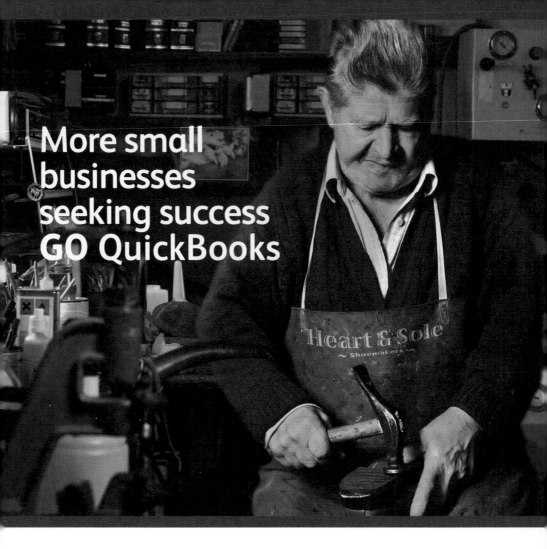

# More small businesses seeking success GO QuickBooks

Managing your new business can be overwhelming, but it doesn't have to be. QuickBooks has been designed to help you manage your company's finances, so you can focus on growing your business. Know exactly how you're getting on with real-time dashboards, plus easily create invoices and reports for your customers and investors.

Thousands of businesses GO with the world's No. 1 online accounting software.[1] Join them today by signing up for our **free 30 day trial**.[2]

For your free trial call **0808 168 4288**
or visit **www.quickbooks.co.uk/start**

30TH EDITION

# The Good Retirement Guide 2016

## EVERYTHING YOU NEED TO KNOW ABOUT HEALTH, PROPERTY, INVESTMENT, LEISURE, WORK, PENSIONS AND TAX

Edited by
Frances Kay and
Allan Esler Smith

KoganPage

LONDON PHILADELPHIA NEW DELHI

**Publisher's note**

Every possible effort has been made to ensure that the information contained in this book is accurate at the time of going to press, and the publishers and author cannot accept responsibility for any errors or omissions, however caused. No responsibility for loss or damage occasioned to any person acting, or refraining from action, as a result of the material in this publication can be accepted by the editor, the publisher or the authors.

The information contained in this book is for guidance only, and does not constitute profes-sional advice. Users should seek appropriate professional adviser concerning specific issues, and their impact on any individual or entity, before making any major decision.

This 30th edition published in 2016 by Kogan Page Limited

Apart from any fair dealing for the purposes of research or private study, or criticism or review, as permitted under the Copyright, Designs and Patents Act 1988, this publication may only be repro-duced, stored or transmitted, in any form or by any means, with the prior permission in writing of the publishers, or in the case of reprographic reproduction in accordance with the terms and licences issued by the CLA. Enquiries concerning reproduction outside these terms should be sent to the publishers at the undermentioned addresses:

2nd Floor, 45 Gee Street
London EC1V 3RS
United Kingdom
www.koganpage.com

© Kogan Page, 2013, 2014, 2015, 2016

The right of Allan Esler Smith to be identified as the author of Chapter 4 'Protection from scams, help from professional advisers and how to complain' and Chapter 7 'Starting your own business' has been asserted by him in accordance with the Copyright, Designs and Patents Act 1988.

The right of Kogan Page to be identified as the author of this work has been asserted by them in accordance with the Copyright, Designs and Patents Act 1988.

ISBN      978 0 7494 7501 7
E-ISBN   978 0 7494 7502 4

**British Library Cataloguing in Publication Data**

A CIP record for this book is available from the British Library.

Typeset by Graphicraft Limited, Hong Kong
Print production managed by Jellyfish
Printed and bound by CPI Group (UK) Ltd, Croydon CR0 4YY

# Contents

**04    Protection from scams, help from professional advisers and how to complain**  84

**05    Your home**  107

**06    Health**  125

## 07   Starting your own business   150

# List of tables

# Chapter One
# Looking forward to retirement and doing the sums

*'Happiness is pretty simple: someone to love, something to do, something to look forward to.'*

**RITA MAE BROWN**

Are you looking forward to retirement? Do you intend it to be a happy, satisfying and enjoyable time of life?

You should, because you have worked for it for many years and now deserve to appreciate to the full this third phase of life. For some there are concerns about the negative aspects of retirement, such as reduced income and reaching the end of working life. However, the positives far outweigh these, for example, having the opportunity to do all the things you've wanted to do for years and never before had the time. Many of us admit to having some fears and reservations as the time for retirement beckons: two of these concern wealth and health. If we have both of these in abundance, happiness should surely follow. But does it?

We can learn a lot about the pursuit of happiness (in retirement) from Tolstoy, according to a recent BBC News article (**www.bbc.co.uk/news/magazine-30536963**). Tolstoy was born in 1828 and died in 1910. His early life was raucous, debauched and violent. However, he gradually adopted a radical, unconventional outlook that shocked his peers. His personal insights reveal several ways to achieve happiness and are a good reminder of what's important for you to consider in this first chapter.

## Tolstoy's keys to happiness

- *Keep an open mind.* The ability to change one's mind based on new experiences is important at any stage of life.

- *Practise empathy.* Tolstoy believed you could never understand the reality of other people's lives unless you had had a taste of it yourself.

- *Make a difference.* Taking practical action to help alleviate others' suffering is something many retirees do, as evidenced by the huge numbers who devote time and effort to volunteering and charitable work.

- *Master the art of simple living.* Tolstoy gave up drinking and smoking and became a vegetarian. He also inspired the creation of communities of simple self-sufficient living. These spread around the world and Gandhi founded an ashram near Johannesburg in 1910, on the appropriately named 'Tolstoy Farm'.

- *Beware your contradictions.* Having preached universal love, it is curious that Tolstoy was constantly at odds with his wife. He lived until old age in a grand house with servants but relinquished copyright to a huge portion of his literary works, thereby sacrificing a fortune.

- *Become a craftsman.* Allowing craft into our lives is an essential part of the creative process. Taking up an interesting hobby is far healthier than spending our leisure time tweeting and texting.

- *Expand your social circle.* Tolstoy's most essential life lesson is that we should spread our conversational wings and spend time with those whose values and experiences contrast with our own. In other words, if you dare, move out of your comfort zone and journey beyond the perimeters of your circle.

Whether or not we agree with the foregoing, in order to obtain maximum fulfillment from our retirement and avoid regrets, we need to think hard and plan before making important decisions. According to a recent website survey (*Saga* magazine, February 2015), the top-five regrets of the over-50s are: not seeing enough of the world; not saving enough for retirement; marrying the wrong person; never telling their parents how much they meant to them and choosing the wrong career. It may not be possible to fix all of these, but some retirement planning should help.

Things to consider include: what standard of living you want, how much money you will need to achieve it and what sort of social life you wish to enjoy. A pre-retirement course should be helpful, if you can find one to suit. Ask friends who have already retired for their advice; they may come up with useful recommendations. Whatever your circumstances, retirement should be anticipated with enthusiasm as it is full of opportunity and choice. Reading *The Good Retirement Guide 2016* is an essential first step because while planning for retirement can be complex, this book is designed to make it easier.

# Pre-retirement planning

There are many ways of accessing information and advice on retirement planning, and the right time to do it is entirely personal. Some people start planning for retirement several years before they give up work, others do it in stages. There is a huge choice of courses, both online and offline. Courses are designed to cover finances, health, housing, leisure and the implications and adjustments needing to be made before or when you retire. If you are considering a residential course, discussions will take place with your partner and others in similar situations, designed to stimulate your planning efforts.

The following websites should enable you to make an informed decision as to what level of retirement planning is appropriate for you:

- **www.activeageplanning.co.uk**;
- **www.life-academy.co.uk**;
- **www.retirement-courses.co.uk**;
- **www.the-retirement-site.co.uk**.

According to recent research (*Saga* magazine, February 2015) the over-50s control 79 per cent of the nation's disposable wealth, and by 2020 will constitute 50 per cent of the population. As we are such a large and important section of society, the amount of information available to us is huge. To gain some idea of how wide ranging this is, here are some of the most useful websites:

- www.ageuk.org.uk;
- www.gov.uk;
- www.npcuk.org;
- www.retirementexpert.co.uk;
- www.retirementlinks.co.uk;
- www.ukretirement.co.uk;
- www.50plusshow.com.

# Doing the sums

One of the biggest challenges when a lifestyle change happens is organizing our personal finances. Putting together a budget can remove a great deal of stress: it takes a little time, but costs nothing and the rewards are immense. Anyone approaching retirement, or who has recently retired, should explore all their financial options. It is essential to know where you are money-wise. Once this has been done, the effects can be life-changing.

There are plenty of sources of advice to help free you from money worries. The *This is Money* website (**www.thisismoney.co.uk**) suggests the following:

1 Get a budget plan as early as possible.
2 Re-assess your debts and outgoings.
3 Make sure you have enough rainy-day savings in a cash ISA.
4 Make or update your will.
5 Fund your company pension to the maximum.
6 Find yourself a fee-based financial planner.

Other websites that offer suggestions for budgeting, finances and retirement include:

- www.adviceguide.org.uk;
- www.financingretirement.co.uk;
- www.moneyadviceservice.org.uk;

- www.moneyexpertise.co.uk;

- www.moneyweek.co.uk;

- www.which.co.uk.

The best way to obtain an objective view of your finances is to draw up a personal budget planner showing your income and outgoings. This comprises several lists:

- expected sources of income on retirement;

- essential outgoings;

- normal additional spending – such as holidays and luxuries;

- possible ways to boost your retirement income;

- spending now for saving later (for example, by paying off your mortgage early).

However well you plan, life is full of uncertainties, and that's not just tax and inflation. The biggest question (to which no one has the answer) is how long you, your partner and any dependants may live. In retirement, what items will still represent a significant percentage of your budget? What areas of expenditure will cease to be important? If you are retiring imminently, doing the sums in as much detail as possible will help you plan your future life with greater confidence. Some people start living on their estimated retirement income six months before they retire, to see whether their calculations are realistic or not.

Here are some tables which should help you budget:

1 Table 1.1. *Possible monthly savings.* Once you stop working a number of expenses should disappear. National Insurance contributions (NICs) cease on retirement, as well as pension payments (unless you choose to invest in a private plan). Be sure to check your tax coding, as you may well move to a lower tax bracket.

NB: You should also take into account reduced running costs if you move to a smaller home; any expenses for dependent children that may cease; other costs such as mortgage payments that may end around the time you retire.

**TABLE 1.1** Breakdown to estimate where monthly savings can be made

| Items | Estimated monthly savings |
|---|---|
| National Insurance contributions | ......................... |
| Pension payments | ......................... |
| Travel expenses to work | ......................... |
| Bought lunches | ......................... |
| Incidentals at work: eg drinks with colleagues, collections for presents | ......................... |
| Special work clothes | ......................... |
| Concessionary travel | ......................... |
| NHS prescriptions | ......................... |
| Eye tests | ......................... |
| Mature drivers' insurance policy | ......................... |
| Retired householders' insurance policy | ......................... |
| Life assurance payments and/or possible endowment policy premiums | ......................... |
| Other | ......................... |
| **TOTAL** | ......................... |

2 Table 1.2. *Estimated extra outgoings.* Looking ahead, home comforts become increasingly important. You may find you are spending more time at home, as a result of which your utility bills rise. You may wish at some point to think about paying other people to do some of the jobs you previously did yourself. NB: If you intend to make regular donations to a charity, or perhaps help with your grandchildren's education, these should be included in this list. The same applies to any new private pension or savings plan that you might want to invest in to boost your long-term retirement income.

**TABLE 1.2** Estimating extra outgoings

| Items | Estimated monthly costs |
|---|---|
| Extra heating and lighting bills | .......................... |
| Extra spending on hobbies and other entertainment | .......................... |
| Replacement of company car | .......................... |
| Private health care insurance | .......................... |
| Longer or more frequent holidays | .......................... |
| Life and permanent health insurance | .......................... |
| Cost of substituting other perks, eg expense account lunches | .......................... |
| Out-of-pocket expenses for voluntary-work activity | .......................... |
| Other | .......................... |
| **TOTAL** | .......................... |

**3** Table 1.3. *Expected sources of income.* These items are listed below, but once you've added the figures you will need to deduct income tax to arrive at the net amount that will be available to you.

**4** Table 1.4. *Unavoidable outgoings.* Since one person's luxury item is another's priority, it is likely you will juggle some of the items between Table 1.4 and Table 1.5.

**5** Table 1.5. *Normal additional expenditure.* You may tend to think in annual expenditure terms for some items, such as holidays and gifts. However, it is probably easier to itemize all the expenditure on a monthly basis for the purposes of comparison.
NB: If you need to save for a special event, such as a luxury holiday or family wedding, it might help to get in the habit of putting some money aside every month.

**TABLE** 1.3 Expected sources of income

| | |
|---|---|
| **A. Income received *before* tax** | |
| Basic state pension | ........................ |
| State graduated pension | ........................ |
| SERPS/State second pension | ........................ |
| Occupational pension(s) | ........................ |
| Stakeholder or personal pension | ........................ |
| State benefits | ........................ |
| Investments and savings plans paid gross, eg gilts, National Savings | ........................ |
| Other incomes (eg rental income) | ........................ |
| Casual or other pre-tax earnings | ........................ |
| **TOTAL** | ........................ |
| **Less:** Personal tax allowance and possibly also married couple's allowance | ........................ |
| Basic-rate tax | ........................ |
| **TOTAL A** | ........................ |
| **B. Income received *after* tax** | |
| Dividends (unit trusts, shares, etc) | ........................ |
| Bank deposit account | ........................ |
| Building society interest | ........................ |
| Annuity income | ........................ |
| Other (including earnings subject to PAYE) | ........................ |
| **TOTAL B** | ........................ |
| **Total A + B** | ........................ |
| **Less:** Higher-rate tax (if any) | ........................ |
| **Plus:** Other tax-free receipts, eg some state benefits, income from an ISA | ........................ |
| Investment bond withdrawals, etc | ........................ |
| Other | ........................ |
| **TOTAL NET INCOME** | ........................ |

**TABLE 1.4** Unavoidable outgoings

| Items | Estimated monthly cost |
|---|---|
| Food | ........................ |
| Rent or mortgage repayments | ........................ |
| Council tax | ........................ |
| Repair and maintenance costs | ........................ |
| Heating | ........................ |
| Lighting and other energy | ........................ |
| Telephone/mobile/internet | ........................ |
| Postage (including Christmas cards) | ........................ |
| TV licence/Sky/digital subscription | ........................ |
| Household insurance | ........................ |
| Clothes | ........................ |
| Laundry, cleaner's bills, shoe repair | ........................ |
| Domestic cleaning products | ........................ |
| Miscellaneous services, eg plumber and window cleaner | ........................ |
| Car (including licence, petrol, etc) | ........................ |
| Other transport | ........................ |
| Regular savings and life assurance | ........................ |
| HP and other loan repayments | ........................ |
| Outgoings on health | ........................ |
| Other | ........................ |
| **TOTAL** | ........................ |

**TABLE** 1.5    Normal additional expenditure

| Items | Estimated monthly cost |
|---|---|
| Gifts | ........................ |
| Holidays | ........................ |
| Newspapers/books/CDs/DVDs | ........................ |
| Computer (including broadband) | ........................ |
| Drink | ........................ |
| Cigarettes/tobacco | ........................ |
| Hairdressing/beauty treatments | ........................ |
| Toiletries/cosmetics | ........................ |
| Entertainment (hobbies, outgoings, home entertaining, etc) | ........................ |
| Miscellaneous subscriptions, membership fees | ........................ |
| Gifts, charitable donations | ........................ |
| Expenditure on pets | ........................ |
| Garden purchases | ........................ |
| Other | ........................ |
| **TOTAL** | ........................ |

# Possible ways of increasing your retirement income

There are probably only three ways to expand your retirement income; these are: from your home, from working or from your investment skills.

- *Your home* offers a number of options, and all possibilities are explored in greater detail in Chapter 5.

- *Working* in your retirement is something many people consider. There is a wealth of information on how to set up in business for yourself and working for others in Chapters 7 and 8.

- *Investing* can be fun and rewarding, even if it is unfamiliar territory. Chapter 2 sets out the various forms investment can take and Chapter 4 gives advice on how to protect yourself from scams and fraudsters.

There is one other possibility which might yield results if you have not already tried it: tracking down lost insurance policies, pensions or share-holdings which can be done quite easily via Experian's Unclaimed Assets Register (**www.uar.co.uk**). There is a £25 charge to run a search but it trawls 4.5 million records from about 80 different companies, saving you the trouble of calling firms directly. Alternatively, try the Government's Pension Tracing Service, which will trace any missing work pensions for you free of charge (**www.gov.uk/find-lost-pension**). For lost or dormant bank accounts, try **www.mylostaccount.org.uk**.

# And finally ...

There are a number of state benefits and allowances available to help pensioners on low to middle incomes. Every year it is estimated that billions of pounds of these go unclaimed. Age UK has produced a helpful booklet entitled 'More money in your pocket', a guide to claiming benefits for people over pension age. This is available via their website: **www.ageuk.org.uk/moneymatters**.

The following publications are aimed specifically at those coming up to retirement and the recently retired:

- *Your Guide to Retirement – Making the most of your money*, published by the Money Advice Service (**www.moneyadviceservice.org.uk**);

- *Wise Guides* – the practical pensioners' handbooks, published by Independent Age (**www.independentage.org**).

# Chapter Two
# Pensions, savings and financing your retirement

*'The question isn't what age I want to retire. It's at what income.'*

**GEORGE FOREMAN**

Pensions can be complicated and misunderstood and for that reason they may be put on the back burner. When the reality becomes apparent it may just be too late to do anything meaningful to make any significant impact. Some of the options to work around the harsh reality of a modest pension and higher living aspirations could be to work longer, start your own small business or raid your savings. Best of all, however, could be to start to remove the complications and misunderstandings and get some pension knowledge and planning in place. Chapters elsewhere in this book can help you with the first two options and leave this chapter to set out some basic information on pensions and savings.

Having started on a relatively negative note, one big cause for optimism is that pensions should become simpler with the 19 March 2014 Budget statement providing the most far-reaching reform to pensions since 1921. This really was a 'fall-off-the-chair' moment for most people in the pensions, savings and tax world. With effect from April 2015, the Chancellor has radically altered the way 'defined contribution' pensions are operated and taxed and this has made sweeping changes to how people can finance their retirement. When combined with new tax-free incentives on income from dividends and interest the combination of pensions and savings into one 'knowledge base' makes a lot of sense and hence this chapter now brings together both pensions and savings for the 2016 edition.

Importantly, this chapter is only a guide and it is neither legal nor financial advice and is no substitute for taking professional advice from an Independent Financial Adviser or other Professional Adviser (see Chapter 4). Any potential tax advantages may be subject to change and will depend upon your individual circumstances and individual professional advice should be obtained. The information outlined in this chapter may, however, assist you in understanding some of the issues you may face, the terminology used and assist you in planning for or achieving a more financially rewarding retirement. This chapter will not incorporate matters arising from the Pensions Tax Relief Consultation Paper, as at the time of writing (Summer 2015) consultation on the paper was due to end on 30 September 2015.

## All you need to know about this chapter and what it contains

- *Understand your state pension entitlement.* Understand any company and private pension entitlement. Ask your current or former employers if they are providing access to any financial advice on pensions – some may do this.

- *Use the free guidance offered by the Government's impartial service* about your defined contribution pension options to get more clarity on your pension pot and how much money you'll have in retirement. Book an appointment via **www.pensionwise.gov.uk**.

- *Think about getting proper financial advice* if you remain unsure or if the sums involved are significant, as the benefits should outweigh fees that you may have to pay. Ask friends and work colleagues if they can recommend a financial adviser or check **www.unbiased.co.uk** but, as a wealth warning, always ensure they are on the Financial Conduct Authority register at **www.fca.org.uk**.

- *Beware of the 'pensions predators'.* There are unauthorized advisers out there trying to help you get your hands on part of your pension before the age of 55. Beware – you will probably get stung. And never deal with an adviser who is not on the FCA register, irrespective of how flash their car is or how impressive they may sound.

- *Split your savings up* so that no more than £75,000 is held per bank or building society and check the institution is covered by the Financial Services Compensation Scheme (the limit reduced from £85,000 to £75,000 from 1 January 2016) and remember that since July 2015 cover after certain life events (selling a house) may get you £1 million coverage for a short period of time.

- *Combine your pensions planning with your savings plan* to finance your retirement. But keep half an eye on the tax implications (which can change) of both as therein lies both opportunities and pitfalls.

The starting point for this chapter is some high-level numbers to scale the pensions challenge. Then we seek to help you build some related knowledge and plans so that some of the complications and misunderstandings around pensions and savings start to be removed.

The Pensions Policy Institute's March 2015 'Pension Facts' demographics show that in 2015 there are 12.3 million people in the UK at state pension age and by 2040 this will increase to 16.3 million. This is an upward shift from 31 per cent of the working age population to 36 per cent. We are living longer with life expectancy at 65 projecting to increase over the same period from 24.3 years for women and 21.6 years for men to 27 and 24.5 years respectively in 2040.

Some other detail from the Pensions Policy Institute's March 2015 'Pension Facts' looking back at 2012:

Weekly national average earnings £607

Compared to an 'average' pension income comprising the four components as follows:

Basic state pension £107.45
SERPS and State Second Pension 'top up' £19.25

Received from an occupational pension scheme £144
Received from a personal pension £70

As with any average some people will have a higher pension income and some will have a lower pension income. One in seven (14 per cent) of people who retired in 2013 were dependent on their state pension as they had no other income, according to research from Prudential, the insurance providers. Analysis also revealed that nearly one in five (18 per cent) of those planning to retire in 2015 would be below the poverty line. The Joseph Rowntree Foundation estimated that in 2013 to be above the poverty line a single pensioner in the UK needed an income of at least £8,254 a year. While the state pension is a valuable source of income for millions of pensioners, it should only represent a part of someone's retirement income, not all of it. So where are you going to fit?

And looking forward the one unknown (and we don't have our crystal ball here) is how the seismic change in the debt levels carried by many of our young people will influence their saving and pension funding plans. This stems from the average student now being saddled with university tuition fees of over £8,000 per annum compared to less than half of that only four years ago. The abolition of cost of living grants and replacing them with even more being added to their student loans could create a debt time-bomb that may never be recoverable – and will parents and grandparents have to step in to assist in a way unheard of before? Time will tell but it is an issue that should be on your radar. The counterbalance could be employers wanting workers to remain in their posts for longer, and a desire among employees to continue working longer. More positively, could today's young be better prepared for retirement and ageing than might previously have been thought by the government's auto-enrolment of employees into pension schemes and compulsory employer and employee contribution levels? Could these contributions be flexed up significantly in the years ahead?

# Understand your state pension entitlement

A new state pension system comes into effect on 6 April 2016. If you reach state pension age (SPA) before 6 April 2016 there are two parts to the state pension – the basic state pension and the additional state pension. Those who qualify for a state pension currently start to receive payments in their 60s. The exact age is being equalized for men and women: to 66 for both sexes by 2020, then to 67 by 2028. The **www.gov.uk** website and a search for '*state pension calculator*' will give the age at which you will receive it.

To qualify for a full basic state pension you currently require 30 years' full National Insurance (NI) contributions. For 2015/16 the full single-person basic state retirement pension rose by £2.85 per week (from £113.10 to £115.95 – or £6,029 per year). If you're married and both you and your partner have built up state pension, you'll get double this amount – £226.20 per week in 2015/16. But if your partner has not built up their own entitlement, they will still be able to claim a state pension based on your record. The maximum is £69.50 per week.

Some people also receive an additional state pension (also called the state second pension or SERPS) which is the government's earnings-related additional pension (see 'State pension top up' below). Further options include deferring your pension (by deferring it you can have a bigger pension when it starts); adult dependency increases (for a husband, wife or someone who is looking after your children); pension credit (an income-related benefit); payments to an overseas address; provisions for married woman and widows, divorce, death and disputes and the Christmas bonus. More detailed information can be found at **www.gov.uk** and at **www.pensionsadvisoryservice.org.uk,** whose help is always free.

If you reach state retirement age after 6 April 2016 the existing two-tier system as described above is to be replaced by a single-tier system from 6 April 2016. To qualify for the new state pension you will need at least 10 qualifying years on your National Insurance record and will need 35 years to get the full new state pension. You will receive a pro-portionate amount of the full new state pension if you have between 10 and 34 qualifying years. The exact value of the new state pension is not yet known. But it is likely to be in the region of £148.40 per week.

## State pension top up

From 12 October 2015 a scheme will be introduced to allow pensioners to top up their additional state pension (also known as SERPS or state second pension – 'S2P' – which is paid along with the basic pension. This new scheme will be called state pension top up.

It will be available to all pensioners who reach state pension age before the introduction of the new state pension on 6 April 2016. The scheme will be open until 5 April 2017.

The state pension top up will give pensioners an option to boost their pension by up to £25 a week, an index-linked return and offer protection to a surviving spouse or civil partner. In particular, it could help some women and those self-employed with low earnings in the past. (More at **www.gov.uk** – search for 'state pension top up' or call 0345 600 4270.)

## Early retirement and your state pension

Because some people retire early, they can mistakenly assume it is possible to get an early pension. While the information is correct as regards many employers' occupational pension schemes, as well as for personal pensions, it does not apply to the basic state pension.

## Next steps – getting that state pension forecast

If you will reach state pension age before 6 April 2016 obtain an online estimate of your basic state pension (BSP) by visiting **www.gov.uk/calculate-state-pension**. To get an estimate of both your BSP and additional state pension, you'll need a state pension statement. You can get a statement online (once you have registered for this service), or you can request a statement by post or by telephone. If you reach your state pension age on or after 6 April 2016 and if you are presently aged 55 or over you can request a pension statement estimating your new state pension based on your current National Insurance record. The statement offers an estimated amount, not a guaranteed amount, as it is based on an individual's current national insurance record and doesn't take into account future national insurance contribution years they may build. If you are under the age of 55 you can only get a statement based on the rules of the existing scheme (that will end on 5 April 2016) and the estimate will be the least amount of state pension that you may get when you reach state pension age so it will still be of use in assembling your pension knowledge. In due course the new state pension statement service will be available to everybody of working age.

## Other sources of help

According to leading charities – Age UK and Elizabeth Finn Care – an estimated 1.5 million people could claim benefits but the means test puts some people off claiming the top-ups they are entitled to. Every year as much as £5.5 billion of benefits that older people are entitled to go unclaimed, despite many of them struggling to make ends meet. Much needs to be done in terms of raising awareness of welfare benefits available and reducing some of the negative perceptions against claiming when times are tough. Don't be afraid to claim.

For help relating to benefits, Turn2Us (**www.turn2us.org.uk**) is a charity set up specifically to identify potential sources of funding for those facing financial difficulty. Individuals can log on to this website for free and in confidence. Also, look at Age UK's website, Britain's leading charity for older people: **www.ageuk.co.uk**.

Community Care grants, Budgeting loans and crisis loans can all help with exceptional expenses if you are facing financial difficulties. These are all dealt with through the government website. See **www.gov.uk** – Jobseeker's Allowance and low-income benefits, for the widest range of online government information for the public, covering benefits, financial support, rights, employment, independent living and much more. For information for disabled people, see **www.gov.uk** – Disability benefits.

## Advice

The Pension Service provides information to current and future pensioners so that making informed decisions about pension arrangements is straightforward: **www.pensionsadvisoryservice.org.uk**.

The Service Personnel and Veterans Agency: **www.veterans-uk.info**.

Citizens Advice: **www.citizensadvice.org.uk**.

# Defined contribution pensions

Defined contribution pension schemes are a pension 'pot' from which future pension income payable to you will depend on the investment growth of your contributions (and those of your employer if it is a workplace scheme). These contrast with defined benefit schemes, which are often known as final salary pension schemes and were the norm until the mid-1980s. Much reduced, these can still be found in the public sector. Defined benefit schemes will pay an income linked to your number of years' service with an organization and your final salary earned at the point of retirement (some schemes have changed to an 'average' rather than final salary.

The game-changing announcement in the 2014 Budget was all about 'pension's liberation'. This changed the pension's world on defined contribution schemes and the changes came into effect in April 2015. In the 'old world' most people bought an annuity with their pension pot on retirement. The annuity paid a fixed income for life. The 'old world' system attracted criticism as it was perceived as representing poor value apart from the 25 per cent tax-free payment available at the start and before investing the remainder in an annuity. Once bought, the annuity could not be changed and the pre-determined rate of income paid was subject to income tax. Some annuities were mis-sold to those in ill-health, or resulted in no financial protection for dependants.

The new world of pensions liberalization resulted in a dramatic change that few expected and caused many in the financial world to – literally – fall off their chairs. Since April 2015 everyone now has a right to access their defined pension pots from age 55; no one is forced to buy an annuity, withdrawals beyond the 25 per cent tax-free cash can be made (in theory) as and when you wish but are subject to income tax. You can take as little or as much as you need and therefore income levels can be varied to take advantage of other income you may be earning (perhaps from a new part-time job, or having started a small business or whilst waiting for the state pension to kick in) to make your tax affairs more efficient. Importantly, the new regime ensures you can now pass on your pension on death to a loved one (perhaps a concern to pensions savings in the old world to those in poor or deteriorating health) and can do so without paying tax.

Most pension experts agree that pensions liberation is a good thing but also add a note of caution. Martin Gorvett, a Chartered Financial Planner says:

> the rules changes have helped enormously in making my clients' retirement
> strategies more efficient. But the new freedom brings temptation and a lot
> of new responsibility. There's a danger that some pension savers will draw
> their pension savings and fritter it all away without any constraints to hold
> them back.

Hints and tips from Martin feature within this chapter.

You can save as much as you like (defined contributions, ie towards your pension) but there is a limit on the amount of tax relief you can get and for that reason linking savings together with pensions is essential for your retirement planning. The lifetime allowance is the maximum amount of pension savings you can build up over your life. If you build up pension savings worth more than the lifetime allowance you will pay a tax charge on the excess. The rules on how much you can contribute have been tightened over recent years. The amount that can be saved into a pension each year (known as the annual allowance) and still receive tax relief is currently £40,000 per year. There are provisions to use three previous years' unused allowance and if this becomes a potential issue the sums involved would justify specific professional advice. The summer 2015 budget introduced a new 'tapered reduction', which reduces the amount of tax relief that can be obtained on pension contributions for taxpayers with 'adjusted income' in excess of £150,000. Adjusted income is a new concept and it reflects recent moves by many employers to use salary sacrifice as part of their pension scheme arrangements. The adjusted income includes any pension contributions funded by a salary sacrifice. Where an individual is subject to the taper, their annual allowance will be reduced by £1 for every £2 by which their income exceeds £150,000, subject to a maximum reduction of £30,000. The annual allowance of £10,000 will, therefore, apply to taxpayers with adjusted income of £210,000 or more. The carry forward of unused annual allowance will continue to be available, but the amount available will be based on the unused tapered annual allowance.

The other big issue that impacts on the tax relief on pension contributions is the 'lifetime allowance'. The lifetime allowance is the maximum amount that can be paid into pensions savings over a lifetime. In 2014/15 this was reduced from £1.5 million to £1.25 million. The Summer 2015 Budget announced that (at the time of writing this chapter) the lifetime allowance is to be reduced from £1.25 million to £1 million from 6 April 2016. It also announced that transitional protection for pension rights already over £1 million will be introduced alongside this reduction to ensure the change is not retrospective. The lifetime allowance will be indexed annually in line with the Consumer Prices Index (CPI) from 6 April 2018. If you are potentially impacted by these changes the period up to 5 April 2016 could be a vital tax planning window and the costs of professional advice should justify the benefits flowing.

It is important to bear in mind that tax rules and tax reliefs can and do change and their exact value depends on each individual's circumstances.

Pension savings are still one of the most tax-effective investments available because you receive income tax relief on contributions at your highest tax rate and the growth in your pension fund is currently totally exempt from income tax and capital gains tax.

Martin Gorvett, Chartered Financial Planner, provides his top five pension tips:

1 *Pensions are still the most tax-privileged savings.* Pensions still offer the best tax breaks for mainstream savings. Where else can

you get tax relief on contributions, tax-free investment returns and take 25 per cent out tax-free? Treat the pension annual allowance of £40,000 like your ISA allowance of £15,240 and save, save, save.

2 *Keeping track of retirement goals*. Retirement is not uniform. Everyone has different expectations. When considering your expenditure patterns split expenses into three categories:

– <u>must</u>-have – food, heating etc;

– <u>like</u>-to-have – a holiday twice a year;

– <u>nice</u>-to-have – a new car, a new kitchen or a legacy for the children.

Consider how these categories interact during the three stages of retirement: active (up to 75), transitional (75–83) and passive retirement (83+). Then formulate a plan to meet your personal retirement goals.

3 *Don't rely on the state.* The state pension is certainly no substitute for private pension provision and other savings but it does provide a secure guaranteed baseline income on which to build.

4 *Understand just how long retirement could last and the effect of inflation.* A 65-year-old can now typically expect to live for another 20 years, and in all likelihood may well live a lot longer. Pensioners are subject to the highest rate of inflation – nationally on average it's 7 per cent per annum. Use the rule of '72' when looking at your income streams.

For example, if inflation is 7 per cent per annum any income that is not inflation proofed will be halved after (72 ÷ 7) 10.29 years. Getting the investment strategy right is integral to achieving sustainability. Professional support will be needed on selecting funds to provide the desired investment returns while limiting volatility.

5 *Retirement isn't just a pension.* You may need professional help to think differently about your goals for later life and how you want to finance them. The traditional view is that your pension provides income and other investments are viewed as 'rainy day' funds.

Retirement income doesn't have to come from the pension alone. Having a variety of different savings and investments can achieve the optimum tax efficient income. Do take professional advice – the benefits arising usually justify any cost.

## *Company pension schemes*

### Types of company pension schemes

The pension that your employer offers may be 'contributory' (you and your employer pay into it) or 'non-contributory', which means that only your employer does. If the scheme offered is a group pension scheme, your employer doesn't have to contribute, so you alone may be putting money in. As set out below, there are four main types of company pension: final salary, career average, money purchase and group/personal pension.

**Final salary**

These are known as a type of defined benefit scheme. You build up a pension at a certain rate – one-sixtieth is quite common – so for each year you've been a scheme member, you receive one-sixtieth of your final salary. In the private sector less than 1.3 million workers are in a final salary scheme and few schemes are open to new employees as it is so expensive for employers. More public sector workers (such as teachers, police, NHS and local government workers) pay into a final salary scheme, but this is still only 5.3 million out of 29 million employed people in the UK. If you work for one of the few remaining employers with a final salary scheme, you would need a compelling reason not to join it or to ever shift the benefits if you have one from a previous employer. Martin Gorvett advises:

> Final salary pension schemes are usually the 'golden goose' of the pensions world as these schemes just keep paying which will be a nice win if you live to over 100. Only in the rarest of exceptions would there ever be a need to shift out of a final salary pension scheme – **if you are unmarried or fear decreased mortality due to health concerns you may wish to seek advice on this topic.** Also there is only modest risk as if a salary-related occupational scheme or the sponsoring employer gets into financial trouble, the Pension Protection Fund can provide some protection. You can normally get a pension of up to 90 per cent of your expected pension, subject to a cap. (See the Pension Protection Fund website for more information: **www.pensionprotectionfund.org.uk**).

**Career average**

This is another type of defined-benefit scheme, because the benefit (your pension) is worked out using your salary and the length of time you have been a member of the pension scheme. The pension you receive will be based on an average of your earnings in the time that you're a member of the scheme (often averaged over the last three years before retirement). What you receive will depend on the proportion of those earnings that you get as pension for each year of membership. The most common are one-sixtieth or one-eightieth of your earnings for each year of membership.

The benefits of such schemes are that the pension is based on your length of membership and salary, so you have a fair idea of how much your pension will be before retirement. Also, your employer should ensure that there is enough money at the time you retire to pay you a pension, and you get tax relief on your contributions. Scheme investments grow generally free of income tax and capital gains tax. Your pension benefits are linked to your salary while you are working, so they automatically increase as your pay rises. Your pension income from the scheme will normally increase each year in line with the consumer price index (CPI) instead of the retail price index (RPI). The rationale for this change is that the Department of Work and Pensions (DWP) believes that CPI better reflects the true cost of living. However, there are also potentially significant savings for the DWP, as CPI has historically tracked lower than RPI.

The Pension Protection Fund again provides some protection. You can normally get a pension of up to 90 per cent of your expected pension, subject to a cap. (See the Pension Protection Fund website for more information: **www.pensionprotectionfund.org.uk**.)

### Money purchase

These are also known as defined-contribution schemes as described earlier. The money paid in by you and your employer is invested and builds up a fund that buys you an income when you retire. Most schemes offer a choice of investment funds.

The fund is invested, usually in stocks and shares and other investments, with the aim of growing it over the years before you retire. You can usually choose from a range of funds to invest in. The Pensions Advisory Service (TPAS) has an online investment choices planner to help you decide how to invest your contributions (see **www.pensionsadvisoryservice.org.uk/online-planners**).

### Group personal pension

These are also money-purchase schemes, ie the pension you get is not linked to your salary. Your employer offers access to a personal pension plan, which you own, and can take with you if you get a new job. Your employer will choose the scheme provider, deduct the contributions you make from your salary and pay these to the provider, along with employer contributions.

# Auto-enrolment

Another big shake up in UK pensions history happened in 2012 when the government introduced 'pensions auto-enrolment'. This was introduced because people in the UK were living longer but were not saving enough to finance their increasing long retirement. Before the introduction of auto-enrolment only 47 per cent of UK employees were enrolled in a qualifying workplace pension scheme. Auto-enrolment was designed to help shift the responsibility away from the state and towards the individual and their employer. Automatic enrolment began in October 2012 and is being phased in so that by 2018, auto-enrolment will cover all employers.

To be eligible an individual must live in the UK and be between 22 and state pensionable age and earn more than £10,000 a year. Each individual will pay 0.8 per cent of their qualifying earnings rising to 4 per cent by 2018. Their employers will pay a minimum of £1 per cent rising to 3 per cent by 2018. The government makes a contribution through tax relief.

The National Employment Savings Trust (NEST) is a national defined contribution workplace pension scheme established by the government to support auto-enrolment. It is transportable between employers and has relatively low changes. It is aimed at low to moderate earners. A company can use NEST as its only workplace pension scheme or can use it alongside another scheme. More at **www.nestpensions.org.uk**.

## Self-invested personal pensions (SIPPs)

If you want to use a pension to save for your retirement, you don't have to give your money to a fund manager. You can manage your own retirement fund with a self-invested personal pension (SIPP). You can either pay a lump sum to a pension provider or drip feed in monthly amounts. The latter can be made via a scheme into which both you and your employer pay. But instead of your employer directing where your money goes, you get free rein over where it's invested. You can buy a range of asset classes, from stocks to bonds to gold bullion (though you can't buy fine wines). Monthly contributions can be as low as £50. You can pay in amounts equal to 100 per cent of your annual salary up to a current ceiling of £40,000 per year. You can access your SIPP from age 55 and draw down however much you want from April 2015. SIPPs are not suitable for everyone; broadly they are for people with larger pension pots and an appetite to play a more active part in their investment strategy. The investments that can be held in the SIPP are quite wide and can even include commercial property and for this reason some owners of small businesses may look at holding their commercial property within their SIPP to good end effect. A specialist pension adviser should be able to assist further. Martin Gorvett advises that 'specialist pension products, SIPPs are becoming a lot more mainstream. If you are venturing away from the more traditional investment routes, especially buying commercial property, it is important to ensure that a "pure" SIPP is used where you are a co-Trustee of the SIPP and hence a co-landlord of the Property'.

As SIPPs are fee-based arrangements, the smaller the fund the more expensive they are. If you are someone who finds the idea of investing your own money daunting, a SIPP may not be for you.

## Flexible drawdown

'Flexible drawdown', became effective since 6 April 2011 and became largely unnecessary following pensions liberation in April 2015. It had allowed some pension investors to take money from their pension as and when they wanted it.

## If you have a small pension pot

If the value of your pension rights is below a certain level, it may be possible to give up those rights in exchange for a cash sum. If all your pension savings in all the pension schemes you belong to are worth no more than £30,000 you may be able to take all your pension pots as a lump sum. You can do this even if one or more of your pension pots is worth more than £10,000 or if you've already started to take one of your pensions.

## *Minimum retirement age*

The minimum age at which you are allowed to take early retirement and draw your pension has been 55 since 6 April 2010 and this is likely to rise in line with state pension age maintaining a 10-year gap. It may be possible to draw retirement benefits earlier if you are in poor health and unable to work.

# Questions on your pension scheme

If you have a query or if you are concerned in some way about your company pension, you should approach whoever is responsible for the scheme in your organization. The questions listed here are simply an indication of some of the key information you may require to plan ahead sensibly.

## *If you want to leave the organization to change jobs*

- Could you have a refund of contributions if you were to leave shortly after joining?
- How much will your deferred pension be worth?
- Should you want to move the transfer value to another scheme, how long would you have to wait from the date of your request? (This should normally be within three to six months.)

## *If you leave for other reasons*

- What happens if you become ill – or die – before pension age?
- What are the arrangements if you want to retire early? Most schemes allow you to do this if you are within about 10 years of normal retirement age, but your pension may be reduced accordingly. Many schemes operate a sliding scale of benefits, with more generous terms offered to those who retire later rather than earlier.

## *If you stay until normal retirement age*

- What will your pension be on your present salary? And what would it be assuming your salary increases by, say, 5 or 10 per cent before you eventually retire?

- What spouse's pension will be paid? Can a pension be paid to other dependants?

- Similarly, can a pension be paid to a partner, male or female?

- What happens if you continue working with the organization after retirement age?

- What are the arrangements if you retire from the organization as a salaried employee but become a retained consultant or contractor?

## If you just want information

- Are any changes envisaged to the scheme? For example, if it is a final salary scheme, is there any chance that it might be wound up and a money-purchase scheme offered instead?

- If there were a new money-purchase scheme, would the company be making the same contributions as before or would these be lower in future?

- Is there any risk that benefits – either members' own or those for dependants – could be reduced?

- Is there a possibility that members might be required to pay higher contributions than at present?

## Should I transfer my long-lost fund?

- Are there any benefits to transferring old pensions into one new scheme?

- One benefit is the saving on fees. However, you should assess the performance and fees for the new scheme into which you want to transfer the funds. Watch out for transfer charges. These are punitive fees that act as a sneaky deterrent for savers trying to integrate their pensions and keep matters simple.

# Beware of predators stalking your pension

Prior to the Budget 2014 announcement about pensions liberation, the Pensions Advisory Service had warned about companies singling out savers and claiming that they can help to cash in a pension early and before you are 55. The risks from the predators stalking your pension remain. Whilst initially attractive, the sting in the tail is that you could face a tax bill of more than half your pension savings. The Pensions Advisory Service warns that this activity is known as 'pensions liberation fraud' and it is on the increase in the UK. The main warning signs are unsolicited text messages and phone calls, a transfer overseas and seeking to access a pension fund before the age of 55 (access to your pension before the age of 55 can only be achieved in rare circumstances) – and the scammers' usual ploy (see Chapter 4 for much more on this) of urgency so that you have no time to think, pause and check it out.

To counter this, always check that any financial adviser is registered with the Financial Conduct Authority (see Chapter 4), obtain a statement about any tax charges and never be rushed into agreeing to a pension transfer. The benefit of dealing with a financial adviser who is registered with the Financial Conduct Authority is that there is a safety net when things go wrong – in the form of the Financial Ombudsman Service – and, if the firm fails and is insolvent the UK safety net, the Financial Services Compensation Scheme, pays up to £50,000 per person per firm (and up to £75,000 per person per institution on savings and deposits).

## *Other help and advice*

### Previous schemes

In addition to understanding your current pension scheme, you may also need to chase up any previous schemes of which you were a member. According to the *This is Money* financial website, an amazing £1.4 billion is estimated to be forgotten and hidden away in accounts worth less than £5,000. At the moment, around 70,000 people get in touch with the Department for Work and Pensions (DWP) for help in finding a lost pension. Hundreds more queries are fielded by the Pensions Advisory Service.

For free help tracking down a pension, contact the Pension Tracing Service, which assists individuals who need help in tracing their pension rights: **www.gov.uk** – Working, jobs and pensions. Choose the link to 'Workplace and personal pensions'. If you have any queries or problems to do with your pension, there are three main sources of help available to you. These are the trustees of your pension scheme, the Pensions Advisory Service and the Pensions Ombudsman.

## Trustees or managers

These are the first people to contact if you do not properly understand your benefit entitlements or if you are unhappy about some point to do with your pension. Pensions managers (or other people responsible for pensions) should give you their names and tell you how they can be reached.

## The Pensions Advisory Service

The Pensions Advisory Service provides members of the public with general information and guidance on pension matters and assists individuals with disputes with personal, company and stakeholder pensions. More information can be found at: **pensionsadvisoryservice.org.uk**.

## Pensions Ombudsman

You would normally approach the ombudsman *only* if neither the pension scheme manager (or trustees) nor the Pensions Advisory Service is able to solve your problem. The ombudsman can investigate: 1) complaints of maladministration by the trustees, managers or administrators of a pension scheme or by an employer; 2) disputes of fact or law with the trustees, managers or an employer. The ombudsman does not, however, investigate complaints about mis-selling of pension schemes, a complaint that is already subject to court proceedings, those that are about a state social security benefit, or disputes that are more appropriate for investigation by another regulatory body. There is also a time limit for lodging complaints, which is normally within three years of the act, or failure to act, about which you are complaining.

There is no charge for the ombudsman's service. The Pensions Ombudsman has now also taken on the role of Pension Protection Fund Ombudsman and will be dealing with complaints about, and appeals from, the Pension Protection Fund. It will also be dealing with appeals from the Financial Assistance Scheme (see below). More information at: **www.pensions-ombudsman.org.uk**.

Some aspects of complaints about pensions can be investigated by the Financial Ombudsman Service (FOS) where the maximum award that the Financial Ombudsman can give is £150,000. A typical example of the type of pension case the FOS investigates is where a consumer complains about the suitability of advice to start a personal pension arrangement (perhaps they would have been better off being advised to join, remain or top-up their employer's company pension scheme). More information is at **www.financial-ombudsman.org.uk** and also see Chapter 4 for The FOS's top tips. The interaction between the FOS and the Pensions Ombudsman can seem confusing but don't worry too much as they have good arrangements to point you in the right direction if you end up with the wrong ombudsman.

## Protection for pension scheme members

The Pension Protection Fund (PPF) helps final-salary pension scheme members who are at risk of losing their pension benefits owing to their employer's insolvency. Members below the scheme's normal retirement age will receive 90 per cent of the Pension Protection Fund level of compensation plus annual increases, subject to a cap and the standard fund rules. See website: **www.pensionprotectionfund.org.uk**.

There is more help too for members who lost pension savings in a company scheme before the introduction of the Pension Protection Fund. The Financial Assistance Scheme (FAS) offers help to some people who have lost out on their pension. It makes payments to top up scheme benefits to eligible members of schemes that are winding up or have wound up. Assistance is also payable to the survivor of a pension scheme member. It is payable from normal retirement age, subject to a lower age limit of 60 and an upper age limit of 65 (see **www.pensionprotectionfund.org.uk**).

Another organization that could help is the National Federation of Occupational Pensioners (NFOP). This is an independent organization that exists to help and support those in receipt of a company pension. For more information see the website: **www.nfop.org.uk**.

## Savings as part of your retirement planning

While the nation has been attempting to extricate itself from the banking crisis and the recession, many pensioners and savers have been left out in the cold. Money in savings and deposit accounts at banks has been earning virtually no interest and the value of capital sums has been eroded by inflation. This has caused real pain to many who have led thrifty lives and saved for old age.

Savings play a critical role in the way that the whole economy works. The more encouragement people have to save, the better it is for new investment, future growth, greater productivity and higher living standards. The £15,240 overall annual investment limit (2015/16) in the new Individual Savings Account (ISA) is for savers most welcome news and allows savers to protect part of their wealth from income tax and capital gains tax. Between a couple and over several years that can equate to a powerful tax-free fund that can help in retirement. From April 2016 the first £1,000 (£500 for higher-rate taxpayers) of interest and the first £5,000 in dividends will not be subject to income tax on your self-assessment return – another useful tax planning tool. The 'fun' of investing up to £50,000 per person in premium bonds provides a tax-free 'average' return that beats many routine savings accounts (but you can do better in ISAs and if you shop around); you can get a return of the capital within days (so easy access if need be) and you may even win a million pounds but the odds are 17 billion to one! These changes put the onus on pension savers to make sensible decisions about how to invest across both savings and pensions and provide for their retirement.

Successful investing has never been easy but for those who are interested in saving for retirement, and for the long term, the principles remain the same: keep the costs down; shelter as much money from the tax office as you can; buy assets when they are cheap and sell when they are expensive (albeit that few people have the financial knowledge or crystal ball to really make a success of this but the motto, generally, is worth remembering). To be a successful investor you have to be disciplined. You need to decide on a strategy, allocate your money to your investment accordingly, then stick with that through the ups and downs that the markets will inevitably bring.

But there's a big difference between 'saving' and 'investing'. Investing is for the long term. It's money you can put away for your retirement, and in the long run it should grow more rapidly than in a savings account. If you are saving for a shorter-term goal, perhaps in less than five years, then you're looking to get the most interest paid on your money. Here are some more tips from Martin Gorvett that you may find useful:

1 *Buy what is right for you and don't believe everything you read or hear.* Just because an investment works well for someone else doesn't necessarily mean it will be right for you. Social Media promotions can be misleading. Ensure that the investment

provider is regulated by the FCA, you don't have to wander off the beaten track just to avoid the herd.

**2** *Diversify and don't put all your eggs in one basket.* Consider spreading your risk by diversifying across a mixture of asset classes, industry sectors and geographical areas. When the value of one asset is falling, another might be rising so could help to compensate.

**3** *Invest for the long term.* Adopt a strategy and stick with it. Investing isn't a matter of 'timing the market', it is about 'time in the market'. Similarly, try not to get emotionally attached to your investments. Review and rebalance your portfolio regularly to ensure you haven't strayed from the original strategy.

**4** *Take professional advice.* Investing is not free. Every avenue to market has a cost. Professional advisers will have a tried-and-tested process, often accessing institutional prices, rather than retail classes available to direct investors.

**5** Lastly, *don't risk investing money that you can't afford to lose.* Investments carry a huge caveat – you may get out less than you put in. So don't over stretch, stick within your means and know when to walk away.

Thanks to the internet, investors have unprecedented opportunity to access information and advice and price comparisons on savings and investment products. These websites are worth saving as a 'favourite':

- The Motley Fool: **www.fool.co.uk**;
- Money Advice Service: **www.moneyadviceservice.org.uk**;
- Money Facts: **www.moneyfacts.co.uk**;
- Money Supermarket: **www.moneysupermarket.com**;
- Money Saving Expert: **www.moneysavingexpert.com**;
- This is Money: **www.thisismoney.co.uk**;
- Which? **www.which.co.uk**.

Since everyone has different financial aims, there is no 'one-size-fits-all' approach to investing. In very simple terms, there are four different types of investment you could consider:

1 *Cash investments*: made into a bank account or cash ISA. These are generally short-term and offer easy access to your money, and lower risk so the potential returns are much less than other types of investment. Your money is secure up to £75,000 (covered under the Financial Services Compensation Scheme limits) but it could lose value due to tax and inflation.

2 *Bonds and gilts*: effectively, an IOU from the government or big companies. When you buy one you are lending money that earns an agreed fixed rate of interest. Government bonds (called gilts) are backed by the state and hopefully are as good as guaranteed. Corporate bonds carry greater risk in the event that the issuing company goes bust or cannot afford to repay you but because of this element of risk they offer the possibility of improved returns.

3 *Investing in property*: directly as a buy-to-let investor or indirectly through certain investment funds carry more risk. Property prices go down as well as up, and it can take time to sell property and get your cash back. Be sure to seek advice beforehand and, even better, don't do anything without reading *Successful Property Letting: How to make money in buy-to-let*, by David Lawrenson, published by Constable & Robinson (2015, website: **www.littlebrown.co.uk/ConstableRobinson**).

4 *Shares*: sometimes referred to as 'equities', this basically means putting money on the stock market. You can do this by buying shares in individual companies or by investing through a professionally managed investment fund, such as a unit trust.

As a rule of thumb, some investors keep an emergency fund equal to at least three months' living costs. Once you work out what you need to have put away for a rainy day and once you have this sum set aside you could consider investing for higher potential returns.

## Sources of investable funds

If you are looking at investment options from your resources, possible sums of quite significant capital include:

- *Commuted lump sum from your pension*: one-quarter of your pension can be taken as a tax-free lump sum. The remainder can be taken as cash, subject to the ordinary rates of income tax.

- *Insurance policies*: designed to mature on or near your date of retirement. These are normally tax-free.

- *Profits on your home*: if you sell it and move to smaller, less expensive accommodation. Provided this is your main home, there is no capital gains tax to pay.

- *Redundancy money, golden handshake or other farewell gift from your employer*: currently you are allowed £30,000 redundancy money free of tax.

- *Sale of SAYE and other share option schemes*: the tax rules vary according to the type of scheme and the rules are liable to change with each Budget statement.

# General investment strategy

Investments differ in their aims, their tax treatment and the amount of risk involved. If you are taking the idea of investing seriously, the aim for most people is to acquire a balanced portfolio. This could comprise a mix of investments variously designed to provide some income to supplement your pension and also some capital appreciation to maintain your standard of living in the long term. Except for annuities and National Savings and Investments, which have sections to themselves, the different types of investment are listed by groups, as follows: variable interest accounts, fixed interest securities, equities and long-term lock-ups.

# Annuities

Until the 2014 Budget this used to be one of the biggest decisions that most people approaching retirement had to make: cashing in their pension and buying an annuity. The headline grabber on Budget day was probably the biggest shake-up to the savings and pension market in the last four decades. In brief, the Chancellor announced that it would no longer be necessary to buy an annuity, giving the individual power to manage their own pension and how it financed their retirement.

The option of purchasing an annuity still remains. When you buy an annuity you hand over a lump sum (usually your pension fund, although you can first withdraw up to 25 per cent of it as a tax-free lump sum) to an insurance company in return for a regular, guaranteed income for the rest of your life. Under the current rules the earliest age you can do this is 55. This income is taxable if it exceeds your personal allowance. If you are retiring today, low annuity rates probably make you wince. That doesn't mean you should necessarily ignore them. Once you have bought your annuity, the income you receive is effectively free of investment risk. That has been transferred to your provider. There is little danger of running out of money, as your provider has to pay you for as long as you live.

When you approach retirement your pension company will contact you about purchasing an annuity and will outline the recently announced changes and options available to you. They will provide you with a quotation, which will tell you the amount of money you have in your 'pension pot', the amount of tax-free lump sum you are entitled to take, and the level of income you will receive each month (should you convert your pension fund to an annuity with them). Check you are getting the correct allowance and that you have the right tax code. This tells the pension company how much tax to deduct, but there is no guarantee that it will be right. For more information, see **www.incometaxcalculator.com**. Specialist help for older people is available from **www.taxvol.org.uk**.

You only get one chance to purchase an annuity, and once you have done so there is no going back. The benefit of shopping around is that you could very well receive more money by doing so. Each annuity provider will have different rates dependent on its own underwriting criteria and your own position. Research shows that by shopping around you may be able to increase the amount of income you receive by up to 20 per cent. Choosing an annuity is a decision that should not be taken without the help of a specialist financial adviser who has experience in this field.

## Types of annuities

There are several different kinds of annuities. The most basic is a *level annuity*. This pays you a fixed income for the rest of your life. If you die, the income usually stops. And – crucially – it will not change if prices rise. So in an inflationary world, your purchasing power will fall every year. For example, if inflation averages 4 per cent per year, the purchasing power of your annuity income will halve in 18 years.

To avoid this you could buy an *increasing annuity*. Here, the amount of income you receive will rise in line with inflation each year, or by a set percentage. And if you are worried about your insurance company keeping a large chunk of your pension fund should you die after only a few years of retirement, you could buy a *guaranteed annuity*. So if you bought a five-year guarantee, and you died after two years, your nominated beneficiary (your spouse perhaps) would receive annuity income for another three years.

Another option is a *joint-life annuity* where your partner can receive some or all of your pension income if you die before them. If you want to take a bit more of a risk, you could choose an *investment-linked annuity*. Here you start with an initial level of income while your fund is invested in an insurance company's with-profits fund. If the fund makes a profit, your income goes up. If it loses money, however, your income goes down.

Your health can also have a significant impact. If you are a smoker or have an illness, you may be eligible for an *enhanced annuity* or *impaired life annuity*. These pay a higher annual income than a standard annuity. In short, the annuity provider is betting that you won't live as long, so it can afford to pay you more.

## Other options

If you don't want to buy an annuity because of low rates, there are a number of strategies you can use. One is known as *phased retirement*. This is where you set up a series of annuities and drawdowns with 25 per cent tax-free lump sums. You will get a lower starting income but if you think annuity rates are going to rise it might be worth considering.

Another possible option is *fixed-term annuities*. Here you set up an annuity for a fixed period (say 5 or 10 years). You get paid an income for the fixed term but at the end of the period you have a guaranteed pot of money to reinvest again. As with phased retirement, your income will be lower than from a standard annuity.

## How to obtain an annuity

The annuity market is large and there is a vast choice of products. A helpful free booklet is Martin Lewis's (MoneySavingExpert.com) *Guide to Annuities* sponsored by Annuity Direct Limited (published March

2013). See Martin Lewis's website: **www.moneysavingexpert.com** or Annuity Direct: **www.annuitydirect.co.uk**.

Other useful websites include:

- Annuity Bureau: **www.annuity-bureau.co.uk;**
- Hargreaves Lansdown: **www.h-l.co.uk/pensions;**
- Origen Annuities: **www.origenfsannuities.co.uk;**
- William Burrows: **www.williamburrows.com.**

You can also buy an annuity direct from an insurance company or via an intermediary, such as an independent financial adviser (IFA) – see Chapter 4. You can also consult these professional advice websites:

- unbiased.co.uk: **www.unbiased.co.uk;**
- The Institute of Financial Planning: **www.financialplanning.org.uk.**

# National Savings and Investments (NS&I)

NS&I Savings Certificates, of which there are two types (fixed interest and index linked), are free of tax. They do not pay much interest but any tax-free investment is worth considering. For non-taxpayers who invest in NS&I products there is no need to complete an HM Revenue and Customs (HMRC) form to receive money in full, as this is automatic. (See the website: **www.nsandi.com.**)

The main NS&I investments are:

- *Easy-access savings accounts*: this is an easy way to build up your savings, with instant access to your money and the option to save regularly by standing order.

- *Income Bonds*: a safe and simple way of earning additional income every month. They pay fairly attractive, variable, tiered rates of interest, increasing with larger investments. Interest is taxable, but paid in full without deduction of tax at source. There is no set term for the investment.

- *Fixed Interest Savings Certificates*: lump-sum investments that earn guaranteed rates of interest over set terms. There are two terms: two years and five years. For maximum benefit, you must hold the certificates for five years.

- *Index-Linked Savings Certificates*: inflation-beating tax-free returns guarantee that your investment will grow in spending power each year, whatever happens to the cost of living. Certificates must be retained for either three or five years. Interest is tax-free.

- *Children's Bonds*: these allow you to invest for a child's future in their own name – and there's no tax to pay on the interest or bonuses. Interest rates are fixed for five years at a time, plus a guaranteed bonus. These are tax-free for parents and children and need not be declared to HMRC.

- *Pensioner Bonds*: became available in 2015 and were quickly snapped up as supply is limited. Pensioners were allowed to save a maximum of £10,000 in each bond, offering a total of £20,000. Interest on the bonds will be taxed in line with all other savings income at the individual's personal tax rate. Watch out for any news on a further release of these attractive investments.

- *Premium Bonds*: one of Britain's most popular savings products with about £55 billion invested. The maximum amount that can be saved into Premium Bonds has now risen to £50,000 and the number of £1 million prizes handed out every month doubled from one to two in August 2014. Prizes range from £25 per month (odds of winning at summer 2015 are about 26,000 to 1 to £1 million (odds are 27 billion to 1). Over 21 million people hold Premium Bonds and prizes are paid out tax-free every month.

# Variable interest accounts

You can save in a wide range of savings accounts with banks, building societies, credit unions and National Savings and Investments (NS&I) – already mentioned. With around 54 million current accounts in the UK, banks and building societies frequently introduce new accounts with introductory bonuses, to attract new customers. Although keeping track may be time-consuming, all advertisements for savings products must now quote the annual equivalent rate (AER). AER provides a true comparison, taking into account the frequency of interest payments and whether or not interest is compounded.

Other than the interest-bearing current accounts described above, these are all 'deposit'-based savings accounts of one form or another, arranged with banks, building societies, the National Savings and Investments Bank, and some financial institutions that operate such accounts jointly with banks. The accounts include instant-access accounts, high-interest accounts and fixed-term savings accounts. Some institutions pay interest annually; others – on some or all of their accounts – will pay it monthly. Although you may get a poor return on your money when interest rates drop, your savings will nearly always be safe. Should the bank or building society get into serious financial difficulty, up to £75,000 (double that if in joint names) of your money will be 100 per cent protected under the Financial Services Compensation Scheme. The limit reduced from £85,000 on 1 January 2016 and remember that from July 2015 the cover can increase for a short period to £1 million to cover certain life events (for instance moving home). More at **www.fscs.org.uk**. As an action point, should you seriously consider splitting your saving up across different banks, you can check that you are covered by listing your banks and building societies at the FSCS website where there is a handy 'check your savings are protected' section.

With the exception of tax-free cash ISAs and of the National Savings and Investments Bank, where interest is paid gross, tax is deducted at source. However, you must enter the interest on your tax return and, if you are a higher-rate taxpayer, you will have additional liability. Basic-rate taxpayers pay 20 per cent on their bank and building society interest. Higher-rate taxpayers pay 40 or 45 per cent. Non-taxpayers can arrange to have their interest paid in full by completing a certificate (R85, available from HMRC or the bank) that enables the financial institution to pay the interest gross. From April 2016 the first £1,000 of interest earned will be tax-free £500 for higher-rate taxpayers and £0 for additional rate taxpayers). If you largely rely on your savings income and believe you are or have been paying excess tax, you can reclaim this from HMRC.

## Choosing a savings account

There are two main areas of choice: the type of savings account and where to invest your money.

### Instant-access savings account

This attracts a relatively low rate of interest, but it is both easy to set up and very flexible, as you can add small or large savings when you like and can usually withdraw your money without any notice. It is an excellent temporary home for your cash if you are saving in the short term. However, it is not recommended as a long-term savings plan.

## High-interest savings account

Your money earns a higher rate of interest than it would in an ordinary savings account. However, to open a high-interest account you will need to deposit a minimum sum, which could be £500 to £1,000. Although you can always add to this amount, if your balance drops below the required minimum your money will immediately stop earning the higher interest rate. Terms vary between providers. Usually interest is only paid yearly but you will be able to identify some providers that pay monthly interest if this is a need.

## Fixed-term savings account

You deposit your money for an agreed period of time, which can vary from a few months to over a year. In return for this commitment, you will normally be paid a superior rate of interest. As with high-interest accounts, there is a minimum investment: roughly £1,500 to £10,000. If you need to withdraw your money before the end of the agreed term, there are usually hefty penalties. If interest rates are still low, your money may be better invested elsewhere.

## Equity-linked savings account

This offers a potentially better rate of return, as the interest is calculated in line with the growth in the stock market. Should the market fall, you may lose the interest, but your capital should normally remain protected. The minimum investment varies from about £500 to £5,000 and, depending on the institution, the money may need to remain deposited for perhaps as much as five years.

# Fixed interest securities

## Gilt-edged securities

Gilts, or gilt-edged securities, are bonds issued by the UK government that offer the investor a fixed interest rate for a predetermined, set time, rather than one that goes up or down with inflation. You can either retain them until their maturity date, in which case the government will return the capital in full, or sell them on the London Stock Exchange at market value. Index-linked gilts are government-issued bonds – glorified IOUs – that you can buy to obtain a guaranteed rate of return over inflation. If you are less worried about preserving your capital and require inflation-linked income then these can still be useful in a balanced portfolio.

Gilt interest is paid gross, which means that you must allow for any tax due before spending the money. A particular attraction of gilts is that no capital gains tax is charged on any profit you may have made, but equally no relief is allowed for any loss.

## Permanent interest-bearing shares (PIBS)

These are a form of investment offered by some building societies to financial institutions and private investors as a means of raising share capital. They have several features in common with gilts including they pay a fixed rate of interest that is set at the date of issue. The interest is usually paid twice yearly; there is no stamp duty to pay or capital gains tax on profits. Despite the fact that PIBS are issued by building societies, they are very different from normal building society investments. In the event of any losses PIBS are not covered by the Financial Services Compensation Scheme.

# Equities

These are all stocks and shares, purchased in different ways and involving varying degrees of risk. They can achieve capital appreciation as well as give you some regular income. Those traded on recognized stock exchanges can allow you to get your money out within a week. Millions of people in the UK invest in shares. Equity securities usually provide steady income as dividends but they fluctuate with the ups and downs in the economic cycle. Investing has never been easier with the growing number of internet-based trading facilities. Equities include ordinary shares, unit trusts, open-ended investment companies (OEICs), investment trusts and real estate investment trusts (REITs).

## Unit trusts and OEICs

Unit trusts and open-ended investment companies (OEICs, a modern equivalent of unit trusts) are forms of shared investments, or funds, which allow you to pool your money with thousands of other people and invest in world stock markets. The advantages are that they are simple to understand, you get professional management and there are no day-to-day decisions to make. Additionally, every fund is required by law to have a trustee (called a 'depository' in the case of OEICs) to protect investors' interests.

Unit trusts have proved incredibly popular because your money is invested in a broad spread of shares and your risk is reduced, but they are rapidly being replaced by the OEIC (pronounced 'oik'). The minimum investment in some of the more popular funds can be as little as £25 per month or a £500 lump sum. Investors' contributions to the fund are divided into units (shares in OEICs) in proportion to the amount they have invested. Unit trusts and OEICs are both open-ended investments. As with ordinary shares, you can sell all or some of your investment by telling the fund manager that you wish to do so. The value of the shares you own in an OEIC, or units in a unit trust, always reflects the value of the fund's assets. The key differences between the two are:

- *Pricing*: when investing in unit trusts, you buy units at the offer price and sell at the lower bid price. The difference in the two prices is known as the spread. To make a return, the bid price must rise above the offer before you sell the units. An OEIC fund contrastingly has a single price, directly linked to the value of the fund's underlying investments. All shares are bought and sold at this single price. An OEIC is sometimes described as a 'what you see is what you get' product.

- *Flexibility*: an OEIC fund offers different types of share or sub-fund to suit different types of investor. The expertise of different fund management teams can be combined to benefit both large and small investors. There is less paperwork as each OEIC will produce one report and accounts for all sub-funds.

- *Complexity*: unit trusts are, legally, much more complex, which is one of the reasons for their rapid conversion to OEICs. Unit trusts allow an investor to participate in the assets of the trust without actually owning any. Investors in an OEIC buy shares in that investment company.

- *Management*: with unit trusts, the fund's assets are protected by an independent trustee and managed by a fund manager. OEICs are protected by an independent depository and managed by an authorized corporate director.

- *Charges*: unit trusts and OEICs usually have an upfront buying charge, typically 3–5 per cent, and an annual management fee of between 0.5 and 1.5 per cent. It is possible to reduce these charges by investing through a discount broker or fund supermarket, but this means acting without financial advice. Charges on OEICs are relatively transparent, shown as a separate item on your transaction statement.

## Investment trusts

One of the biggest benefits that investment trusts offer is to income investors. While open-ended funds must pay out all the income they receive, investment trusts can hold some back in reserve. This allows them to offer a smoother and more certain return. There are four major advantages that an investment trust has over a unit trust:

1 *Cost*. The initial charges on unit trusts typically range from 4 to 6 per cent but there is also the annual fee costing in the region of 1.5 to 2 per cent. An investment trust also levies annual fees, but on average they are lower because most investment trusts don't pay commission to financial advisers.

2 *Gearing*. Like other companies, investment trusts are fairly free to borrow for investment purposes. Unit trusts, however, are usually restricted by regulation. But when markets are rising and the trust is run well, gearing will deliver superior returns.

3 *Size*. Investment trusts tend to be smaller than unit trusts on average, and so are less unwieldy and more focused on their investment objectives. To grow beyond their initial remit, they need permission from shareholders. Many also have a fixed life expectancy. Conversely, unit trusts are called 'open ended' because they can expand and contract to meet demand – 'big' is not always beautiful.

**4** *Discounts.* Because their shares are listed and traded freely (unlike a unit trust), investment trusts can end up with a market capitalization that is greater than (at a 'premium'), or lower than (at a 'discount') its assets under management (the 'net asset value', or NAV). If the discount narrows after you buy, you'll make a small gain on top of any increase in the trust's NAV.

## Ordinary shares listed on the London Stock Exchange

Public companies issue shares as a way of raising money. When you buy shares and become a shareholder in a company, you own a small part of the business and are entitled to participate in its profits through a dividend, which is normally paid six-monthly. It is possible that in a bad year no dividends at all will be paid. However, in good years, dividends can increase very substantially. The money you invest is unsecured. This means that, quite apart from any dividends, your capital could be reduced in value – or if the company goes bankrupt you could lose the lot. The value of a company's shares is decided by the stock market. The price of a share can fluctuate daily, and this will affect both how much you have to pay if you want to buy and how much you will make (or lose) if you want to sell.

See the London Stock Exchange website, **www.londonstockexchange.com**, to find a list of brokers in your area that would be willing to deal for you. The securities department of your bank or one of the authorized share shops will place the order for you, or you can do it online. Whichever method you use, you will be charged both commission and stamp duty (the latter is currently 0.5 per cent). Unless you use a nominee account (see below), you will be issued with a share certificate that you or your financial adviser must keep, as you will have to produce it when you wish to sell all or part of your holding. It is likely, when approaching a stockbroker or other share-dealing service, that you will be asked to deposit money for your investment up front or advised that you should use a nominee account to speed up and streamline the share-dealing process.

All UK shares pay dividends net of 10 per cent corporation tax (the 1/9 tax credit as it is sometimes called. Prior to April 2016 the position is that basic-rate and non-taxpayers have no further liability to income tax. Higher-rate 40 per cent taxpayers must pay further income tax that works out at 25 per cent of the net dividend received and for additional rate taxpayers (earning over £150,000) the amount of tax works out at

30.5 per cent of the dividend received. After April 2016 the situation changes significantly as a result of changes introduced in the summer 2015 budget and the proposal is that:

- There will be a new annual dividend allowance of £5,000 that is tax-free.
- The 1/9 tax credit will disappear.
- The new rates of tax on dividend will then be 7.5 per cent if the dividend falls in the basic rate tax band, 32.5 per cent if it falls in the higher-rate tax band (£42,785 to £150,000) and 38.1 per cent if it falls in the additional rate tax band (£150,000 plus).

An important wealth warning on shares. The financial pages of the Sunday newspapers carry regular stories about investors who have been scammed into buying worthless shares traded on some obscure stock exchange. Don't be caught out by the scammers and read Chapter 4 of this book (Protection from scams, help from professional advisers and how to complain). That chapter is packed with useful hints and tips.

## Individual savings account (ISA)

ISAs prove popular because of the tax breaks as you do not pay any tax on the interest or the profits you make and there is no capital gains tax. It is important to shop around for the best rates and take full advantage of your annual allowance. There are two types of ISA: cash ISAs, and stocks and shares ISAs.

You can put up to £15,240 into a new, simpler type of tax-free savings account. In this new account, savers will be able to move their money easily between the stock market and regular high-street deals in a bid to get the best possible return from their nest eggs. ISAs can be held in any mix of cash and stocks and shares – and entirely in cash if desired. The rules covering switching ISAs have also been relaxed. For the first time, savers can now transfer the previous years' funds from stocks and shares ISAs into cash ISAs.

## Enterprise Investment Scheme and Seed Enterprise Investment Scheme

Unquoted companies (ie those whose shares are not traded on a recognized stock exchange) can face problems when trying to raise finance.

The Enterprise Investment Scheme and Seed Enterprise Investment Scheme offer tax relief at 30 per cent and 50 per cent and for amounts up to £1,000,000 and £100,000 respectively if the shares are held for three years. The risk level of such investments is high and specialist advice and recommendations should be secured before venturing down this path. Albeit the tax breaks prove enticing to some with the appropriate risk attitude and, perhaps, with specialist knowledge of the business concerned (perhaps through family or other connections). Another variant is **Venture Capital Trusts** where tax relief can be secured at 30 per cent on new shares up to £200,000 in any tax year providing the shares are held for five years.

## Other tax incentives for interest and dividends

*The £5,000 dividend allowance*: In the Summer 2015 Budget the Chancellor proposed that from April 2016 there will be a significant change to the way dividends are taxed in your self-assessment and this follows an earlier announcement in the Spring 2015 Budget about a new £1,000 allowance on savings interest.

The proposal (at Summer 2015) is that:

- There will be a new annual dividend allowance of £5,000 that is tax-free.

- The 1/9 tax credit will disappear.

- The new rates of tax on the net dividend income will then be 7.5 per cent if the dividend falls in the basic rate tax band, 32.5 per cent if it falls in the higher-rate tax band (£42,785 to £150,000) and 38.1 per cent if it falls in the additional rate tax band (£150,000 plus). This compares to existing rates of 0 per cent, 25 per cent and 30.56 per cent on the net income.

There will be winners and losers as a result of this change. Presently the higher-rate taxpayer with dividends of £9,000 a year (net amount) will pay less tax of around £950 in 2016/17 compared to 2015/16 and thus dividend income may start to be more actively considered as part of financing your retirement. The counter-balance is that shares carry more risk than interest as noted elsewhere in this chapter – both in terms of income variability and credit risk (and without the fallback of FSCS protection if a bank/building society should fail). This tax saving will be offset by individuals with a small business paying more in tax where they take the majority of their income as dividends rather than salary.

*A £1,000 interest allowance*: In the Spring 2015 Budget the Chancellor announced the separate £1,000 allowance for basic rate taxpayers (£500 for higher-rate taxpayers) upon which no tax would be payable from April 2016. A welcome addition for many who previously had to scramble around to count up small levels of interest to ensure they were disclosed in your self-assessment.

*Getting your interest paid tax-free*: From April 2015, the 10 per cent 'savings rate' band was abolished and replaced with a £5,000 tax-free (0 per cent) savings income band on top of the personal allowance.

To check that you have not overpaid tax on your interest (which may have been deducted at source by your bank or building society) in 2015/16, first of all set your tax-free personal allowance against any non-savings income. If there is any tax-free allowance left, deduct this from your savings income. Any remaining savings income figure should then be set against the £5,000 band. If it all falls within this, the whole sum is eligible for a 20 per cent tax refund or you could use form R85 to register to receive the interest without any tax deducted in 2015/16. If the savings income exceeds the band, any further interest is taxed at 20 per cent.

If your non-savings income exceeds your personal allowance, deduct the excess from the £5,000 figure to see how much of the 0 per cent band you have left. Set your savings income against whatever is left of the £5,000 band. If it all falls within the residue, the whole sum is eligible for a 20 per cent tax refund or, again, you could use form R85 to register to receive the interest gross. If the savings income exceeds what's left, only the amount within the reduced band is tax-free, with any further interest being taxed at 20 per cent. More information at **www.gov.uk** and search 'Getting your interest without tax taken off (R85)'.

## *Investing for your grandchild*

### Children's savings account

All you need to set this up is the child's birth certificate. The interest on money deposited by grandparents isn't subject to tax, and interest rates are currently as high as 4 to 6 per cent if you shop around.

## Junior ISA (JISA)

You can't open a Junior ISA for your grandchild – that's one for the parents – but you can make contributions up to the JISA's annual limit. You can currently save up to £4,080 a year into a JISA. Junior ISAs are available to all children born on or after 3 January 2011, or born before September 2002, or are under 18 and do not have a child trust fund. The fund is locked until the child is 18 when they get control of the money.

## Help-to-buy ISA

These new accounts will be available from banks and building societies for four years from the autumn of 2015 and can be opened by individuals who are at least 16 years old. Help-to-buy ISAs are available to prospective first time buyers purchasing properties in the UK and are only paid when purchasing the first home (on purchases up to £250,000 outside London and £450,000 in London). Deposits can then be made of up to £1,000 when the account is opened followed by deposits up to £200 each month. The government will then boost the young person's savings by 25 per cent ie £50 for every £200 saved. The maximum bonus is £3,000 on £12,000 of savings.

## Child Trust Funds (CTF)

All babies born between September 2002 and 2 January 2011 got £500 or more free from the Government to save in a CTF. Children born after December 2010 are not eligible for a child trust fund. However, accounts set up for eligible children will continue to benefit from tax-free investment growth and you can still add £4,080 a year tax-free. Withdrawals will not be possible until the child reaches 18. These are now a defunct product and with less competition the interest rates tend not to be as good as a JISA. You are allowed to transfer these accounts to a new JISA and **www.moneysavingexpert.com** has a good article entitled 'Should you switch to a Junior ISA?' which may help your children/ grandchildren.

## Children's Bonds

Unlike the lottery of Premium Bonds – which require a minimum investment of £100 – Children's Bonds offered by National Savings and Investments (NSI) offer a guaranteed rate of return, with only a £25 minimum investment; the best five-year deal currently pays 2.5 per cent.

## Pension

For really long-term saving, pay into a pension. Your grandchild takes control at 18, but can only access the money aged 55. Tax relief currently applies so the government will top up a payment of £2,880 to the limit of £3,600.

## Useful reading

*How the Stock Market Works*, by Michael Becket of the *Daily Telegraph*, published by Kogan Page; see website: **www.koganpage.com**.

# Long-term lock-ups

Certain types of investment, mostly offered by insurance companies, provide fairly high guaranteed growth in exchange for your undertaking to leave a lump sum with them or to pay regular premiums for a fixed period, usually five years or longer. The list includes life assurance policies, investment bonds and some types of National Savings Certificates.

## Life assurance policies

### Definition

Life assurance can provide you with one of two main benefits: it can either provide your successors with money when you die or it can be used as a savings plan to provide you with a lump sum (or income) on a fixed date. There are three basic types of life assurance: whole-life policies, term policies and endowment policies:

1 *Whole-life policies* are designed to pay out on your death: you pay a premium every year and, when you die, your beneficiaries receive the money. The insurance holds good only if you continue the payments. If one year you did not pay and were to die, the policy could be void and your successors would receive nothing.

2 *Term policies* involve a definite commitment. As opposed to paying premiums every year, you elect to make regular payments for an agreed period, for example until such time as your children have completed their education, say eight years. If you die during

this period, your family will be paid the agreed sum in full. If you die after the end of the term (when you have stopped making payments), your family will normally receive nothing.

**3** *Endowment policies* are essentially savings plans. You sign a contract to pay regular premiums over a number of years and in exchange receive a lump sum on a specific date; this could be from 10 to 25 years. Once you have committed yourself, you have to go on paying every year (as with term assurance).

An important feature of endowment policies is that they are linked to death cover. If you die before the policy matures, the remaining payments are excused and your successors will be paid a lump sum on your death. The amount of money you stand to receive, however, can vary hugely, depending on the charges and how generous a bonus the insurance company feels it can afford on the policy's maturity. Over the last decade payouts have been considerably lower than their earlier projections might have suggested.

Both whole-life policies and endowment policies offer two basic options: with profits or without profits:

- *Without profits*: sometimes known as 'guaranteed sum assured'. The insurance company guarantees you a specific fixed sum, you know the amount in advance and this is the sum you – or your successors – will be paid.

- *With profits*: you are paid a guaranteed fixed sum plus an addition, based on the profits that the insurance company has made by investing your annual or monthly payments. The basic premiums are higher and the profits element is not known in advance.

- *Unit linked*: a refinement of the 'with profits' policy, in that the investment element of the policy is linked in with a unit trust.

Premiums can normally be paid monthly or annually, as you prefer. The size of premium varies enormously, depending on the type of policy you choose, the amount of cover you want and any health underwriting that may be required – you may be required to have a medical check if large sums are involved. More usually, you fill in and sign a declaration of health. If you make a claim on your policy and it is subsequently discovered that you gave misleading information, your policy could be declared void and the insurance company could refuse to pay.

Under current legislation, the proceeds of a qualifying policy – whether taken as a lump sum or in regular income payments – are free of all tax. If, as applies to many people, you have a life insurance policy written into a trust, there is a possibility that it could be hit by inheritance tax rules affecting trusts if the sum it is expected to pay out is above the £325,000 IHT threshold. Check matters with an IFA or solicitor.

Policies are usually available through banks, insurance companies, independent financial advisers (IFA) and building societies. Be careful with the small print: terms and conditions that sound very similar may obscure important differences that could affect your benefit. To be sure of choosing the policy best-suited to your requirements, consult an IFA. For more information about IFAs and help when things go wrong see Chapter 4.

### Alternatives to surrendering a policy

If you wish to terminate an endowment policy before the date of the agreement, and avoid the punitive costs, you could sell the policy for a sum that is higher than its surrender value. See the Association of Policy Market Makers website: **www.apmm.org**. For those looking for investment possibilities, second-hand policies could be worth investigating. Known as traded endowment policies (TEPs), they offer the combination of a low-risk investment with a good potential return. A full list of appropriate financial institutions and authorized dealers that buy and sell mid-term policies is obtainable from the Association of Policy Market Makers. It can also arrange for suitable policies to be valued by member firms, free of charge.

## *Bonds*

The London Stock Exchange operates a retail bond platform designed to make trading corporate bonds as easy as trading listed shares. Since March 2011 nearly £1.7 billion has been raised by companies in the market. Bonds generally offer less opportunity for capital growth; they tend to be lower risk as they are less exposed to stock market volatility; but they have the advantage of producing a regular guaranteed income. The three main types of bonds are:

- *Gilts*: (government bonds) explained earlier in this chapter, are the least risky. They are secured by the government, which guarantees both the interest payable and the return of your capital in full if you hold the stocks until their maturity.

- *Corporate bonds*: these are fairly similar to gilts except that you are lending to a large company, rather than owning a piece of it, as you do with an equity. The company has to repay the loan at some point, known as the bond's redemption date. It will pay out the 'face value' of the bond and the company also has to pay interest on the loan, known as the 'coupon'. After they are issued, bonds trade in the secondary market, just like shares. Bond prices are driven by two main factors: interest rates and credit risk. Most bonds have a fixed income; the longer the time to maturity, the more sensitive the bond is to changes in interest rates.

One reason to hold bonds is for income. Should corporate profits stall, companies might have to cut dividends. But unlike dividends, bond coupons can't be suspended, so your income is more predictable. The main risks to bonds are rising interest rates and credit risk.

## Investment bonds

Not to be confused with debt-based investments, they are tax wrappers, rather than specific investment instruments. They are a method of investing a lump sum with an insurance company over the long term.

Available in both onshore and offshore variants, both offer life assurance cover as part of the deal, although this is usually only 101 per cent of the fund value at time of death.

The underlying investment of any type of Investment Bond will be retail Units Trusts and OEICs – similar to those available under ISA or SIPP wrappers. The manager/adviser will be able to tailor the investment strategy to meet your risk/reward. They are generally used to produce long-term capital growth and can generate regular (tax deferred) income.

The tax position of an Investment Bond depends on whether it is onshore or offshore. Whilst both types can offer the investor withdrawals of up to 5 per cent of the initial investment each year without creating a liability to tax, the amount drawn does remain restricted to the value of the original investment and can therefore be deemed to reduce in line with inflation each year.

Onshore Investment Bonds are subject to a special rate of corporation tax (roughly 18.4 per cent) on any growth or income within the Bond so basic rate taxpayers are deemed to have no further liability on surrender or encashment (known as a chargeable event).

Any further tax liability for higher- and top-rate taxpayers is calculated using complicated 'top slicing' rules – where in short the overall growth is annualized and then assessed alongside the recipient's other income for the tax year in question. If this pushes the recipient into the higher-rate threshold or top rate of tax threshold, further tax will be due.

Offshore Investment Bonds on the other hand are only subject to a nominal withholding tax, so all investors will be subject to tax at their marginal rate on any growth achieved on repatriation of the funds to the UK – including the value of the permitted 5 per cent withdrawals drawn, which are added back in.

Any gain on an Investment Bond is subject to Income Tax, therefore your personal allowance can be used to reduce any tax payable but your capital gains allowance cannot be used to offset tax.

There has been much interest in Offshore Bonds from high earners looking for an alternative to pensions for their retirement savings. These can provide significant tax savings because of the 5 per cent withdrawals, with no immediate tax to pay.

Ongoing charges for offshore bonds are high: typically an extra 0.4 per cent per annum in addition to usual investment costs. Professional adviser charges on top means that bonds are generally best for investments greater than £100,000.

It should also be noted that any ongoing professional adviser charges deducted from the Bond will either create a chargeable event each year, or reduce your 5 per cent withdrawals. So a Bond with a 1 per cent annual fee will only provide net 4 per cent withdrawals.

## Structured products

A structured product is a fixed-term investment where the payout depends on the performance of something else, typically a stock market index eg FTSE 100 or S&P 500. They are complex and can carry hidden risk because they can appear on the surface to be an alternative to cash.

There are two main types of structured product – Structured Deposit and Structured Investments.

1 *Structured Deposits* are savings accounts but they are certainly not cash based. The rate of interest (or rate of annual return) provided depends on how the underlying stock market index

performs. So if the stock market index rises you receive a predetermined rate of interest, if it falls you will get nothing.

**2** *Structured Investments* offer either an annual rate of return, or a return over a fixed term. They are typically comprised of two underlying investments, one designed to protect your capital and another to provide the bonus/'kicker'. The return you get will be stated at outset and depend on how the underlying stock market index performs. If it performs badly, or the counterparty fails (the counterparty is the company providing the stated return), you may lose some or all of your original investment.

Be careful to peel back the label on these investments. The use of the word 'guaranteed' in the literature does not mean what you may first think! It means you are 'guaranteed' to get the returns stated *only* if the stock market index performs as required in the product's terms and conditions – noting that fees and charges may ultimately mean you get back less than you put in and professional advice would be recommended for anyone seeking to make this type of investment.

# Investor protection

As we say in Chapter 4, most financial transactions involving banks, investments, pensions and insurance take place without any problems but sometimes things go wrong. This is where the UK's regulatory regime steps in. As it is vitally important to your protection part of that chapter is repeated here.

The **Financial Conduct Authority (FCA)** is accountable to the Treasury and aims to make sure the UK financial markets work well so that consumers get a fair deal. It registers individuals and companies that are suitable to work in the industry and checks that they are doing their job properly and fines them if they do a bad job. The FCA has a range of helpful guides and factsheets to help consumers understand the UK's financial markets and the role of the FCA. More at **www.fca.org.uk**.

The **Financial Ombudsman Service (FOS)** is a free service set up by law with the power to sort out problems between consumers and registered financial businesses. It is an impartial service and will investigate your complaint if you have been unable to resolve matters with the registered individual or company (ie registered with the Financial Conduct

Authority as above). If the ombudsman considers the complaint justified it can award compensation. More at **www.financial-ombudsman.org.uk**.

The **Financial Services Compensation Scheme (FSCS)** is the body that can pay you compensation if your financial services provider goes bust. The FSCS is independent and free to access. The financial services industry funds the FSCS and the compensation it pays. There are limits on how much compensation it pays and these are different for different types of financial products. To be eligible for compensation the person or company must have been registered by the Financial Conduct Authority (FCA). More at **www.fscs.org.uk**.

In addition, and for your protection when dealing with company and certain other pensions the protection may come from a different route. Although this may appear complicated the relevant ombudsman is very good at pointing you in the right direction if you end up in the wrong place. The further help on pensions comes from:

Information and assistance from the Pensions Advisory Service (more at **www.pensionsadvisoryservice.org.uk**).

Protection comes from the Pensions Ombudsman (more at **www.pensions-ombudsman.org.uk**) and the Pension Protection Fund (more at **www.pensionprotectionfund.org.uk**).

Finally, possibly the biggest change and issue for many are the decisions to be taken about defined pension schemes and the new regime of pensions liberation. The final plug therefore goes to the free and impartial government service where you can obtain guidance on what you can do with your pension pot, how to shop around and what to look out for on taxes and fees and how to avoid pension scams. The service is at **www.pensionwise.gov.uk** and as Pension Wise says, hopefully they can help you make sure your money lasts as long as you do.

# Chapter Three
# Tax

*'I like to pay taxes. With them I buy civilization.'*

**OLIVER WENDELL HOLMES JR**

Tax in the UK is unnecessarily complicated and we can't promise to cut through it all in the one chapter that we have devoted to this important subject. We will, however, highlight some key aspects for retirement planning. Most importantly, we plead that our new government finally and properly delivers on the majority of UK taxpayers' one wish – to massively reduce red tape on taxation. The tax rulebook needs to be put on a four-foot-high bonfire and the process started afresh again. In 2009, an article in the *Daily Telegraph* (Jonathan Russell, 6 September 2009) drew our attention to an announcement by LexisNexis, publishers of *Tolley's Tax Guide*, that:

> The UK now has the longest tax code in the world ... the handbook of tax legislation now runs to 11,520 pages, a 10 per cent increase on last year and more than double the number of pages from 12 years ago.

Fast forward six years and for a sense of balance we turn to the *Guardian* newspaper's Marina Hyde (13 February 2015), who was also scratching her head over the well-posed question: 'Why does the UK have the longest tax code in the world?' Hyde observed:

> The Hong Kong tax code, widely held by tax lawyers to be the most admirably efficient in the world, is 276 pages long. The British tax code, rapidly beginning to look like the most disingenuous in the world, is currently in excess of 17,000 pages. It has more than trebled in size since 1977.

Taxes are necessary. Few would disagree with the view of Oliver Wendell Holmes Jr (one of the most widely cited United States Supreme Court

Justices, quoted at the beginning of this chapter) and seek to disown the schooling, roads, health service, security and rescue services that our taxes pay for (in one way or another). But with taxes can't we do more to 'keep it simple stupid' (or KISS – to use another quote from the United Sates, this time from the 1960s US Navy)?

Maybe we can then strive to earn more in retirement and not engage expensive lawyers and accountants to weave around the 17,000 pages to either (a) just make sure we are doing things correctly or (b) spot gaps, holes and t's that are not crossed if that happens to be your thing. Time will tell but the trend line on the page count in the big tax book does not look promising. So how about a target: no more than 1,000 pages in the big tax book by the time the 2018/19 *Good Retirement Guide* is published?

In our current low-interest rate environment financing your retirement from savings has been difficult ground to find crumbs of comfort. However, there has been some good news for savers and imminent or new pensioners in recent Budgets. Tax restrictions on interest and dividends have been improved for most people; the increase in the tax-free limit on all ISAs has helped, there was the introduction of pensioner bonds with attractive interest rates and then the introduction of significant new access arrangements on defined contribution pension schemes was ground-breaking.

With the longest tax book in the world, tax knowledge and planning around these recent improvements in the UK remains essential. Understanding the broad principles of taxation can help you save money. This is not 'dodgy' – it is simply knowing the rules and applying them. The problem is not in this planning activity – the problem is the long and complicated rule book. It is not the effect, it is the cause that is the real problem.

On the other hand, there is tax evasion which you can always remember because E is for *E-legal*. This shorthand might help reinforce that it is *illegal*. That is the work of the tradesperson who takes cash and does not declare it to the taxman. And it is the individual who forgets that the reason they had a few flights to some offshore tax jurisdiction was to hide money offshore to try and evade tax on the interest they were earning. HMRC's own definition of tax evasion is 'when people or businesses deliberately do not pay the taxes that they owe and it is illegal.' (Source: **www.gov.uk**.)

HMRC's own definition of tax avoidance is:

bending the rules of the tax system to gain a tax advantage that Parliament never intended. It often involves contrived, artificial transactions that serve little or no purpose other than to produce tax advantage. It involves operating within the letter – but not the spirit – of the law.

It is also the crook in a suit who resides in the UK and takes an income and routes it round the world, writes it off through loans and puts it in and out of trusts and ends up spending the same money in the UK and, hey presto, there is a rich lifestyle and no tax paid. But then again on this later 'category' there is probably a barrister's opinion that is produced showing that 'technically' the scheme has navigated the 17,000 pages and the route to tax-free money is not E-legal. The individual concerned would probably dismiss Oliver Wendell Holmes Jr's quote at the head of this chapter while still enjoying the benefits of society. HMRC are targeting just this sort of person with increased resources and commitment (and powers) – more later.

Importantly this chapter is only a guide and it is neither legal nor taxation advice and is no substitute for taking professional advice from a Professional Adviser (see Chapter 4). Any potential tax advantages may be subject to change and will depend upon your individual circumstances and individual professional advice should be obtained. The information outlined in this chapter may, however, assist you in understanding some of the issues you may face, the terminology used and assist you in planning for and achieving a more financially rewarding retirement.

### All you need to know about this chapter and what it contains

- If you are a higher-rate taxpayer because of a pension and other employed or business income, take professional advice. Consider using your pension allowance to contribute to a defined benefit pension, receive extra income tax relief and then manage your defined benefit pension fund withdrawals to keep within a lower tax rate band.

- If you do not use your £15,240 ISA allowance by 5 April 2016 the tax shelter for that amount will be lost forever. If you have a spouse or civil partner the amount doubles if they also have not used their allowance.

Then open up and start funding your 2016/17 ISA and you can start saving more tax from 6 April 2016.

- Use up gains of £11,100 by 5 April 2016 without paying tax if you hold shares outside a tax wrapper (like an ISA or SIPP) which have gained by less than £11,100. Consider selling them and using the proceeds to fund an ISA or SIPP.

- Reduce your inheritance tax liability by gifting using the reliefs set out in this chapter. Larger gifts are normally tax-free if the giver survives a further seven years. New inheritance tax rules could result in unmarried couples with children and a house worth more than £650,000 walking down the aisle after April 2017.

- Remember the new reliefs coming in from 6 April 2016 to allow you £5,000 of dividend income tax-free and £1,000 of interest tax-free (for basic rate taxpayers and for higher-rate taxpayers the amount reduces to £500). If married or in a civil partnership you should consider how best to structure who holds investments and bank deposits.

- From 6 April 2015 you may be able to transfer part of your personal allowance if you are a married couple or in a civil partnership.

- Review and update your will.

# But it's all so complicated – and what about Betty down the road?

*The Good Retirement Guide 2016* will try and help but remember you are not alone; here's our pick of free further help (which could be all that Betty down the road needs after she lost her husband and has no relatives close by, so don't keep these tips to yourself):

- *Tax Help for Older People* (TOP) is a charity that is an independent, free tax-advice service for vulnerable and unrepresented people on low incomes – **www.taxvol.org.uk**.

- *Tax Aid* is a charity that advises only those people on low incomes whose problems cannot be resolved by HMRC – **www.taxaid.org.uk**.

- *The Money Advice Service* provides free and impartial advice and guides on tax and benefits to help you improve your finances and support in person over the phone – **www.moneyadviceservice.org.uk**.

- *The Citizens Advice Service* has a very useful website to help you understand tax and how it is collected and what to do if you have a tax problem. They can also provide face to face and telephone support – **www.citizensadvice.org.uk**.

# Self-assessment

Self-assessment is the system HM Revenue and Customs (HMRC) uses to collect income tax. Income tax is usually deducted automatically from wages, pensions and savings but people with other income must report it in a tax return. The tax you have to pay depends on allowances you have, the income tax band you're in and also there are different rates for capital gains tax and inheritance tax. Self-assessment forms are sent out in April, and the details you need to enter on the form you receive in April 2016 are those relating to the 2015/16 tax year ie 6 April 2015 to 5 April 2016. Not everyone has to complete a self-assessment form but one is required for a number of specified circumstances which include: the self-employed; being a company director; having income from savings and investments of £10,000 or more; having employment income on PAYE above £100,000; and having Capital Gains Tax to pay. All taxpayers have an obligation to keep records of all their different sources of income and capital gains. These include:

- details of earnings plus any bonus, expenses and benefits in kind received;
- bank and building society interest;
- dividend vouchers and/or other documentation showing gains from investments;
- pension payments, eg both state and occupational or private pensions;
- income and costs of any trading or other business activity;
- rental income from letting a property and associated costs;
- taxable social security benefits (for instance job seekers' allowance and carers' allowance);

- gains or losses made on selling investments or a second home;
- payments against which tax relief can be claimed (eg charitable donations or contributions to a personal pension).

If you don't voluntarily disclose the fact that you may owe tax and HMRC finds out about untaxed income and launches an inquiry (or investigation) into your tax affairs you could face stiff penalties as well as paying any tax due and interest (more on this later).

# Income tax

This is calculated on all (or nearly all) of your income, after deduction of your tax allowances. The reason for saying 'nearly all' is that some income you may receive is tax-free; types of income on which you do not have to pay tax are listed a little further on in this chapter.

Most income counts, however. You will be assessed for income tax on your pension; interest you receive from most types of savings (some relaxation from 6 April 2016); dividends from investments (some relaxation from 6 April 2016); any earnings (even if these are only from casual work); plus rent from any lodgers, should the amount you receive from a room exceed £7,500 (up from £4,250 in April 2016). Some social security benefits are also taxable. The tax year runs from 6 April to the following 5 April, so the amount of tax you pay in any one year is calculated on the income you receive (or are deemed to have received) between these two dates. Points to note – with effect from 6 April 2016 and the new tax year 2016/17:

- The point at which most people start paying income tax will be the personal allowance of £11,000 (this will increase from £10,600 on 6 April 2016). Then in 2017/18 it is set to increase again to £11,200. The target of the current government is to increase this to £12,500 by the end of the current parliament. Once the personal allowance has reached £12,500, legislation will apply so that it increases automatically in line with the equivalent of 30 hours a week at the national minimum wage for employees aged over 21.

- The 20 per cent basic-rate tax is payable on further income beyond the personal allowance up to £32,000 (this will increase from £31,765 on 6 April 2016). Then in 2017/18 it is set to increase again to £32,400).

- The combined effect of the above measures is that the 40 per cent income tax threshold rises from £42,385 in 2015/16 to £43,000 in 2016/17 and then to £43,600 in 2017/18. The target of the current government is to increase this to £50,000 by the end of the current parliament.

- The top rate of 45 per cent is levied on incomes in excess of £150,000.

The current government has pledged a lock on these 20 per cent, 40 per cent and 45 per cent rates of income tax and will not raise them in the current parliament. This lock will also apply the standard (20 per cent) and reduced (5 per cent) rates of VAT and employer (13.8 per cent) and employee (12 per cent) class 1 national insurance rates. This is good news but there remains scope to increase other taxes and, for instance, in the Summer 2015 budget increases in insurance premium tax from 6 per cent to 9.5 per cent were announced and we could expect an increase to the current self-employed national insurance rate of 9 per cent (given it was not 'locked' and the disparity with employed national insurance levels).

# Tax allowances

## Personal allowance

Your personal allowance is the amount of money you are allowed to retain before income tax becomes applicable. The headline rates both now and in the future were stated in the immediately prior section.

Since 2010 as part of the 'tax the rich' measures introduced in that era the personal allowance is reduced by £1 for every £2 of income over £100,000. The personal allowance will therefore disappear if your income in 2015/16 is above £122,000.

---

**Tax tip**

For 2015/16 you may still be able to preserve your part or all of your personal allowance by making pension contributions but due to other potential restrictions professional advice should be sought. See also Chapter 2 for further information and possible opportunities around pensions and financing your retirement.

When calculating how much tax you will have to pay in any one year, first deduct from your total income the amount represented by your personal allowance. You will not have to pay any income tax if your income does not exceed your personal allowance (or total of your allowances), and you may be able to claim a refund for any tax you have paid, or that has been deducted from payments made to you, during the year. You should add any other tax allowance to which you may be entitled (further information can be found at **www.gov.uk** and also **www.moneyadviceservice.org.uk**) and such other allowances include:

- Married Couple's Allowance of £8,355 (2015/16) is available to people born before 6 April 1935. Tax relief for this allowance is restricted to 10 per cent.

- A widowed partner, where the couple at the time of death were entitled to Married Couple's Allowance, can claim any unused portion of the allowance in the year he or she became widowed.

- Registered blind people can claim an allowance (the Blind Person's Allowance) of £2,290 per year (2015/16). If both husband and wife are registered as blind, they can each claim the allowance.

**Tax tip**

Transferable tax allowances between married couples and civil partnership came into effect on 6 April 2015 and this could reduce your tax in 2015/16 and can make sure you don't lose out on the personal allowance. From 6 April 2015 a spouse or civil partner who is not liable to income tax above the basic rate can transfer £1,050 of their personal allowance to their spouse/civil partner, provided that the recipient of the transfer is not liable to income tax above the basic rate.

## Same-sex partners

Same-sex couples in a civil partnership are treated the same as married couples for tax purposes.

# Tax relief

Separate from any personal allowances, you can obtain tax relief on the following:

- a covenant for the benefit of a charity, or a donation under the Gift Aid scheme;
- contributions to occupational pensions, self-employed pension plans and other personal pensions (more later);
- £1,000 of interest (£500 for a higher-rate taxpayer) and £5,000 of dividends (more later);
- rental income of up to £4,250 (increasing to £7,500 from 6 April 2016) per year from letting out a room in your home.
- mortgage interest relief in respect of loans secured on an older person's home to purchase a life annuity. However, to qualify, the loan must have been taken out (or at least processed and confirmed in writing) by 9 March 1999. Borrowers in this situation can continue to benefit from the relief for the duration of their loan. As before, the relief remains at 10 per cent on the first £30,000 of the loan;
- some maintenance payments on arrangements set up prior to 5 April 2000. Individuals in receipt of maintenance payments are not affected and will continue to receive their money free of income tax. Those who had to pay tax under the pre-March 1988 rules now also receive their payments free of tax. Most individuals paying maintenance no longer get any relief at all. An exception has been made in cases where one (or both) of the divorced or separated spouses was aged 65 or over at 5 April 2000. Those paying maintenance are still able to claim tax relief – but only at 10 per cent.

# Tax-free income

Not all income is taxable and the following list indicates some of the more common sources of income which are free of tax:

- Attendance Allowance;
- Child Benefit (NB: Child Benefit cuts introduced in 2013 result in a partial tax clawback if one parent earns more than £50,000 and

child benefit was received and results in all child benefit being repayable via a tax assessment for those on £60,000 or more);

- Child Tax Credit;
- Disability Living Allowance and Personal Independence Payment;
- Housing Benefit;
- Industrial Injuries Disablement Pension;
- Income-related Employment and Support Allowance;
- Income Support (in some circumstances, such as when the recipient is also getting Jobseeker's Allowance, Income Support benefit will be taxable);
- pensions paid to war widows (plus any additions for children);
- certain disablement pensions from the armed forces, police, fire brigade and merchant navy;
- the Winter Fuel Payment (paid to pensioners);
- Working Tax Credit;
- National Savings Premium Bond prizes;
- winnings on the National Lottery and other forms of betting;
- rental income of up to £4,250 (increasing to £7,500 from 6 April 2016) per year from letting out a room in your home;
- income received from certain insurance policies (mortgage payment protection, permanent health insurance, creditor insurance for loans and utility bills, various approved long-term care policies) if the recipient is sick, disabled or unemployed at the time the benefits become payable;
- income and dividends received from savings in an individual savings account (ISA);
- dividend income from investments in venture capital trusts (VCTs);
- virtually all gifts (in certain circumstances you could have to pay tax if the gift is above £3,000 or if, as may occasionally be the case, the money from the donor has not been previously taxed);
- a redundancy payment up to the value of £30,000 (note that the Summer 2015 Budget announced that the government wished to consult on this long standing relief so things may change);

- a lump sum commuted from a pension;
- a matured endowment policy.

If in doubt take professional advice on any 'unusual' income that you have received or further information is available at the Citizens Advice Bureau website: **www.adviceguide.org.uk** – taxable and non-taxable income.

# Income tax on savings and investments

## Savings

In the Spring 2015 Budget the Chancellor announced the separate £1,000 allowance for basic rate taxpayers (£500 for higher-rate taxpayers) upon which no tax would be payable on savings interest from April 2016. There is no allowance for additional (45 per cent) rate taxpayers. This will provide a welcome additional £200 tax break for many. In addition time could be saved for those who remember when they had to scramble around to count up small levels of interest to ensure they were disclosed in their self-assessment. Another change (this time from April 2015) saw the 10 per cent 'savings rate' band abolished and being replaced with a £5,000 tax-free (0 per cent) savings income band on top of the personal allowance. More information on this is set out in Chapter 2 and the section 'Other tax incentives for interest and dividends'.

> **Tax tip**
>
> These changes will increase the number of savers who are not required to pay tax on savings income. It may also represent a good tax-planning opportunity for a husband and wife (or partners in a civil partnership) on different tax rates.

## Investments

Again the situation is changing from April 2016. Previously, and for the 2015/16 self-assessment most UK-based equity investments on which you are likely to receive dividends, basic-rate tax will have been deducted before the money is paid to you. If you are a basic-rate taxpayer, the money you receive will be yours in its entirety. If you pay tax at the higher rate of 40 per cent you will have to pay 25 per cent of the net dividend received on the amount received that takes you above the higher-rate threshold (£42,285 in 2015/16) and should allow for this in your budgeting. In the Summer 2015 Budget the Chancellor proposed that from April 2016 there will be a significant change to the way dividends are taxed in your self-assessment and introduced a new £5,000 dividend allowance which would take dividends up to this value to be taken 'tax-free'. Higher dividend taxes would then be levied on amounts above £5,000 and more information on this is set out in Chapter 2 and the section 'Other tax incentives for interest and dividends'.

**Tax tip**

Again this may also represent another good tax-planning opportunity for a husband and wife (or partners in a civil partnership) on different tax rates.

**Tax tip**

If you are a few years from retirement and currently employed think about investing in your employer. Shares acquired under share incentive plans or sharesave schemes usually provide price discounts and tax breaks for taking part. Think about and plan your annual contribution limits so that there could be a steady flow of share sales in the future so you can maximize your capital gains tax exemption (see below).

## Income received gross

Exceptionally, there are some investments where the income is paid to you gross – without the basic-rate tax deducted. These include NS&I income bonds, capital bonds, the NS&I Investment Account and all gilt interest (albeit people who prefer to receive gilt interest net can opt to do so.) This can lead to a surprise tax liability for the unwary.

This is similar to higher- and additional-rate taxpayers who have to play 'catch-up' every 31 January on the difference between the tax they have paid on their interest at source (charged at 20 per cent basic rate tax and deducted at source) and the tax due at the higher rate (40 per cent) and/or additional rate (45 per cent). If appropriate you will need to save sufficient money to pay the additional tax due by 31 January after the end of the tax year.

## Stopping or reclaiming tax on savings income

Banks and building societies automatically deduct basic-rate (20 per cent) tax from interest before it is paid to savers. As a result, most working people, except higher-rate taxpayers, can keep all their savings without having to worry about paying additional tax. While convenient for the majority, a problem is that some 4 million people on low incomes – including in particular many women and pensioners – are unwittingly paying more tax than they need. Those most affected are non-taxpayers (anyone whose taxable income is less than their tax allowances) who, although not liable for tax, are having it taken from their income before they receive the money.

### Tax tip

Non-taxpayers can stop this happening quite simply by requesting their bank and/or building society to pay any interest owing to them gross, without deduction of tax at source. Request form R85 from the institution in question and completion of this will enable interest to be paid to you with the deduction of basic rate income tax. More information is also available at **www.gov.uk** and search 'Getting your interest without tax taken off (R85)'.

## Reclaiming tax overpaid

If you are a non-taxpayer and have not yet completed an R85 form (or forms), you are very likely to be eligible to claim a tax rebate. To claim tax back you will need to fill in HMRC's form R40 Tax Repayment Form. More information at **www.gov.uk** and search 'Claim for repayment of tax deducted from savings and investments (R40)'.

## Mis-sold PPI compensation 'interest'

Millions of consumers have been receiving refunds after being mis-sold payment protection insurance (PPI) with credit cards and personal loans. Successful claimants are also being paid interest on the refunds to compensate for being without their money all that time. *But*, while there is no tax to pay on the refund element, which simply returns your own money to you, you may have to pay tax on the interest, just as you do on earned interest in a savings account. If you have received a compensation payment check what the lender advises and whether they have deducted basic tax at 20 per cent already (which non-taxpayers can reclaim and higher-rate payers report to HMRC on their self-assessment).

# Mistakes by HMRC

HMRC does sometimes make mistakes. Normally, if it has charged you insufficient tax and later discovers the error, it will send you a supplementary demand requesting the balance owing. However, a provision previously known as the 'Official Error Concession' and now labelled 'Extra Statutory Concession A19' provides that, if the mistake was due to HMRC's failure 'to make proper and timely use' of information it received, it is possible that you may be excused the arrears.

Undercharging is not the only type of error. It is equally possible that you may have been overcharged and either do not owe as much as has been stated or, not having spotted the mistake, have paid more than you needed to previously. If you think there has been a mistake, write to your tax office explaining why you think the amount is too high. If a large sum is involved it could well be worth asking an accountant to help you. If HMRC have acted incorrectly you may also be able to claim repayment of some or all of the accountant's fees (your accountant will be able to advise you on this).

As part of the Citizen's Charter, HMRC has appointed an independent adjudicator to examine taxpayers' complaints about their dealings with HMRC and, if considered valid, to determine what action would be fair. Complaints appropriate to the adjudicator are mainly limited to the way that HMRC has handled someone's tax affairs (perhaps unduly delays, errors and discourtesy). Before approaching the adjudicator, taxpayers are expected to have tried to resolve the matter with their tax office.

Where the taxpayer has made a mistake and owes more tax they will need to convince officials at HMRC that they had not been careless in completing their returns otherwise they could be at risk of incurring a penalty of 30 to 100 per cent of the tax involved, plus the tax owed itself and interest, and potentially HMRC widening its focus on you and your tax affairs.

### Important dates to remember

The deadline for filing paper self-assessment forms for the 2015/16 tax year is 31 October 2016. Those filing online will have until 31 January 2017.

The penalty for breaching these deadlines is £100. If your return is more than three months late an automatic penalty of £10 per day commences up to a maximum of £900. If your return is still outstanding after a year another penalty arises based on the greater of £300 or 5 per cent of the tax due. In serious cases of delay a higher penalty of up to 100 per cent of the tax due can be imposed.

One final key date – you can amend your self-assessment at any time in the 12 month period after the latest 31 January deadline.

# Tax rebates

When you retire, you may be due a tax rebate because tax has been collected using PAYE assuming you will earn your salary for a whole year and rebates usually arise for Summer or Autumn leavers. The tax overpayment would normally be resolved automatically, especially, if you are getting a pension from your last employer or move into part-time employment. The P45 (tax form for leavers) should be used by the pension payer or new employer and, normally, the tax sorts itself out. If not and the potential reclaim is for a previous tax year HMRC may be ahead of you as they may spot it (usually by the end of July following the tax year) and send you a P800 tax calculation if they know you have paid too much tax. You will then get your refund automatically within 14 days of the P800.

If you have not received a P800 or can't wait to the end of the tax year you may make a claim to HMRC for any of the 4 previous tax years. You will need to know your national insurance number, your P45 if you have one and details of the jobs or state benefits you were getting at the time. HMRC will then send you a cheque or explain what further information they need. Use this address for all income tax correspondence with HMRC: Pay As You Earn and Self-Assessment, HM Revenue and Customs, BX9 1AS (telephone 0300 300 3300).

# Capital Gains Tax (CGT)

You may have to pay capital gains tax if you make a profit (or, to use the proper term, 'gain') on the sale of a capital asset. CGT applies only to the actual gain you make. There is an exemption limit of currently £11,100 per year. This means that in 2015/16 a married couple or a couple in civil partnership can make gains of £22,200 that are free of CGT. However, it is not possible to use the losses of one spouse to cover the gains of the other. Transfers between husband and wife or civil partners usually remain tax-free, although any income arising from such a gift will of course be taxed in due course in the hands of the recipient.

Any gains you make are taxed at 18 per cent for basic-rate taxpayers and 28 per cent for higher-rate and additional-rate taxpayers. Company owners benefit from further tax breaks, including 'entrepreneurs' relief', which can get relief limits on CGT down to 10 per cent (professional advice should be sought on this).

The following assets are not subject to CGT and do not count towards the gains you are allowed to make:

- your main home (but see the note below);
- your car;
- personal belongings up to the value of £6,000 each, such as jewellery, paintings or antiques;
- proceeds of a life assurance policy (in most circumstances);
- profits on UK government loan stock issued by HM Treasury;
- National Savings certificates;
- gains from assets held in an individual savings account (ISA and older PEPs);
- Premium Bond winnings (maximum holding was increased to £50,000 in 2015/16);

- betting and lottery winnings and life insurance policies if you are the original owner;

- gifts to registered charities;

- usually small part-disposals of land (limited to 5 per cent of the total holding, with a maximum value of £20,000);

- gains on the disposal of qualifying shares in a venture capital trust (VCT) or within the Enterprise Investment Scheme (EIS) and Seed Enterprise Investment Scheme provided these have been held for the necessary holding period (see below). These are complex and tax-efficient investment schemes and carry risk but are outside the scope of this book. Further information can be gained from **www.hmrc.gov.uk**, and professional advice should be sought.

## *Your home*

Your main home is usually exempt from CGT. However, if you convert part of your home into an office or into self-contained accommodation on which you charge rent, the part of your home that is deemed to be a 'business' may be separately assessed and CGT may be payable when you come to sell it (CGT would not usually apply if you simply take in a lodger who is treated as family, in the sense of sharing your kitchen or bathroom.)

If you leave your home to someone else who later decides to sell it, then he or she may be liable for CGT when the property is sold (although only on the gain since the date of death). There may also be inheritance tax implications, so you are strongly advised to consult a solicitor or a chartered accountant. If you own two homes, only one of them is exempt from CGT, namely the one you designate as your 'main residence', although there may be some overlap opportunities and, providing a dwelling home has been your only or main home for a period, the final period of ownership that qualifies for relief can be useful. In the 2014 Budget it was announced that from 6 April 2014 the final period of ownership of a private residence that qualifies for relief was reduced from 36 months to 18 months. HMRC's helpsheet 283, 'Private Residence Relief', available from **www.gov.uk** provides more information.

Tax tip

If you have two homes and have lived in both consider taking professional advice on whether to make a main residence election for your second home if it is standing at a large gain or you are thinking of selling it first. One of the tests used by HMRC when considering the availability of such reliefs is the actual period of residence and the quality rather than quantity of that residence.

## Selling a family business

CGT is payable if you are selling a family business, and is 28 per cent for higher-rate and additional-rate taxpayers, but the reduced level of 18 per cent for basic-rate taxpayers. There are a number of CGT reduction opportunities or deferral reliefs allowable including the potential to attain entrepreneurs' relief which could produce a tax rate of 10 per cent. This, however, is a complex area and timing could be vital, so well before either retiring or selling shares you should seek professional advice.

# Inheritance Tax (IHT)

Inheritance tax (IHT) is the tax that is paid on your 'estate'. The tax threshold (the level at which you'll need to pay tax) is set at £325,000 and frozen at this rate until 2020/21. The threshold amount for married couples and civil partners is £650,000. The value of estates over and above this sum is taxed at 40 per cent.

There is no immediate tax on lifetime gifts between individuals. The gifts become wholly exempt if the donor survives for seven years. When the donor dies, any gifts made within the previous seven years become chargeable and their value is added to that of the estate. The total is then taxed on the excess over £325,000. Chargeable gifts benefit first towards the £325,000 exemption, starting with the earliest gifts and continuing in the order in which they were given. Any unused balance of the £325,000 threshold goes towards the remaining estate.

The £325,000 threshold allows married couples or civil partners to transfer the unused element of their IHT-free allowance to their spouse or civil partner when they die, giving an attractive effective threshold of £650,000. IHT will, however, still be levied at 40 per cent above £325,000 on the estate of anyone who is single or divorced when they die.

One of the biggest fanfares in the Summer 2015 budget was for the 'main residence nil rate band' which will be an extra relief planned to commence from April 2017. It will be an extra relief available where the value of the estate is above the IHT threshold and contains a main residence which is being passed on to 'lineal descendants'.

There will be a consultation on this in September 2015, with the legislation in Finance Bill 2016 so much remains uncertain at the time of writing this chapter but, for the moment, the key aspects appear to be:

- The relief will be introduced in April 2017, for deaths on or after that date.

- It will be phased in, starting at £100,000 in 2017/18, rising to £125,000 in 2018/19, £150,000 in 2019/20 and £175,000 in 2020/21. For a couple, the £175,000 plus the existing £325,000, each, makes the £1 million maximum relief quoted by the government.

- The relief will then increase in line with CPI from 2021/22 onwards.

- The relief applies only on death, not on lifetime transfers.

- The amount available will be the lower of the net value of the property and the maximum amount of the main residence nil rate band. The net value of the property is after deducting liabilities such as a mortgage.

- The property will qualify if it has been the deceased's residence at some point.

- The property must be left to lineal descendants: children, grandchildren, great-grandchildren, etc. Children include step-children and adopted children.

- The relief is transferable, so the estate of the second spouse to die can benefit from the main residence nil-rate band of their deceased spouse, regardless of when that spouse died.

- The relief will be tapered away for estates with a net value over £2 million, at the rate of £1 for every £2 over that limit, so will be reduced to zero on an estate of £2.35 million.

> **Tax tip**
>
> Could these new inheritance tax rules result in unmarried couples with children and a house worth more than £650,000 walking down the aisle after April 2017?

Other relatively recent changes to capital gains tax are also worth a reminder. The government changed the tax law in April 2012 to encourage donating to charities, and reduced the inheritance tax payable on estates that give at least 10 per cent to charity. The remainder is taxed at 36 per cent against the usual 40 per cent inheritance tax rate. Existing wills can be amended by codicil to include this 10 per cent provision. There is no such benefit to those whose estate falls below the current IHT threshold.

Gifts or money up to the value of £3,000 can be given annually free of tax, regardless of the particular date they were given. Additionally, it is possible to make small gifts to any number of individuals free of tax, provided the amount to each does not exceed £250. And £5,000 can be given to your children on their marriage.

> **Tax tip**
>
> Planning and longevity go hand-in-hand as most lifetime gifts to individuals that are not covered by one of the exemptions mentioned do not trigger inheritance tax if you survive for seven years.

Recent budgets also created new and welcome provisions to enable the tax and other advantages of ISAs and pensions to be passed onto the deceased's spouse (for instance in the case of ISAs that funds could remain in the ISA tax effective wrapper). Could it be tax-efficient to ensure that your spouse inherits your ISA under your will rather than the investments passing to other family members?

It follows that one final and vital consideration relating to IHT is the need to make a will and keep it up to date so that it is both effective and efficient from both a legal and a tax perspective. For further information, see 'Wills', in Chapter 11.

More at **www.gov.uk** (search 'probate and inheritance tax') or the HMRC helpline is 0300 1072.

## Tax treatment of trusts

There may be inheritance tax to pay when assets – such as money, land or buildings – are transferred into or out of trusts when they reach a 10-year anniversary. There are complex rules that determine whether a trust needs to pay IHT in such situations. This is a particularly complex area and professional advice is highly recommended. Further information is available on the website: **www.hmrc.gov.uk** – Inheritance tax and trusts.

## Help in dealing with a tax investigation

HMRC is increasing its investigation capability armed with more staff and more power. If HMRC believes your errors were deliberate they can go back 20 years. Add in interest on any late tax and further additional penalties of up to 100 per cent of the tax shortfall and you could be facing an eye-watering tax assessment.

HMRC will listen carefully to facts that may mitigate any penalty due – and if you are looking at serious amounts of tax due then early discussion with a professional adviser will assist you in dealing with the unwelcome situation you may find yourself in. You should also check whether any insurance or professional association memberships that you have can provide free tax investigation cover. This is a very useful piece of cover.

Abbey Tax has one of the leading tax consultancy teams in the UK, which is headed by Guy Smith, a former HMRC tax inspector. Indeed, all of Guy's team are ex-tax inspectors and cumulatively have spent over 125 years working for HMRC.

We asked Guy for his views on the compliance landscape and how HMRC has been performing:

> In many ways, the transformation of HMRC over the five years of the coalition government was remarkable. Against a backdrop of falling staff numbers and the closure of tax offices, HMRC consistently produced higher compliance yields year after year, as processes were streamlined and digital systems developed. During 2014/15 alone a record £26.6 billion was

delivered in compliance revenue, which was an increase of £2.7 billion on 2013/14.

Since the Conservative government was elected, a further £1.3 billion of investment in HMRC has been approved by the Chancellor, with the objective of raising an additional £5 billion a year on top of that already being achieved. £300 million of that pot of money is to allow HMRC to pursue small- and medium-sized enterprises (SMEs), as well as wealthy individuals.

You may well be wondering why there is such a focus on the sole trader, partnership or professional person. According to HMRC's calculations the current tax gap is some £34 billion with 44 per cent of this down to SMEs and 12 per cent down to individuals failing to declare and pay the right amount of tax.

HMRC has responded by transferring more staff into enforcement and compliance work from a base of 38 per cent of the workforce at March 2011 to 46 per cent at March 2015. Over 26,000 HMRC officers out of circa 57,000 are now actively involved in delivering the yield results demanded by the Treasury.

Many people 'in the know' are now aware of HMRC's award-winning 'Connect' technology which helps identify risks across a wide variety of sources including tax returns, third-party data, tax evasion reports made by the public, social media activity and information reported by other government agencies, including the Land Registry.

HMRC is now exploiting this data even further. It is moving all of its information into a single storage space called the 'enterprise data hub', where tax staff will see everything they need to know about an individual in one place. HMRC intends to make this information available to all operational teams who need it, from contact centres to debt-management staff.

The new hub will give HMRC the capacity to store 960 terabytes of data – ten times more than the current capacity and 20 times more what the Hubble Space Telescope has collected in the last 20 years.

In addition, HMRC is seeking an extension of its data gathering powers. In 2013, HMRC obtained new powers to collect data from merchant acquirers – businesses that process credit and debit card transactions. The government has now announced its intention to legislate to extend access to data held by 'business intermediaries' and 'electronic payment providers'.

Business intermediaries include booking and reservation companies such as those that take payment for hotel and holiday accommodation, restaurants supplying take-away food and outlets reselling tickets for music concerts, theatre productions and other similar performances.

Electronic payment providers facilitate different ways of paying, such as via digital wallets, which can be used in conjunction with mobile payment systems that allow individuals to make purchases with their smart phones. HMRC has proposed that the new legislation is 'future-proofed' so similar data can be requested from new business models as they emerge.

The landscape has therefore changed significantly and HMRC not only has the intention to narrow the 'tax gap' but the targeted resources and a much more focused capability. Apart from deploying extra staff and closing tax loopholes, we sought Guy's views on what we should be looking out for in the year ahead.

With all the background information HMRC now holds on SMEs and individuals, it is uncommon for a tax investigation to begin as a 'fishing trip'. The tax inspector will usually have been provided with a package of information that HMRC has collated and risk-assessed, which identifies potential issues either with the business accounts which have been declared and filed, where there is believed to be 'hidden wealth', online trading or even undisclosed rental income.

Examples

Potential issues with the business accounts declared and filed: We see a lot of tax enquiries launched when business losses are declared year after year. HMRC will often ask for proof that the business is being run as a commercial venture and ask for sight of business and marketing plans. The tax inspector will also ask how the losses are being sustained, which will usually be followed by a request to see personal bank statements to judge how the individual's lifestyle is being funded, whilst business losses are being incurred.

*Hidden wealth* – HMRC operates a series of taskforces every year, where a specific risk is identified in a designated geographical area. One of the taskforces which has been running recently involves HMRC staff calling upon individuals it believes have hidden wealth. HMRC may have information of an offshore bank account held, or an expensive asset like a yacht or aeroplane or luxury car, or aerial photos from Google Earth showing extensive external improvements to the residential property. Put simply, after looking at the tax returns filed by those individuals, HMRC may be unable to ascertain how the assets acquired or home improvements have been funded, or where the money has come from to be deposited in the offshore account.

*Online trading* – This is a typical paragraph from a letter from HMRC: 'eBay records show that you became a business seller on 1 June 2010 and you have sold at least 19,251 items since that date. When submitting your business accounts, please also provide copies of your PayPal accounts to substantiate the figures shown.' We anticipate this will continue to be a tactic used by HMRC to dispute the turnover declared by businesses with a significant online presence.

*Rental income* – HMRC receives information from the Land Registry outlining when properties have been bought and sold, can access the voters list records to check for multiple occupancy properties and can also analyse housing benefit payments made. This data enables HMRC to check the accuracy of rental income being declared by known landlords, but also helps HMRC identify 'ghost' landlords who have not registered to pay tax. HMRC has been running the Let Property Campaign to encourage landlords who may have understated their rental income to come forward, to settle on favourable terms.

If HMRC discovers an error during an investigation, it can reopen other closed years as well. For example, if a careless error is discovered, HMRC can include up to six years within any settlement negotiations. If a deliberate error is uncovered, HMRC can include up to 20 years in the most serious cases. In addition to settling any tax owed you will have to pay interest on that tax and a penalty which can be up to 100 per cent of the tax owed. Needless to say, tax investigations can prove to be extremely stressful and very expensive. So we turned to Guy for his concluding hints and tips:

1 *Engage an accountant.* Make sure the accountant is a chartered accountant and a member of one of the tax professional bodies. In other words, get an accountant who has passed their exams and has qualifications.

2 *Keep good records.* Although there is an obligation to keep business records, it is always sensible to keep personal records as well. Dividend vouchers and interest certificates will always need to be retained for completing the self-assessment tax return, but it is wise to keep records relating to house moves and monies received from third parties, whether from an inheritance or savings maturity.

**3** *Talk to your accountant.* It is always surprising how many people simply give their business records to their accountant and then sign their tax return when it is presented, without asking any questions. The danger is that the accountant may have to make assumptions when preparing the accounts and introduce estimates to get the accounts to balance. If a tax inspector finds estimated or other balancing figures during a tax investigation, it calls into question the accuracy of the business records and can lead to all sorts of problems.

**4** *Get tax investigation insurance cover.* Many accountants will offer this type of insurance; specialist providers such as Abbey Tax do too, as well as trade membership bodies such as the Federation of Small Businesses. It is always worth comparing prices and benefits before taking out fee protection insurance, as it is often called.

**5** *Be discreet.* HMRC views social media websites so, for example, if your business has had a bad year and made low profits, don't start posting pictures of an expensive foreign holiday on Facebook or a luxury car on Instagram.

# Retiring abroad

A vital question is the taxation effects of living overseas. There are many examples of people who retired abroad in the expectation of being able to afford a higher standard of living and who returned home a few years later, thoroughly disillusioned. If you are thinking of retiring abroad, do thoroughly investigate the potential effects this will have on your finances in order to avoid unpleasant surprises.

Tax rates vary from one country to another: a prime example is VAT, which varies considerably in Europe. Additionally, many countries levy taxes that don't apply in the UK. Wealth tax exists in quite a few parts of the world. Estate duty on property left by one spouse to another is also fairly widespread. There are all sorts of property taxes, different from those in the UK, which – however described – are variously assessable as income or capital. Sometimes a special tax is imposed on foreign residents.

Apart from the essential of getting first-class legal advice when buying property overseas, if you are thinking of retiring abroad the golden rule must be to investigate the situation thoroughly before you take an irrevocable step, such as selling your home in the UK.

Many intending emigrants cheerfully imagine that, once they have settled themselves in a dream villa overseas, they are safely out of the clutches of the HMRC. This is not so. You first have to acquire non-resident status. If you have severed all your ties, including selling your home, to take up a permanent job overseas, this is normally granted fairly quickly. But for most retirees, acquiring unconditional non-resident status can take up to three years. The purpose is to check that you are not just having a prolonged holiday but are actually living as a resident abroad. During the check period, HMRC may allow you conditional non-resident status and, if it is satisfied, full status may be granted retrospectively.

At a very high level and start point is HMRC's Statutory Residence Test, which states that you are likely to be treated as UK resident if you spend more than 183 days in the UK in any one tax year, or have a home in the UK and don't have a home overseas or work full time in the UK over a period of 365 days. An online tool, the 'Tax Residence Indicator', can provide more guidance and is available by searching **www.gov.uk**.

Even if you are not resident in the UK, some of your income may still be liable for UK taxation, so, as with previous suggestions above, profes-sional advice should be sought. In the meantime, more information can be found via **www.gov.uk** and search for 'Guidance Note: Residence, Domicile and the Remittance Basis'.

### Double tax agreement

A person who is a resident of a country with which the UK has a double taxation agreement may be entitled to exemption or partial relief from UK income tax on certain kinds of income from UK sources, and may also be exempt from UK tax on the disposal of assets. The conditions of exemption or relief vary from agreement to agreement. It may be a con-dition of the relief that the income is subject to tax in the other country.

# Further information

- HMRC has closed all of its enquiry centres which used to give face-to-face help to people with tax queries. This service has been replaced by an enhanced information service via **www.gov.uk** and a telephone support service. The most frequently used telephone line is the self-assessment: general enquiries number 0300 200 3310.

- Use this address for all income tax correspondence with HMRC: Pay As You Earn and Self-Assessment, HM Revenue and Customs, BX9 1AS.

- Contact the Adjudicator's Office for information about referring a complaint about HMRC: **www.adjudicatorsoffice.gov.uk**.

- The TaxPayers' Alliance campaigns towards achieving a low-tax society: **www.taxpayersalliance.com**.

- Tax Help for Older People (TOP) is a charity that is an independent, free tax-advice service for vulnerable and unrepresented people on low incomes: **www.taxvol.org.uk**.

- Tax Aid is a charity that advises only those people on low incomes whose problems cannot be resolved by HMRC: **www.taxaid.org.uk**.

- The Money Advice Service provides free and impartial advices and guides on tax and benefits to help you improve your finances and support in person over the phone: **www.moneyadviceservice.org.uk**.

- The Citizens Advice Service has a very useful website to help you understand tax and how it is collected and what to do if you have a tax problem. They can also provide face to face and telephone support: **www.citizensadvice.org.uk**.

Useful tax forms that can help you pay less tax:

- R40. If you want to claim back tax paid on savings and investments, you need to complete this form.

- R85. Getting your interest paid without tax being taken off: if you are not a taxpayer, this form will save you having to claim tax back each year.

- P161. Are you going to be 65 (61 for a woman) in this tax year? Or is your income changing – for example, if state pension and private pensions are due to start. If yes, this form will inform HMRC of your age and income, allowing it to give you your age allowance and your new tax codes.

- P53. If you have recently taken a lump sum rather than buying an annuity (pension), an enormous amount of tax was deducted before you received it. To claim this back immediately you should complete a P53.

- P45. You should receive one of these when you finish work with an employer. If you start a new job in the same tax year it is important that you give it to your new employer. It will ensure you are given the correct tax code and the right tax is deducted.

- P46. As important as the P45. If you start a new job and you do not have a P45 you must complete a P46. Your employer should prompt you to do this. If not, ask for one. This form also sorts out your tax codes.

- Forms 575 and 18. If you are thinking of transferring some of your Married Couples' Allowance, form 575 allows you to transfer the excess at the end of the tax year. Form 18 allows you to transfer the minimum amount.

Most forms can be obtained via the HMRC website: **www.hmrc.gov.uk**.

## Useful reading

*The Daily Telegraph Tax Guide* 2016 by David Genders, published annually by Kogan Page; see website: **www.koganpage.com**.

# Chapter Four
# Protection from scams, help from professional advisers and how to complain

'Greed is the root of [all] evils.'

'THE PARDONER'S TALE', ONE OF THE *CANTERBURY TALES* BY GEOFFREY CHAUCER

Having worked so long to build up a wealth and asset base we want to protect it and enjoy the benefits of our decades of hard work or perhaps lucky opportunities over the years. There are, however, predators out there who may want a slice of our cake. Intelligent, honest people don't fall victim to scammers, do they? And do we know how to spot a professional reputable adviser from a 'crook in a suit'. And, finally, do we need to be a little bit un-British and get better at complaining?

## All you need to know about this chapter and what it contains

- Scammers employ sleight of hand, fast talk and a few back-up techniques such as vanity and knowing that people never want to admit to being stupid. You will never spot what they have done in the same way as a good magician really will leave you believing that they made someone 'float' on stage. Smoke, mirrors, sleight of hand and anything can be made to look possible.

- So how can we protect ourselves? First of all forget the 'it could never happen to me' line. How many times have we read a story and thought the victim should have known better? However, many of the victims are just like you but have encountered very professional scammers who have employed all their tricks and, before you know it, a payment has been made. If it was a few pounds you might write it off to bad luck and experience, but what if it was a few hundred pounds, a few thousand, or even more?

- The main solution is all about knowledge and awareness and looking after each other. Our five 'tests' and the further tips from the very best in the industry will help you. Taking professional advice and ensuring that the person really is a 'professional' will help reduce the risk of falling victim to a scammer or a 'crook in a suit' and this chapter will guide you through some of the professionals that can help.

- Inevitably, however, things do sometimes go wrong in life. If you do lose out and have encountered a genuine business that is at fault there is also a section in this chapter on complaints and 'how to and how not to' complain.

# The five tests for staying safe from the scammers

## *The duck test*

A respected detective superintendent summed up the duck test rather neatly. The test flows from cutting short a debate over the identification of a crook (duck) and, out of pure frustration, is drawn to a close by: 'It looks like a duck, it walks like a duck, it quacks like a duck – it is a (expletive deleted) duck!' It's a simple common-sense approach – ignore the smoke and mirrors and sleight of hand that crooks and scammers are so capable of pulling off – anything that is used to distract you from the real issue. Does it look, feel, and 'smell' like a scam? If so walk away, put the letter in the bin or put down the phone.

## *The granny test*

Trust your instincts, especially after you ask yourself the rather telling question about whether you would let the character you are dealing with anywhere near an elderly relative on the subject of money or financial advice. Instincts have been honed in the human species over thousands of years – if they have served you well in the past, learn to trust them.

## Actions speak louder than words

Scammers, generally, are all talk (unsurprisingly, they are very good at it) and no action. Any reasonable person should be able to deliver against what they promise or apologize and explain before you have to ask 'what's going on'. If the actions don't happen, then just walk away and don't give them a second or third chance to take advantage of you if you have to keep chasing.

## Too good to be true?

Scammers know that greed can get the better of many people and employ it to their purposes. If it sounds too good to be true, it is probably a scam. Walk away.

## Thank you, but I'll just check with...

We have great financial institutions in the UK and this goes to the very heart of the UK economy. Our regulatory system is sound. You should therefore check precisely who you are dealing with and more on this follows in the professional advisers section of this chapter. If it is a company and it is not a high-street name check out the company at Companies House (**www.companieshouse.gov.uk**) to see how long it has been in existence and whether it has filed its accounts on time. This will never be definitive but it is something you can check for yourself – and it can be very telling if the company involved has only been around for a year. For more definitive assurance and for investments you really must check that the firm is regulated by the Financial Conduct Authority (**www.fca.org.uk**). After all, the FCA says: 'Our aim is to help firms put the interests of their customers and the integrity of the market at the core of what they do.' If it is an investment and it is not regulated by the FCA then, again, this tells its own story and, if things go wrong, you are more likely to be on your own.

Also linked to the 'I'll just check with...' tip is the simple fact that crooks have one other objective in addition to taking your hard-earned cash – and that is not getting caught out. This is where nosy neighbours are brilliant – and a stroll over and a few questions can be of great assistance. The scammers quickly move on. If you only do one thing as a result of this chapter do this: require any friend or relative that is over 70 to learn this tip and apply it and nosy neighbours are just what they need!

# Some common scams

## *Advance fee fraud*

This is one of the scammer's favourites and has been dressed up in a hundred different guises. The spine is remarkably simple. A payment is made by you with the promise of a bigger pay-out in return. Perhaps it is cloaked in terms of funds left to you by a mystery relative, where you pay a processing fee of £50, then maybe you are asked to pay another release fee of £150 and on it goes with a promise of £10,000 sucking you in (which, of course, you will never actually receive). Walk away.

## *The surprise prize-ballot win*

There is usually a premium-rate telephone number to call in order to claim the prize and the ultimate actual prize is probably worthless or trivial. File anything like this under 'B' for bin. It is, however, sometimes fun to read the small print in such 'prizes' in order to spot the scam or the impossibility of winning the surprise big win. This is how it works: there will be a token nominal prize for which there may be 10,000 or more winners and it will probably take you more than £15 in phone or other charges to 'win' and the prize will be pretty useless. As a final deterrent if you do reply, you are likely to be put on a 'suckers list' and will be bombarded by even more junk ballots and scams. Remember... just file under 'B' for bin.

## *Romance scams*

The new lover or someone showing you interest or attention who, and unremarkably, shows you the attention you crave just when you need it or are at a low point. Maybe then they need some money for a sick mother or child. Scammers can be very clever and know how to manipulate you to get the response they want. They usually want you to keep things 'secret' as they know that any friend you confide in will tell you to run a mile. Sadly, emotional involvement and shame prevent people from acting rationally – and the scammers know this. Smoke, mirrors, sleight of hand and, just like a magician, your money is gone before you know it. Be brave and confide in someone you really trust.

## Credit and bank card cloning or snatching

This can be the jackpot for the scammers, but how can they actually get your credit or bank card? The cloning devices that they attach to a bank's cash machine are not so far-fetched these days. But how about the scammer who calls you and pretends to be from the police, explaining that they have just arrested someone who 'apparently' was caught with a clone of your card. They arrange for a courier to call and collect your actual card as part of their investigations. Unfortunately it is all just another scam and the supposed police officer is just another scammer. These guys really do have balls, but the bottom line is never ever be worried about feeling made to look silly.

Follow our five tips – and then if you spot a scam or have been scammed, report it and get help. Contact the Police Action Fraud team on 0300 123 2040 or online at **www.actionfraud.police.uk**, or contact the police in your area – unless a crime is in progress or about to be, the suspect is known or can be easily identified, or the crime involves a vulnerable victim, in which case dial 999 if it is an emergency or 101 if it isn't.

But don't just take my word for it. The Metropolitan Police are at the forefront of fighting fraud with their fraud prevention team – 'Sterling' – now part of FALCON (**F**raud **A**nd **L**inked **C**rime **On**line) Organized Crime Command. We asked them about current trends. Their spokesperson set the scene very neatly:

> MP: The over-70s are a more trusting generation and therefore more likely to be taken in by fraudsters and they tend to have more money at their immediate disposal and more that can be readily accessed.
>
> We are seeing individuals who have been arrested for burglary, robbery and drug dealing in the past being arrested in connection with fraud. Criminals follow the money. Where some have had success, others will follow.

> Good Retirement Guide (GRG): So what are the current scams?

> MP: Courier fraud is a particular type of fraud that is sweeping the country. It originated in London – at the time of writing the Metropolitan Police Service has had over 4,000 offences – but there have been incidents in every force area. In London, the average age of the victim is 72 years and the average loss over £3,000 but we have seen a number of incidents where victims have lost significant amounts of money.

> GRG: This is part of the credit or bank card cloning or snatching we highlighted above, isn't it?

MP: Basically, yes, that's right. It's a real hotspot in 2015, we want everyone to watch out for it, so I will give you some more detail on this one. Also as you say earlier in this chapter the very best thing someone reading this chapter can do is to pass this information on to family and friends that are aged over 70. The crime has evolved over time but typically a fraudster will phone you at home pretending to be a police officer or a bank employee. He or she will be reading from a well-rehearsed script – they may be making hundreds of telephone calls a day until they succeed. They may say that they have arrested an individual with a cloned copy of your bank card or if pretending to be a bank, say that there has been some recent unusual spending on your card and they need to confirm your personal and banking details.

To engender trust they typically ask you to dial 999/ 101 or the telephone number on the back of your bank card and ask to be put back through to the police officer or bank employee. However, the fraudster keeps the line open at their end so no matter who you call, you end up speaking to the fraudster or their 'colleague'.

They then proceed to ask for your personal and banking details and will often ask you for your PIN or ask you to type it using your phone keypad. The fraudster uses special technology to decipher the keypad number tones. As a result they have all your details, including your PIN.

They will then say that they need your card for evidence or if from the bank they may say that they need it for their investigations and will send out a replacement and will send someone, typically a taxi or courier to collect your card and they may ask you to cut the card in half but to avoid the CHIP on the card. When the suspect gets the card they will glue or tape the card back together. They often ask you to place it in a greetings card and then into an envelope. This is to disguise what the letter contains when it is picked up. They may get you to write a fake reference number on it – again, to engender trust but in fact the reference number means nothing. They sometimes get the victim to pay for the cost of the collecting taxi driver who will then take the card to the fraudster typically on a street corner and the fraudster will then go on a spending spree as he or she has your card and PIN.

GRG: It seems strange that people are taken in by this, doesn't it?

MP: The suspects are very convincing and work from scripts and make the victim panic that their card was being used. There has been a common variation with fraudsters claiming to be a police officer and asking for your help to investigate a bank employee at a particular branch. You may be asked to go to your local branch and ask to withdraw a large amount of cash – sometimes thousands of pounds. You are told that the objective is to help in the investigation to identify the corrupt bank staff and you are told not to tell anyone else about what you are doing, as it may compromise the investigation. They will give the victim a cover story to use if they are challenged by bank staff asking why they are taking out so much money. Examples of which are they may tell you to say you are buying a car for your daughter or for a family wedding. This is to make the request more plausible when asked by the bank staff. They may say you are being watched by undercover police and you may get a reward. They have also used this method to get people to remove Euro currency from Bureau de Change supposedly testing that they are passing out counterfeit currency. The victim then returns home and the cash is collected from them.

On other occasions they have got victims to purchase high-value watches from jewellery/watch shops and department stores. Again they tell the victims a number of stories along the lines that the shop is selling fake watches and that they are helping in a Police investigation. There have been variations where the fraudster, pretending to be the police, scams the victim into thinking that their house is being targeted by burglars and persuades you to hand over valuables such as jewellery and electronics.

GRG: We have set out some tests and tips earlier but this emerging scam sounds very sinister. Do have you any further tips?

MP: Your bank or the police will never ask for your PIN, your bank card or ask you to withdraw cash. Never share your PIN with anyone. Never give your bank card or any goods you have purchased as a result of a phone call to anyone who comes to your front door.

The Metropolitan Police Service has highlighted to OFCOM (the phone company regulators) the ability of fraudsters (or anyone else) to hold telephone lines open and, as a result, changes to the telephone systems are being introduced. However, to ensure safety if you are asked to phone back via 999 or a bank to confirm a caller's identity, wait at least five minutes or use a phone that has a different line for instance a mobile phone or neighbour's phone and talk immediately about this to someone you trust.

The Metropolitan Police spokesperson then returned to another of the common scams we featured earlier – the surprise prize-ballot win. Scam lotteries, fake inheritance scams are becoming a real menace and people are losing out. If you reply to just one of these letters you risk being inundated by more and the police spokesperson agreed that your name will form part of a 'suckers list'. This list is then traded amongst scam-mail fraudsters. Genuine lotteries will not ask you to pay a fee to collect your winnings. For more information, please see the links below to the third edition of the little book of big scams: **http://www.met.police.uk/docs/ little_book_scam.pdf**.

The Metropolitan Police also have an audio version and a business edition on their website: **http://content.met.police.uk/Site/fraudalert**.

Advice about scam mail can be found at **www.thinkjessica.com**. The fraud prevention team 'Sterling' is also working with the Royal Mail to prevent scam mail entering the UK and being delivered to UK residents. You can help by reporting it at **scam.mail@royalmail.com** or report concerns by calling 08456 113413.

# Keeping safe from telephone cold calls, e-mail scammers and online fraud

The above examples are just some of the higher-profile and potentially higher-value scams, but there are many more. Some of them you may encounter over the phone and internet on a weekly basis.

Cold callers on the telephone can be irritating at best and sometimes downright scary. They may not take 'no' for an answer. The way these calls are intruding into our life is becoming a real problem.

'Good afternoon, it's John from UK Lifestyle Survey' and he cheer-fully explains that he is representing UK leading energy suppliers and wants to know who your energy supplier is. These calls are just seeking to gather marketing data from you. The data are then sold on and you will be bombarded with more calls and literature after you are put on a 'suckers list'.

'Good morning, we are opening a home improvement shop in the local area and we would like to send you a £1,000 voucher': calls like these are also just seeking to gather marketing data and replying will just cause you to get more and more calls. Use the magic words 'I am signed up to the Telephone Preference Service and you should not be calling this number,' which helps them 'go away'.

The Telephone Preference Service (TPS) is a free service. It is the official central opt-out register on which you can record your preference not to receive unsolicited sales or marketing calls. It is a legal requirement that all organizations (including charities, voluntary organizations and political parties) do not make such calls to numbers registered on the TPS unless they have your consent to do so. You can register your phone number with the telephone preference service by calling 0845 070 0707 or you can do this online at **www.tpsonline.org.uk**. If you are worried about an elderly relative, neighbour or friend who is on their own and could be vulnerable the best thing you could do is talk to them and buy them a telephone that displays the inbound number and, even better, blocks certain numbers including overseas numbers (other than those you want to receive).

## E-mail scammers

The ingenuity and creativity of the e-mail scammers is reaching new heights. Someone somewhere has gathered thousands of e-mail addresses, including yours, and mass-mails them with a piece of information – designed with only one purpose in mind. That purpose is to gain your attention and engagement. All scam e-mails end up the same way, which is you losing out. Maybe they offer a refund from HMRC or it is a bank indicating that the security of your account has been compromised. The e-mail asks you to click on a link and then follow the instructions. The quality of the websites you link to is usually convincing, with lots of branding and official-looking information. Unfortunately, the reality is that they have been built by scammers and they want to steal your money. Never click on any refund links and always check with the organization directly.

Generally try to protect yourself by restricting yourself to known organizations and deal directly with their websites. If it is a UK business they must clearly show the company or business operating the website (usually in the 'contact us' or 'about us' section), which you can then check out. The watchwords here are 'if in doubt... leave them out'.

## Online fraud

The online world offers rich pickings for crooks as the criminal can engage with the victim without having to meet them. They can be sat in an internet café on the other side of the world! This makes it increasingly difficult for law enforcement to trace the suspects' victims who are frequently scammed when trying to make purchases online including vehicles, event tickets and holiday lettings. Criminals also prey on people through dating sites, trying to win the victims' trust and engineer them to send money.

The Metropolitan Police has just investigated a case involving 3,500 victims across the country and indeed the world with a total combined loss of over £10 million. Victims had transferred thousands of pounds into UK bank accounts in the belief that they were buying a vehicle or some other valuable item (maybe a ticket to a prized event) which never turns up. As knowledge is the key in the fight against the scammers a Metropolitan Police spokesperson explained:

MP: Often, there are a series of e-mails going between the suspect and the victim when the victim believes they are building a relationship with the suspect and levels of trust are increased. The criminal uses a name they think will engender trust and a scripted cover story as to why the victim cannot see the vehicle before they buy, ie it is in storage in Scotland. Often the victim is persuaded that any money will go into an escrow/holding account and will only be released once the vehicle has been delivered. They want you to believe the money is safe in the event that anything goes wrong. In reality the bank account the victim pays into has been opened purely for the purpose of receiving fraudulent funds. The victim pays the money but the vehicle is never delivered. When the victim realizes their mistake the money is gone as it gets withdrawn from the account on the same day and you will eventually find out it was opened with false documents using a false address.

GRG: So what can we do to protect ourselves?

MP: Read and follow the fraud prevention advice given on the auction websites themselves. Do not be tempted to stray from that advice. Pay by credit card as that offers some degree of protection for amounts over £100. If the seller refuses to talk over the phone and/or meet with you walk away from the deal. Two of the techniques of the scammers are rushing you (take time out and think) and wanting you to keep things secret (talk it over with a trusted friend). Never let the excitement of a bargain get in the way of applying good common sense and caution. And our most important tip – wealth can be replaced or insured but always consider your personal safety before meeting with someone you have had contact with over the internet – take a friend along or walk away.

The Metropolitan Police Service's Organized Crime Command 'Sterling' has published *The Little Book of Big Scams*. This is now in its third edition and can be viewed online. It has also been given to other forces who are printing their own copies. The booklet can be seen and printed by visiting **http://www.met.police.uk/fraudalert/**. The booklet provides further information on a variety of common frauds and advice on how to prevent you from falling victim.

Reporting fraud can be done online at **www.actionfraud.police.uk** or over the telephone on 0300 123 2040. In an emergency, dial 999. Be assured that the most effective method to combat fraud is to prevent it in the first place. Awareness of common frauds and taking simple action to prevent yourself from falling victim is the most vital thing you can do. We are delighted to be able to help *The Good Retirement Guide 2016* and its ability to spread the word so pass on your copy to an elderly friend or relative so we can all keep people that little bit safer as knowledge is the key to protecting yourself.

### The Financial Ombudsman Service's top tips to fight back against the financial predators that are stalking your wealth

Co-author of this book Allan Esler Smith worked with David Cresswell two decades ago at the then Investors Compensation Scheme (now the Financial Services Compensation Scheme). Allan undertook the investigations and David looked after communications, and his invaluable hints and tips helped to keep investors safe back then. David is now Director of Communications and Insight at the Financial Ombudsman Service and his knowledge on keeping your wealth safe is second to none. David Cresswell's top five tips for our readers are listed below and will continue to help keep investors safe.

1 *Are they regulated?* The Financial Ombudsman Service and Financial Services Compensation Scheme are there to help if the person or company you are dealing with is on the official Financial Conduct Authority (FCA) register and things go wrong.

Because of this added protection you should always check if you are offered investments or pension products or advice if they are on the register at **www.fca.org.uk/register** or phone 0800 111 6768. Both organizations are unlikely to be able to help if the business you think you have been scammed by isn't registered but if you're not sure, call the Ombudsman to ask. But often prevention is better than cure so the further four tips below will help you steer a safer course.

2 *Out of the blue.* They say you have more chance of being repeatedly struck by lightning than you have of winning the lottery. And yet every day hundreds of us receive e-mails claiming that we've won money from a mysterious foreign country, or that we've been selected by a strange organization for a random prize.

Most of us know better than to fall for this. But, in recent years, fraudsters have invested time and effort into making fake e-mails and letters from official organizations look more convincing. These could be messages from your bank, HMRC or even the ombudsman, all asking for you to confirm your personal details. Recently, we've even seen pleas for help that look like they've been sent to you by friends in trouble who need you to send them cash. Don't fall for them. Watch out for questionable e-mail addresses that are either from personal accounts (Gmail, Hotmail) or other countries (check the letters after the 'dot' – as in '.ru' for Russia) and e-mails or letters that fail to address you by your name.

3 *Too much information.* Phone or online banking passwords are often the source of much frustration – but they are a necessary hassle in many ways. Your bank will ask you for random letters, numbers or characters from your password. But they will not ask you to confirm your full password on the phone or ask to know your PIN number. If you're asked for this information, this should be a clear warning that something is wrong. If you're struggling to remember a password – or you're worried your existing ones are too simple, try getting creative, like taking the first letter of each word in a line of your favourite song.

Many people are concerned about 'chip-and-PIN' cards – the ombudsman gets lots of enquiries from people suggesting their card has been cloned. This is extremely unusual. In fact, the most common form of PIN fraud is the most low-tech. Shoulder-surfing – peering over your shoulder at an ATM or when typing in your pin at the local supermarket.

4 *Pry before you buy* – Every year, the number of things we buy online increases dramatically. Crowded shopping centres and stuffy shops mean many of us are going online and bargain hunting. But sometimes we let down our guard when surfing the web. Websites are always competing to offer you the best possible price and it's tempting to think that 'cheapest is best'.

   If you've never used a website before, before you confirm the purchase you should run a quick internet search to check out reviews and see what your fellow consumers are saying. If it seems too good to be true, be sceptical. Regardless, use a form of payment that offers you some protection, such as PayPal or MoneyGram. Alternatively, if you're making a larger payment, your credit card gives you some rights under the Consumer Credit Act if something goes wrong.

5 *Look after yourself.* The easiest way to spot something untoward with your money is to know your finances inside out. Reading your bank statements and knowing what you've got coming in and going out each month is the best way to avoid any cashflow surprises. Most importantly, trust your instincts. If something doesn't feel right it's probably because it isn't.

Hopefully, these tips will help you keep one step ahead of the scammers. But, if something does go wrong, the most important thing is to keep calm. Contact your bank straight away and it may be able to sort things out. If you don't feel like it's being helpful or you're not sure what it should be doing to help, call the ombudsman – they might be able to help. Financial Ombudsman Service: 0300 123 9123; **www.financial-ombudsman.org.uk**.

# Professional advisers

## Choosing an independent financial adviser (IFA)

The role of IFAs has become more important since the number of investment, mortgage, pension protection and insurance products has multiplied and financial decision making has become increasingly complicated. An IFA is the only type of adviser who is able to select from all the investment policies and products on offer in the market-place. It is his or her responsibility to make sure you get the right product for your individual needs. This means they have to gain a full understanding of your circumstances and requirements before helping to choose any financial products.

Common areas where you might want expert help include:

- annuities;
- financial and tax planning and structuring;
- investments;
- mortgages;
- pensions and pension transfers.

Advisers are divided into one of two types:

1 *Independent financial advisers*: IFAs are unbiased and can advise on, and sell, products from any provider right across the market. They are obliged to give 'best advice'.

2 *Restricted advisers*: they specialize in particular providers' products or specific areas of advice. Their 'restricted' status means they can only sell and advise on a limited range of products, or from a limited number of firms.

   Since 31 December 2012, independent and restricted advisers have to charge a fee for investment and pension advice rather than accepting commission. You can pay up front for the adviser's time, rather like an accountant or solicitor, or you can agree a commission-like fee that is deducted from the money you invest in a product purchased through them. Don't worry about asking up front what the cost will be – it is vital – so just take a deep breath and ask the question so that you can compare different IFAs.

When choosing an IFA ask for and consider their qualifications, FCA registration, fee structure, how long they have been in business (and with whom) and convenience. Ask family or friends who they would recommend. Or try talking to some of an IFA's existing clients and don't be afraid to ask for references. Most reputable professionals will be delighted to assist, as it means that the relationship will be founded on a basis of greater trust and confidence.

Most importantly (and worth repeating) check whether your IFA is registered on the FCA's Central Register website: **www.fca.org.uk/register** or phone 0800 111 6768.

To find an IFA near you, look at the Unbiased.co.uk website: **www.unbiased.co.uk**.

Also remember:

- *Get it in writing.* Be sure to get their recommendations in writing. Read them through carefully, and if you don't understand, ask.

- *Final checks.* The decision is yours alone. You do not have to do what they tell you. Make sure their advice is really right for you.

## For your protection

Most financial transactions involving banks, investments, pensions and insurance take place without any problems but sometimes things go wrong. This is where the UK's regulatory regime steps in.

The **Financial Conduct Authority (FCA)** is accountable to the Treasury and aims to make sure the UK financial markets work well so that consumers get a fair deal. It registers individuals and companies that are suitable to work in the industry and checks that they are doing their job properly and fines them if they do a bad job. The FCA has a range of helpful guides and factsheets to help consumers understand the UK's financial markets and the role of the FCA. More at **www.fca.org.uk**.

The **Financial Ombudsman Service (FOS)** is a free service set up by law with the power to sort out problems between consumers and registered financial businesses. It is an impartial service and will investigate your complaint if you have been unable to resolve matters with the registered individual or company (ie registered with the Financial Conduct Authority, as above). If the ombudsman considers the complaint justified it can award compensation. More at **www.financial-ombudsman.org.uk**.

The **Financial Services Compensation Scheme (FSCS)** is the body that can pay you compensation if your financial services provider goes bust. The FSCS is independent and free to access. The financial services industry funds the FSCS and the compensation it pays. There are limits on how much compensation it pays and these are different for different types of financial products. To be eligible for compensation the person or company must have been registered by the Financial Conduct Authority (FCA). More at **www.fscs.org.uk**.

# Other types of advisers

## *Accountants*

Accountants are specialists in matters concerning taxation. Many accountants can also help with raising finance and offer support with the preparation of business plans. Additionally, they may be able to advise on the tax implications of your pensions and investments but are unable to advise on the products themselves unless they are registered with the FCA. When choosing an accountant ask for and consider their qualifications, registration with one of the relevant professional bodies (see below, and did you know that anyone can set themselves up as an accountant without holding any qualifications so this check can be important), fee structure and hourly rate, how long they have been in business (and with whom) and convenience. Check they hold professional indemnity insurance. If you need help in locating a suitable accountant the following will have registers of their members:

- Association of Chartered Certified Accountants (ACCA), website: **www.accaglobal.com**;
- Institute of Chartered Accountants in England and Wales (ICAEW): website: **www.icaew.co.uk**;
- Chartered Accountants Ireland (for both N Ireland and the Republic of Ireland): **www.charteredaccountants.ie**;
- Institute of Chartered Accountants of Scotland (ICAS): website: **www.icas.co.uk**.

Anyone with a complaint against an accountancy firm should contact the company's relevant professional body for advice and assistance – see ACCA, ICAEW, CAI or ICAS, above.

## *Solicitors*

Solicitors are professional advisers on subjects to do with the law or on matters that could have legal implications. Their advice can be invaluable in vetting any important document before you sign it. Often the best way to find a suitable solicitor (if you do not already have one) is through the recommendation of a friend or other professional adviser, such as an accountant. If you need a solicitor specifically for a business or professional matter, organizations such as your local Chambers of Commerce, small business associations, your professional institute or trade union may be able to put you in touch with someone in your area who has relevant experience.

Two organizations to contact for help are: The Law Society, website: **www.lawsociety.org.uk**; and Solicitors for Independent Financial Advice (SIFA), which is the trade body for solicitor financial advisers: **www.sifa.co.uk**.

Unlike accountants where literally anyone can set themselves up as an accountant (hence the importance of the check points outlined above) only solicitors regulated by the Solicitors Regulatory Authority can describe themselves as a solicitor and trade as such (others may seek to skirt around this with such terms as legal services and the like). If you are unhappy about the service you have received from your solicitor, you should first try to resolve the matter with the firm through its complaints-handling partner. If you still feel aggrieved you can approach the Solicitors Regulation Authority: **www.sra.org.uk**.

For practical assistance if you are having problems with your solicitor, you can approach the Legal Services Ombudsman. See the Legal Services Ombudsman website: **www.legalombudsman.org.uk**.

For queries of a more general nature, you should approach the Law Society; see website: **www.lawsociety.org.uk**. For those living in Scotland or Northern Ireland, see The Law Society of Scotland; website: **www.lawscot.org.uk** or The Law Society of Northern Ireland; website: **www.lawsoc-ni.org**, respectively.

## Banks

Banks can provide comprehensive services in addition to the normal account facilities. These include investment, insurance and tax-planning services, as well as how to draw up a will. Regulation and protection is via the FCA, FOS and FSCS regime outlined above.

## Insurance brokers

The insurance business covers a very wide area, from straightforward policies – such as motor or household insurance – to rather more complex areas, including life assurance and pensions. Whereas IFAs specialize in advising on products and policies with some investment content, brokers primarily deal with the more straightforward type of insurance, such as motor, medical, household and holiday insurance. Some brokers are also authorized to give investment advice. A broker will help you to choose the policies best suited to you, assist with any claims, remind you when renewals are due and advise you on keeping your cover up to date.

Regulation and protection is via the FCA, FOS and FSCS regime outlined above.

## Stockbrokers

A stockbroker is a regulated professional broker who buys and sells shares and other securities through market makers or agency-only firms on behalf of investors. A broker may be employed by a brokerage firm. A transaction on the stock exchange must be made between two members of the exchange.

There are three types of stockbroking service:

- *Execution only*: which means the broker will carry out only the client's instructions to buy or sell.

- *Advisory dealing*: where the broker advises the client on which shares to buy and sell, but leaves the financial decision to the investor.

- *Discretionary dealing*: where the stockbroker ascertains the client's investment objectives and then makes all the dealing decisions on the client's behalf.

Roles similar to that of stockbroker include investment adviser and financial adviser. A stockbroker may or may not be an investment adviser. While some stockbrokers now charge fees in the same way as a solicitor, generally stockbrokers make their living by charging commission on every transaction. You will need to establish what the terms and conditions are before committing yourself, as these can vary quite considerably between one firm and another. Nearly all major stockbrokers now run unit trusts.

To find a stockbroker: you can approach an individual through a recommendation or visit the London Stock Exchange website: **www.londonstockexchange.com**, or the Association of Private Client Investment Managers and Stockbrokers (APCIMS) website: **www.apcims.co.uk**.

Regulation and protection is via the FCA, FOS and FSCS regime outlined above.

## Estate agents and letting agents

Some of the biggest financial transactions we entrust to professional advisers are around possibly the biggest asset we own – the house. Things can go wrong and protection and industry standards have been hit-and-miss in the past. The Property Ombudsman is penetrating into this area and has the power to make awards of compensation for loss and/or aggravation, distress and inconvenience. The service is free of charge for the public. Their website at **www.tpos.co.uk** contains all the information that you need for making a complaint to an agent and then bringing that complaint to the the Property Ombudsman if you remain dissatisfied. The website also lists all agents that are members. If an agent is not a member then you are not covered, so why would anyone want to risk one of their biggest transactions to an agent that was not a member? So stay away from any agent (estate agent, letting agent) that is not a member.

# Complaints and 'how to complain'

Things in life inevitably go wrong and sometimes you lose out when it was not your fault. It is always satisfying when you explain your complaint and an organization says: 'We are terribly sorry for the inconvenience we have caused you. Thank you for taking the time to set out your concerns. We have now fixed the issue and it will not happen again and we would like you to accept a bunch of flowers as our way of saying sorry.'

This sort of response is rare and we find it irritating the way more and more companies hide behind websites and it is almost impossible to find someone to speak to directly. Perhaps some businesses will see the benefit of reverting to two-way communications and proper customer care. Many consumers are willing to pay that little bit more for decent service and the assurance that when something goes wrong there will be someone there to do something about it. Perhaps that is one of the reasons for the success of companies such as the John Lewis Partnership.

While *The Good Retirement Guide*'s campaign for better customer service continues, our hints and tips on complaints might just help you to get a better outcome:

- When something goes wrong contact the firm or organization responsible straight away and give them a chance to sort out the problem. It is only fair that they have a chance to look into your complaint as there are usually two sides to any story and perhaps you have simply misunderstood the situation. Clearly state your complaint. Spend time thinking about this beforehand so that you can be clear and concise about what has happened and what you expect. If you are vague and unclear when you complain then you can expect a vague and unclear reply. If you want compensation, state how much and why.

- When you complain, keep a note of who you spoke to, the date and time, and what they said will happen next and by when. Ask whether it would help if you put your complaint in writing.

- If the issue is not resolved, take steps to make it a formal complaint. Ask the organization for the name, address, telephone number and e-mail of the person or department that deals with complaints. Write a letter and head it up 'FORMAL COMPLAINT' in capitals. Spend time getting it factually correct and attach supporting evidence. If it goes beyond two pages it sounds like you could be rambling. Don't worry – we all do this when we feel aggrieved – but it probably means you need to set it aside and come back to it. Reread it and relegate some information to an attachment if it goes beyond two pages. Send it by recorded delivery and keep a copy, together with the post office tracking receipt.

- Take the case further if the organization rejects your complaint and you believe they have not addressed your concerns. Unfortunately some customer relations teams really don't seem to care what you say or how unfairly you have been treated and will just go through a formula approach. At best they may say 'Here are some discount vouchers to use against your next booking...' or words to that effect.

- If you remain dissatisfied, say so, and ask how you can escalate your complaint. Some organizations will try to get rid of you by sending you a 'go away' letter. This needs some explanation. They will say that they have 'fully considered' your complaint and have now exhausted all opportunities to reach a conclusion. The punchline is that they will no longer respond to any further letters or communications from you and they will close their file. At this stage it is up to you to decide whether to give up (that is what they want) or take them to court (but this could be expensive and is it really worth it?).

- But there may be another route. Some organizations have independent assessors and their service is completely free (for instance, Companies House and other quasi government agencies). Some have a free ombudsman service (banks, financial advisers and estate agents as we have signposted above). Others have regulating bodies (solicitors, surveyors and chartered accountants) that may be able to intervene on your behalf. Others have oversight organizations such as Ofcom (mobile phones) or Ofgem (utilities). Help could also be at hand from Citizens Advice, who also have very useful template letters and advice for complainants at **www.adviceguide.org.uk**.

- If there is no external organization, you could choose to use a complaints management service. These, however, charge a fee, so make sure you understand the costs you will have to pay. You could also consider legal proceedings, but again consider the costs you will pay including, perhaps, the other side's costs if the court decides you are wrong.

- Another useful route is to consider if mediation or arbitration is possible. The ABTA arbitration scheme, for example, deals with alleged breaches of contract and/or negligence between consumers and members of ABTA, the travel organization, and has been in operation for over 40 years. The scheme is provided so that consumers can have disputes resolved without having to go to court and without having to go to the expense of instructing solicitors. It is important to understand that arbitration is a legal process; this means that if you do go through arbitration, but are not happy with the outcome, you cannot then go to court. You have to choose one or the other when pursuing your complaint.

- The final and perhaps most important tip is to consider whether or not your complaint is really worth the effort of pursuing. Perhaps an organization has been wrong and you have been dealt with unfairly. You should, of course, think about taking the first step as outlined above. But then do you just vote with your feet and go elsewhere – and tell your friends about it? Sadly I have to report that I have seen complainants who just went on and on (and on) making the same points that had been dealt with by the organization they are complaining against. The complainants then availed themselves of all appeal mechanisms, including involving their MPs. Perhaps they just didn't fully understand the issues or maybe they had too much time on their hands but they just managed to dig themselves into a rut. Obviously, this is to be avoided but then again some organizations create so much havoc with their 'customer don't care' attitude that perhaps we as a Nation should be better at holding them to account, telling our friends and then voting with our feet and being a little bit more un-British from time to time.

We hope this section tunes up your ability to complain more effectively or helps you just to drop the matter and move on. In addition to the Citizens Advice help, mentioned above, there is some further free help available (including letter templates) at the government-funded The Money Advice Service at **www.moneyadviceservice.org.uk** or on the Money Advice Line at 0300 500 5000.

# Further reading

Our top six recommendations for further help, guidance and support on scams and complaints are:

1 *The Little Book of Big Scams*, published by the Metropolitan Police Service, PSNI and other forces. You can download the booklet at **www.met.police.uk/docs/little_book_scam.pdf**.

2 BBC's 'Rip Off Britain' via **www.bbc.co.uk** then 'Rip Off Britain' and then their section on consumer advice.

3 The Money Advice Service offering free, unbiased and independent help via **www.moneyadviceservice.org.uk**.

4 Citizens Advice: **www.adviceguide.org.uk**.

5 The Financial Ombudsman Service website and their 'How to complain' section to help you tackle financial organizations that cause you loss, inconvenience and distress: **www.financial-ombudsman.org.uk/consumer/complaints**.

**6** The Property Ombudsman Service and their consumer guide which sets out what Estate Agents and Letting Agents should do and what you can do if they cause you loss, inconvenience and distress: **www.tpos.co.uk** and search for their Consumer Guide.

# Chapter Five
# Your home

'After my work in the city I like to be at home.
What's the good of a home if you are never in it?'

**CHARLES POOTER, FROM *THE DIARY OF A NOBODY***

**D**id you know that a quarter of all UK property wealth in the UK is owned by the over-60s? This amounts to around £993 billion, according to a survey by a leading insurer, and the value of the average property owned by this section of the population is £272,000 (£6,000 more than the national average). This information was published in a recent edition of *Saga* magazine. Surprised by these statistics? You shouldn't be, housing ownership lies at the very heart of middle-class ambition and for most people in their 50s and 60s their home is their most highly prized possession.

## All you need to know about your home

The three most important issues for those reaching retirement are money, health and property. As a quick guide, this chapter covers in detail all aspects of home and property that you might want to consider now you've reached that point in life. It could be the most important chapter in this book, if you feel that entering retirement is the beginning of the rest of your life. If nothing else, look at the following points which are vital to consider before reading the whole chapter.

- Most important of all is future-proofing your home. In essence this means taking an in-depth look at where you currently live and deciding if you can make it work for you in your retirement.

- If you decide your current home is where you wish to remain, do you have any idea of what to do if you are staying put? Suggestions and help are provided.

- Say you are keen on moving to a new home – there is a helpful list of the pros and cons of taking this course of action.

- You may decide that living in leasehold is right for you, if so, you can find out all about it and other options in this chapter.

- There is much publicity about energy companies and how to keep your bills in check. You'll find lots of help and information and practical suggestions for reducing energy bills here.

- What if your home requires repairs and improvements? There's a section on this and home safety, which could save you time, trouble and money.

- It's never been more important to be up to date on home security and insurance matters. You will find help and advice to steer you through these complex areas.

- Should it be necessary/helpful to use your home to earn money, there are some great ideas on how you can do this. Perhaps this is something that interests you?

- Finally, it is well worth while being informed on available benefits and the issues of taxes. This section is important should any of the information be applicable to your circumstances.

If you read through to the end of the chapter, you could be surprised – it is brimming with ideas and suggestions.

# Future-proofing your home

This is essentially deciding on a plan for the next ten or more years. With life expectancy rising in the UK on average to 78.7 years for men and 82.6 years for women, today's retirees are living longer and staying fitter than previous generations. Most are aware of the need to keep fit and are looking for opportunities to maintain an active and healthy lifestyle. Rather than assuming that retirement means you should contemplate 'downsizing', the current buzzword is now 'rightsizing'.

The way we consider our living environment as we get older is changing. It is important that the property you live in is right for you for the next phase of your life. Ask yourself the following questions:

1 Can you get around your current home safely and manage its upkeep?

2 Do you have good support networks in the area – family, friends and neighbours?

3 Can you get to the places you need and want to go easily – by car, on foot, or by public transport?

4 Are you reasonably confident that this will still be the case in 10 or 15 years, or if your health and other circumstances change?

If the answer is 'no' to some of these questions, it might be the right time to investigate possible alternatives. Even if you don't want to move now, thinking about the possibility will make things easier, should your circumstances change.

## What to do if staying put

Recent **Office for National Statistic** (ONS) figures show that the over-60s are no longer moving to idyllic seaside towns that a decade or more ago seemed to be their ultimate dream. Instead there are powerful reasons why they are choosing to stay put in the same area where they have lived for years. Being close to where they used to work, or near their families for whom they provide 'grandsitting' support (enabling their children to work), staying within reach of friends, where their networks are. Not least being known to your local medical practice (which could prove a blessing in later life when more support may be needed). In essence, it is sometimes wise to respect your roots.

Things you can do to improve your property and maximize its potential include:

- *Extending your property.* If you're considering doing building works, make sure you apply for planning permission if you are adding an extension, and make it as big as permitted. Smaller extensions to the rear or side of a property can often be built without having to make a planning application, provided that the design complies with the rules for permitted development (see **www.planningportal.gov.uk**). Obtain three quotes from contractors and check with friends for recommendations before going ahead. Keep things in proportion – extra bedrooms are no good if there aren't enough bathrooms. Remember, any new work must comply with building regulations. It is wise always to check with your local authority first before committing to any work.

- *Buying the property next door.* If your budget allows, becoming your own neighbour is a great way to increase your property's value. Knocking through allows more space than an extension, without incurring moving costs or leaving the neighbourhood. This option is neither cheap nor simple and professional advice from an architect is essential. Even if you live in a flat you might be able to buy the adjoining unit or the one above or below, then knock through or install a staircase to achieve double living space. Any construction work being undertaken must, of course, adhere strictly to planning and building regulations and you must ensure the project is completed properly. If you can continue to live at the property while work is progressing, this often makes for a smoother and swifter conclusion to the project.

- *Garage conversion.* This is another popular way to increase space in your home and is reasonably simple. If you propose to add a room above your garage, any scheme would be subject to appropriate planning permission being granted. This is needed because of the extra height and alteration to the roof line. Whether your garage is single size or double, attached or detached, this type of extension is one of the quickest 'wins' because you are working with what you've got and you are spared the necessity of digging new foundations. Rooms above a detached garage make an ideal guest suite, office, study, granny or nanny flat (or somewhere to carry on a noisy hobby).

## Moving to a new home – pros and cons

It may sound obvious but many people don't really consider the reasons why they are moving in the first place. Instead they are swayed by seeing a lovely property without thinking how usefully it is situated. You may have bought and sold properties in the past, but when buying possibly your last home it is essential to get things right. There is no *typical* last-time buyer. Some people wish to upgrade because they can afford it and want more space now they are retired, to be able to put up friends, family and grandchildren. Many downsize to release equity and help fund retirement, while others are motivated by lower running costs. If there are mobility issues, bungalows become attractive, as do retirement apartments in buildings with lifts.

**Don't overstretch yourself** on your last purchase because if things go wrong and you have to sell your property in a hurry there's no guarantee you will get the price you want for it.

**Consider downsizing** if your home really is too big for you or you are bored with the gardening. The easier it is for you to get around your property the longer you will be able to stay in it should you get ill or your mobility becomes impaired. It makes sense to consider a property that will last you beyond the next few years.

**Location, location, location** – because it's important to consider access to public transport as you get older. Remember the old saying: 'when you've one foot in the grave make sure the other is on a bus route'? A property within a thriving community gives you access to other people, shops, libraries, doctors and local amenities.

**Get advice** – when it comes to your last-time property purchase it's crucial to seek professional financial, legal and tax advice. There is more about this in Chapter 4.

**Do your research carefully.** Should you decide that a move is for you, even if you think you know an area well, check it out properly before coming to a final decision. If possible, take a self-catering let for a couple of months, preferably out of season when rents are low and the weather is bad. For more information on the area you are interested in look at the Office for National Statistics neighbourhood statistics website: **www.neighbourhoodstatistics.gov.uk**. Another good website to check for potential properties is: Rightmove: **www.rightmove.co.uk**.

**Moving abroad.** If you're planning to retire abroad, you should seriously consider the financial implications. Pensions, tax, buying property in another jurisdiction in a foreign language can be fraught with difficulty. However taken you may be by a location, a great place for a holiday is not always a good place to live permanently.

Some ways of protecting yourself when buying property abroad include:

- Get all documents translated.
- If you are given something to sign, make sure you have a 14-day cooling-off period.
- Take the documents home to the UK and speak to a lawyer and financial adviser over here rather than in the country overseas.
- Make sure the lawyer you use is independent and not involved in the sale in any way.
- Do not use a lawyer recommended by the seller.
- If you are buying a repossessed property, find out what happened.
- If you are borrowing money, go to a reputable bank. The bank manager will want to be sure that the deal is sound – this adds another layer of checks and protection.

There are many websites offering advice and information on retiring abroad. Have a browse through the following:

- **www.gov.uk** – Britons preparing to move or retire abroad;
- **www.propertyinretirement.co.uk** – section on retiring abroad;
- **www.buyassociation.co.uk** – section on advice on retiring abroad and homes abroad;
- **www.retirementexpert.co.uk** – section on retiring abroad and popular locations;
- **www.shelteroffshore.com** – information on living abroad;
- **www.expatfocus.com** – provides essential information and advice for a successful move abroad.

For more information on the financial implications of living overseas, see the section 'Retiring abroad' in Chapter 3.

## Counting the cost

It is estimated that the cost of moving is between 5 and 10 per cent of the value of a new home, once you have added in search fees, removal charges, insurance, stamp duty, VAT, legal fees and estate agents' commission. HM Revenue and Customs' website **www.hmrc.gov.uk** gives information on **Stamp Duty Land Tax** (SDLT). When buying a new home, especially an older property, a full building (structural) survey is essential before committing yourself. This costs upwards of £500 depending on the type and size of property, but it will provide you with a comeback in law should things go wrong. Also helpful to homebuyers, the Land Registry allows members of the public to seek information directly about the 23 million or so properties held on its register via the Land Registry website: **www.landregistry.gov.uk**.

## For your protection

The Property Ombudsman scheme provides an independent review service for buyers or sellers of UK residential property in the event of a complaint. It also covers lettings agents and residential leasehold management. As with most ombudsman schemes, action can be taken only against firms that are actually members of the scheme. See The Property Ombudsman website: **www.tpos.co.uk**.

## Removals

Professional help is essential for anyone contemplating a house move. A reputable firm of removers and shippers will eliminate many of the headaches. A full packing service can save much anxiety and a lot of your time. Costs vary depending on the type and size of furniture, the distance over which it is being moved and other factors, including insurance and seasonal troughs and peaks. The British Association of Removers (BAR) promotes excellence in the removals industry; for approved member firms all of whom work to a rigorous code of practice, see their website: **www.bar.co.uk**.

# Living in leasehold

An ever-increasing number of people move into a flat in retirement. If acquiring a leasehold flat, the freeholder of the building may be an investment company, a private investor, or ideally the leaseholders themselves in the form of a management company. With the advent of 'right to manage', leaseholders do not need to own the freehold but will be able to manage the building as if they were the freeholder.

Leaseholders need to be aware of their responsibilities, such as keeping the inside of their flat in good order, paying their share of the cost of maintaining and running the building, behaving in a neighbourly manner and not contravening things as set out in the lease, such as subletting their flat without the freeholder's prior consent, or keeping a pet when the lease clearly states this is not permitted.

The leaseholder has the right to expect the freeholder to maintain the building and common parts for which the leaseholder will be required to pay a 'service charge' to the freeholder (or their managing agent) to maintain, repair and insure the building as well as to provide other services, such as lifts, central heating or cleaners. These charges must at all times be 'reasonable'. Leaseholders have a right to challenge the service charge if they feel it is 'unreasonable' via the Leasehold Valuation Tribunal (LVT). For further information, see Leasehold Advisory Service (LAS): **www.lease-advice.org** and Association of Retirement Housing Managers (ARHM): **www.arhm.org**.

## Other options

### Caravans or mobile homes

If you want to live in a caravan on land you own, or other private land, you should contact your local authority for information about any planning permission or site licensing requirements that may apply. If you want to keep it on an established site, there is a varied choice. Check carefully, whichever you choose, that the site owner has all the necessary permissions. All disputes, since 30 April 2011 are, under the Mobile Homes Act 1983, being dealt with by residential property tribunals in place of the county court.

### Park mobile homes

These are modern, bungalow-style residential properties, usually sited on private estates. Impartial advice can be obtained from the NCC, the trade body that represents the UK tourer, motor home, holiday home and park home industries (**www.thencc.org.uk**). Before entering into a commitment to purchase a park home, it's well worth visiting an exhibition dedicated to park homes to gain useful information, of which there are several held annually. For further information see websites: **www.parkhomemagazine.co.uk** or **www.parkhome-living.co.uk**.

## Retirement housing and sheltered accommodation

The terms 'retirement housing' and 'sheltered accommodation' cover a wide variety of housing but are designed primarily to bridge the gap between the family home and residential care. There are many well-designed, high-quality private developments of 'retirement homes' now on the market, for sale or rent, at prices to suit most pockets. As a general rule, you have to be over 55 when you buy property of this kind. For full details see Chapter 10 (Taking care of elderly parents).

## *Practical suggestions for reducing your energy bills*

You can save hundreds of pounds on your energy bills according to *Which* magazine (**www.which.co.uk/energy/saving-money/guides/how-to-cut-your-energy-bill**). This is an excellent article, full of vital information, and well worth reading.

Another article which has some great tips for reducing costs is found on the *This is Money* website: **www.thisismoney.co.uk/money/bills/article-2218782/Cut-energy-bills**.

In summary:

- Switching suppliers: it is no longer sensible to be a loyal customer. It really does pay to switch suppliers to save on energy bills.

- Don't forget that just a simple thing like turning down your thermostat can save you money. It is cheaper to wear an extra jumper! According to Age UK, 21 degrees centigrade is the magic number to keep your living room warm, the ideal bedroom temperature is 18 degrees centigrade. For more information see the Age UK website, **www.ageuk.org.uk** and search for 'keeping warm'.

- Turning off the lights when you go out of a room and replacing light bulbs with energy saving ones sounds simple enough. It really can save you money and if you think you might have got into some bad habits, try this tip to see what you can save.

- Closing curtains can cut draughts, so don't let heat disappear through cracks. Check on your windows, doors, chimneys and get draught blockers in place. Find out about the Green Deal and other Government schemes. Visit **www.gov.uk/energy-grants-calculator**.

- If you have to replace any appliances, make sure you choose the most energy-efficient models. Also replacing a gas boiler may be expensive, but it could save you money if it is uneconomical to repair it.

- Check whether you are eligible to claim the winter fuel payment, this is an annual, tax-free benefit paid to people over the age of 61, irrespective of how much they earn. A separate benefit, the cold weather payment, is paid in the event of exceptionally cold weather.

- For further research on saving energy, see Energy Saving Trust: **www.energysavingtrust.org.uk**.

Other organizations which could help:

- Age UK: **www.ageuk.org.uk/keepingwarm**;
- British Standards Institution: **www.bsigroup.co.uk**;
- Cavity Insulation Guarantee Agency (CIGA): **www.ciga.co.uk**;
- Draught Proofing Advisory Association: **www.dpaa-association.org.uk**;
- Glass and Glazing Federation: **www.ggf.org.uk**;
- National Insulation Association: **www.nia-uk.org.uk**.

## Structural repairs and improvements

Having home improvement work done in your home can be a stressful, costly business. Whether the work you are contemplating is complex or simple, here are some top tips to help avoid some of the pitfalls.

- *If your house needs structural repairs* – the Royal Institution of Chartered Surveyors can help you find a reputable chartered surveyor. See website: **www.rics.org**.

- *Before work starts* – Don't forget to contact your Local Authority Planning and Building Control Departments to check if there are any restrictions on what changes can be made.

- *Budgeting, quotes and specifications* – Make a detailed list of everything you would like to have included; compare quotes and check whether value-added tax (VAT). is included in the final cost. Include costs for labour and parts in your overall budget and agree with contractors who will purchase items and have responsibility for their delivery.

- *Finding a trader* – Check your local authority Trading Standards website for details of approved trader schemes. Be clear about whether you need building regulations certificates for any of the work you are doing. Never use anyone who comes to your door cold calling.

- *Contractual information* – Written quotations are essential; they should be broken down to itemize price of work and materials. List work you wish to have done and agree who is responsible if there are delays and who pays. Agree a timetable for the work and how payments will be made.

- *During work* – Agree a single point of contact for the project, and raise issues as they arise. If your local authority Building Control Department has to sign off key stages of the work, check they have done so.

- *Finishing work* – Agreement must be clear as to when the project is to be completed, and when the final payment is required and what it covers. Some money is usually withheld to cover snagging.

With regard to structural work, here are some other useful websites:

- APHC Ltd (Association of Plumbing and Heating Contractors Ltd) holds a national register of licensed members. See website: **www.aphc.co.uk**.

- Chartered Association of Building Engineers can supply names of qualified building engineers/surveyors. See website: **www.cbuilde.com**.

- Building Centre can give guidance on building problems. See website: **www.buildingcentre.co.uk**.

- Federation of Master Builders (FMB): lists of members are available from regional offices. See website: **www.fmb.org.uk**.

- Guild of Master Craftsmen supplies names of all types of specialist craftspeople. See website: **www.guildmc.com**.

- Chartered Institute of Plumbing and Heating Engineering lists professional plumbers. See website: **www.ciphe.org.uk**.

- Royal Institute of British Architects (RIBA) will recommend up to three suitable architects. See website: **www.architecture.com**.

- Scottish and Northern Ireland Plumbing Employers' Federation (SNIPEF) is the national trade association for plumbing and domestic heating contractors in Scotland and Northern Ireland. See website: **www.snipef.org**.

- Trustmark Scheme, which finds reliable, trustworthy tradespeople. See website: **www.trustmark.org.uk**.

- Trading Standards, where you can search for trusted traders in your area. See website: **www.tradingstandards.gov.uk**.

## Safety in the home

Sadly, accidents are most likely to occur at home. The Royal Society for the Prevention of Accidents has some excellent advice and tips, which can be found on the RoSPA (Royal Society for the Prevention of Accidents) website: **www.rospa.com/home-safety/advice/general/preventing-accidents-in-the-home**.

In brief, their advice covers:

- *Fire* – this can damage you, your home and possessions. Better to prevent them from starting. Many fires start in the kitchen. Never leave a pan unattended. Having approved smoke detectors is vital. If a fire starts, RoSPA advises: '... Get out, stay out and call the fire brigade out.'

- *Electricity* – wiring should be checked at least every five years by an approved contractor. If an appliance appears to be faulty, stop using it. When buying electrical equipment look for the CE mark. Don't overload sockets.

- *Heating and cooking* – air vents or airbricks should be kept clean and clear. Did you know that a gas flame normally burns blue? If it burns orange, this may be a build up of carbon monoxide. Appliances should be regularly checked. Be aware of signs of CO poisoning such as drowsiness and flu-like symptoms. If purchasing gas appliances look for the BS safety mark. Should you suspect a gas leak, open windows, turn off supply and call your gas supplier.

  If you smell gas or suspect a carbon monoxide leak – call free on the National Grid 24-hour emergency line free: 0800 111 999.

- *Safety with medicines and cleaners* – medicines and chemicals should be kept in a safe, locked container or cupboard, where children can neither see nor reach them. Leftover medicines should be returned to the pharmacist for destruction.

- *DIY and garden safety* – Enthusiasm and inexperience can be fatal. Wear appropriate protective gear (when barbecuing) or sturdy shoes when mowing the grass. All electrical appliances and tools should be disconnected before working on them. Barbecues should be at a safe distance from trees, buildings and fences. Never pour petrol on a barbecue. Remember some plants and berries are poisonous or can cause an allergic reaction.

The RoSPA *Home Safety Book* (ref HS 178) can be purchased via their online shop. See: **www.rospa.com**.

# Home security

In terms of home security, it pays everyone to ensure they are not at risk from crime. Your local police station will have a crime prevention officer who can advise on home security arrangements and they will be able to tell you whether there are any local Neighbourhood Watch Schemes in operation.

If you are going away, the Royal Mail's 'Keepsafe' service will store your mail so as to avoid it piling up and alerting potential burglars to your absence. There is a charge for the service. See: **www.royalmail.com**.

There is some excellent security advice to be found on the website of The Master Locksmiths Association – see **www.locksmiths.co.uk/faq/ security-advice-for-your-home-top-13-tips**. In brief, these include:

- *Home exterior* – check any broken windows and access via garages or conservatories. Tools and ladders should be locked away.

- *Door and window locks* – all windows and doors should have locks that are in good condition, properly fitted to comply with insurance requirements.

- *Beware opportunist thieves* – should your home look unoccupied, using time switches to control inside lighting is a good deterrent.

- *Sensor lights* – dusk-to-dawn or sensor lighting to the front and rear of your home will deter potential thieves.

- *Security alarms* – remember to regularly change the code as this gains you the maximum benefit.

- *Security grilles or bars* – can protect side windows, or use reinforced glass if window cannot be blocked.

- *Key replacement* – if you haven't replaced locks recently it's possibly time you did. If you ask a professional locksmith to fit a patented system, you will have the reassurance that keys can only be copied with proof of ownership.

- *Garden shed* – A good quality lock or padlock will protect your garden shed and its contents.
- *Car keys at risk* – thieves often break into homes to steal car keys. Don't make it easy for them – put your keys out of sight.

If you want to know of a reputable locksmith, you should contact the Master Locksmiths Association; website: **www.locksmiths.co.uk**. The BBC *Crimewatch* Roadshow (**www.bbc.co.uk/crimewatchroadshow**) also offers tips on staying safe.

Age UK Advice provides a booklet *Staying Safe*. See website: **www.ageuk.org.uk**.

# Insurance

According to recent research, 7 out of 10 householders are under insured. Reassessing your policy makes sense for two reasons: first, because the number of burglaries has risen, so the risks are greater; second, you may be able to obtain better value than you are getting at present. A number of insurance companies now give discounts on house contents premiums if proper security precautions have been installed.

If you are planning to move into accommodation that has been converted from one large house into several flats or maisonettes, check with the landlord or managing agent that the insurance on the structure of the total building is adequate. When buying a new property you are under no obligation to insure your home with the particular company suggested by your building society.

Owners of properties in flood-prone areas in the UK have difficulty getting insurance. It is advisable to check whether you live in a high-risk area and, if so, take steps to protect your property. Information on flood-risk areas and how to get help in obtaining insurance can be found on the Environment Agency website: **www.environment-agency.gov.uk**.

## Buildings Insurance

If your buildings and contents insurance was originally arranged through your building society, it may cease when your mortgage is paid off. If you buy a house with cash – for instance when moving to a smaller home – it is advisable to get a qualified assessor to work out the rebuilding costs and insurance value of your new home. The cost of replacing the fabric of your house, were it to burn down, could possibly be significantly greater than the amount for which it is currently insured. Remember, you must insure for the full rebuilding cost: the market value may be inappropriate. Your policy should also provide money to meet architects' or surveyors' fees, as well as alternative accommodation for you and your family if your home were completely destroyed by fire.

If you rent your home, it is up to your landlord to arrange buildings insurance. If you own your own home, it is up to you. Even if you no longer have a mortgage, make sure your home is insured. The Royal Institution of Chartered Surveyors' (RICS) Building Cost Information Service (BCIS), provides cost information on all aspects of construction. It has an online calculator at **www.rics.co.uk** to estimate how much cover you need.

## Contents Insurance

It is important to have the right level of cover. Once you stop work, you may need to review the value of your home contents. With older possessions, you should assess the replacement cost and make sure you have a 'new-for-old' or 'replacement as-new' policy. Cancel items on your contents policy that you no longer possess and add new valuables that have been bought or received as presents. In particular, do check that you are adequately covered for any home improvements you may have added.

Where antiques and jewellery are concerned, a professional valuation is wise. See British Antique Dealers' Association (BADA) website: **www.bada.org**; or Association of Art and Antiques Dealers (LAPADA), website: **www.lapada.org**. Photographs of particularly valuable items can help in the assessment of premiums and settlement of claims. Property marking, for example with an ultraviolet marker, is another useful ploy, as it will help the police trace your possessions should any be stolen.

Further advice can be obtained from the Association of British Insurers: **www.abi.org.uk**. and the British Insurance Brokers' Association **www.biba.org.uk**. Some insurance companies offer home and contents policies for older people at substantially reduced rates. Such as:

- www.rias.co.uk;
- www.castlecover.co.uk;
- www.ageuk.org.uk;

- **www.staysure.co.uk;**
- **www.50plusinsurance.co.uk;**
- **www.saga.co.uk.**

Financial institutions are keen on 'loyalty marketing' but loyalty should work both ways. Don't stay with a provider out of loyalty. Nowadays *disloyalty* pays because the winners are those customers who constantly switch from one provider to another.

## Using your home to earn money

Your home doesn't have to be a drain on your finances, if you need some spare cash or a regular source of income, there are several ways you could make money from your home. Some good ideas can be found on the Moneywise website: **www.moneywise.co.uk/work-wages/make-more-money/10-ways-to-turn-your-home-into-a-goldmine.**

Very briefly, here are some ideas to consider:

- *Rent a room scheme* – the Government's 'Rent a Room' scheme allows you to earn up to, from 6 April 2016, £7,500 a year tax-free for letting out a room in your main home. £625 a month is the maximum rental income you can receive in rent without having to fill in any tax forms. If you earn more than that, you will have to fill out a self-assessment form and pay income tax on the rent above that amount. For more information see: HMRC website: **www.hmrc.gov.uk.** If you live in a suitable area, you could find a commuting lodger who only wants the room on week nights, see websites such as **Monday to Friday.**

- *Rent out your drive* – some areas of the UK are chronically short of available parking for people going to work or travelling from a nearby airport. You can rent out your drive using websites like **Park At My House, Just Park** or **Park On My Drive.** Top parking spaces can make several hundred pounds a month, though £50 or thereabouts is more usual.

- *Your home in lights* – it is possible to rent out your home as a film or TV set, particularly if it is quirky or charming. You can list your home via an online agency, **Film Locations** or **Amazing Space,** though it will take a fee if your home is used.

- *Host students* – offer your home as a base for a foreign language or exchange student. This pays typically £100 per week. Contact your local language schools, colleges and universities to see if they offer a pairing service for would-be lodgers and hosts.

- *Holiday lets* – If you own a home in the country, renting it out for holiday lets can be profitable as long as certain conditions are met. To qualify, the property must be in the UK, be available for at least 140 days during the tax year and actually be let for at least 70 days. For more information on financial responsibilities see Money Advice Service.

    Further information on this subject can be found in *The Complete Guide to Letting Property*, by Liz Hodgkinson, published by Kogan Page (website: **www.koganpage.com**).

# Benefits and taxes

## Housing Benefit

If you rent your property and have less than £16,000 in savings you may be able to get financial help from your local council. For advice contact your Local Authority or Citizens Advice Bureau. The amount of benefit you receive depends on several factors: the number of people in the household, your eligible rent, your capital or savings, your income and your 'applicable amount' (which is the amount the government considers you need for basic living expenses). If you think you may be eligible, contact your Council for an application form or apply on line. For further information see **www.gov.uk** – Benefits.

## Council Tax

This is based on the value of the property you live in and also consists of a personal element. Most domestic properties are liable for council tax, including rented property, mobile homes and houseboats. The value of the property is assessed according to a banding system. Not everyone pays council tax. The bill, which is sent out in April each year is normally sent to the resident owner or to the tenant. The valuation of each property assumes that two adults are resident. The charge remains the same if there are more adults. However, if there is a single adult only living in the property, the bill is reduced by 25 per cent. For further information see **www.gov.uk** – Council Tax.

Exemptions from Council Tax include:

- property that has been unoccupied and unfurnished for less than six months;
- the home of a deceased person; the exemption lasts until six months after the grant of probate;
- a home that is empty because the occupier is absent in order to care for someone else;
- the home of a person who is or would be exempted from council tax because of moving to a residential home, hospital care or similar.

Empty properties in need of major repairs or undergoing structural alteration can be exempt for an initial period of six months, but this can be extended for a further six months. After 12 months, the standard 50 (or possibly full 100) per cent charge for empty properties will apply.

Granny flats that are part of another private domestic dwelling may be exempt, but this depends on access and other conditions. To check, contact your local Valuation Office.

## Disputes

If you are responsible for paying the council tax on a property that you feel has been wrongly banded, you have six months to appeal and can request that the valuation be reconsidered. If you have grounds for appeal, you should take up the matter with the Valuation Office. If the matter is not resolved, you can then appeal to an independent valuation tribunal. For advice and further information, contact your local Citizens Advice Bureau.

## Council Tax Benefit

This may be available to you if you are on a low income and cannot afford to pay council tax. People on Pension Credit (Guarantee Credit) are entitled to rebates of up to 100 per cent. Even if you are not receiving any other social security benefit, you may still qualify for some Council Tax Benefit. The amount you get depends on your income, savings, personal circumstances, who else lives in your home (in particular whether they would be counted as 'non-dependants') and your net council tax bill (ie after any deductions that apply to your home). For further information see: Citizens Advice Bureau: **www.citizensadvice.org.uk**.

# Chapter Six
# Health

'If you want a cure for a cold, put on two pullovers, take up a baton, poker or pencil, tune the radio to a symphony concert, stand on a chair, and conduct like mad for an hour or so and the cold will have vanished. It never fails. You know why conductors live so long? Because we perspire so much.'

**SIR JOHN BARBIROLLI**

Did you know that life expectancy for men in the 1950s was 65? So six decades ago men didn't have much time to enjoy their retirement. Women lived slightly longer, but didn't have the benefits that pensioners have today. The average person now lives about a third longer than 50 years ago. Since the establishment of the National Health Service in 1945 things have changed enormously – for the better. Some examples of major developments in healthcare in the last 70 years include new drugs, organ transplants, micro, keyhole and joint replacement surgery. Diseases that would have been fatal in 1945 are now usually treatable, and in many cases curable. New retirees should be more satisfied with life as they are probably wealthier and healthier than previous generations. Research shows that as our standard of living rises, so does our generosity. We now give more of our earnings to charity than our grandparents did, compared with any time in the past half century. Would you not agree that there are many reasons to be cheerful in retirement today and much to be grateful for?

## All you need to know about your health, and how to maintain it

This chapter is important reading – if for no other reason than that if you take on board some of the advice it contains, it could literally add years to your happy retirement. As we age, it gets harder to change one's habits. However, if we do as we've always done, we'll get what we've always got. So for starters, have a think about what you would like to do differently now you are in retirement. As the saying goes, use it or lose it!

- *Keep fit at all costs.* Get moving as much as you can. Exercise is one of the greatest benefits to good health, so fight the urge towards a sedentary lifestyle in retirement. This chapter shows you what options and choices you have and how achievable they are.

- *You are what you eat.* Is this true of you? Be honest! There is a great section on health and diet and tips and hints on how to eat more healthily now that you have more time to spare. Don't avoid the issue, taking action could add years to your life.

- *Be weather wise.* Tips included in this chapter cover what to do in the heat and tips on food safety. All sensible advice and well worth adopting some of these suggestions if you value your health and wellbeing.

- There are sections on *drink (alcohol) and smoking, as well as accident prevention.* You can never be too careful. Aches, pains and other abnormalities highlight some areas well worth paying attention to. Prevention is always better than cure.

- If you already have, or are considering taking out, *health insurance*, there is some good advice on this topic. In addition there is information about long-term care insurance, and income protection insurance too.

- You may already have had some *health screening checks*. If not, when new to retirement this may well give you some peace of mind. There are also sections on the NHS and advice about going into hospital.

- *Complementary and alternative medicine* may not be for you, but if you want to find out more about it, there are sections on this which might prove interesting reading.

- It pays to look after what you've got: so pay attention to the sections on eyes, feet, hearing, sleep, teeth, and personal relationships.

- Finally, this chapter covers the issue of depression (which can affect a large number of newly retireds) and also gives information on some common disorders.

Why not get reading? You should soon start feeling a lot healthier.

'If you always do what you've always done, you'll always get what you've always got' are words attributed to Henry Ford. There's nothing wrong with doing what we've always done if it's enjoyable, but if we're not careful, remaining in our comfort zone can become a rut. We need variety, stimulation and challenge to get the most out of life. Fitness trainers advise gym users to vary their workout routines to avoid reaching a plateau and getting stuck there.

In retirement, one of the most important things is to keep fit and healthy for as long as we can. According to the website **nidirect.gov.uk** guide to health and fitness for the over-50s, making sure you exercise regularly and keep an eye on what you eat is of real importance. So perhaps a few changes in your daily routine (now that you've retired and have a little more time) could go a long way to improving your physical and mental health. It makes sense for all of us to look after ourselves and not take our health for granted.

# Keeping fit

Staying physically active improves our health and quality of life, and can help us live longer. Physical activity can include everyday tasks, like housework, gardening or dog walking or can involve specific exercise like swimming, golf, gym-based activities or sports such as tennis or football. Anything that makes you a bit out of breath, and gets your heart and pulse pumping faster than usual is beneficial.

The benefits of keeping active include a reduced risk of developing a life-threatening disease; a better chance of maintaining or reaching a healthy weight; improved sleep and increased daytime energy; feeling happier and keeping your brain sharp. The more physically active you are, the longer you are likely to remain independent. Exercise makes you stronger, boosts confidence and increases a sense of well-being.

If you haven't done any exercise for years, speak to your doctor before starting any fitness programme. It is best to start slowly and build up gradually. Experts recommend thirty minutes of moderate exercise a day about five times a week. It's easy to boost your physical activity by incorporating some of the following into your everyday life:

- walking up stairs (don't use the lift or escalator);
- get off the bus a stop or two earlier and walk home;

- vacuum the house;
- clean the car by hand;
- play games with the grandchildren;
- take a walk with friends.

(*Source:* **nidirect.gov.uk.**)

# Organized activities

There are lots of ways of staying fit and lots of classes to help you do it. In some local areas there may be free, or cut-price sessions at your local sports or leisure centre. The following three websites are where you can find online exercise classes if this appeals to you:

- Fitness Blender offers more than 400 free workout videos, ranging from high-intensity interval training to yoga: **www.fitnessblender.com.**
- Crunch Live is the online outpost of New York's Crunch Gym. The classes put a premium on high-energy 'entertainment' but they also cover more sensible basics, including aerobics and core fitness: **www.crunchlive.com.**
- Pilatesology covers classes for all needs; the only kit required is a mat: **www.pilatesology.com.**

(*Source: The Sunday Times*)

The following websites will give you information on classes and other choices available to you:

- Extend: **www.extend.org.uk;**
- Fitness League: **www.thefitnessleague.com;**
- Keep Fit Association: **wwwkeepfit.org.uk;**
- Medau Movement: **www.medau.org.uk;**
- Pilates Foundation: **www.pilatesfoundation.com;**
- British Wheel of Yoga: **www.bwy.org.uk;**
- Yoga for Health and Education Trust (YHET): **www.yoga-health-education.org.uk;**
- Yoga Village UK: **www.yogauk.com.**

# Healthy eating

If you want to improve your quality of life and avoid diseases associated with ageing, sensible eating is the best way forward. As we age our metabolic rate slows down so age-related weight gain will occur if we don't adjust our diet or increase the amount we exercise. We need fewer calories in our 50s and 60s than we did in our 30s. Eating a balanced diet and not overeating is important. To get the best from your diet, follow these suggestions:

- Eat at least five portions of fruit and vegetables a day.
- Base meals on starchy foods like bread, potatoes, rice or pasta.
- Drink plenty of water and cut out fizzy, sugary drinks.
- Limit consumption of saturated fats.
- Eat more fish.
- Drink less alcohol.
- Limit your salt intake.

(*Source:* **nidirect.gov.uk**.)

Should you be advised to lose weight, there are weight loss programmes to help you. Here are two websites, should you want to kick-start a weight-loss regime:

Slimming World: **www.slimmingworld.com** and Weight Watchers: **www.weightwatchers.com**.

# How to keep healthy in the heat

In the very hot weather there are certain groups of people who are at risk: the very young, the elderly and the seriously ill, as heat can make heart and breathing problems worse. As long as we take sensible precautions, most of us can safely enjoy hot weather. The main risks posed by a heatwave are: dehydration (not having enough water), overheating, heat exhaustion and heatstroke. The website **www.nhs.uk/Livewell/Summerhealth** offers some tips for coping in hot weather:

- Shut windows and pull down blinds when it is hot outside.
- Stay inside during the hottest time of the day.

- Take cool baths or showers.

- Drink cold drinks regularly: avoid tea, coffee and alcohol.

- Wear loose, cool clothing and take a sun hat when outdoors.

- Keep an eye on friends, relatives and neighbours who may be less able to look after themselves.

# Food safety

One disadvantage of age is that we become more vulnerable to bugs and germs from incorrectly prepared food. As our immune system weakens, it is harder to fight off bacteria and serious illness. Once a foodborne illness is contracted, the infections can be difficult to treat. Many such illnesses have virus-like symptoms, which could lead to dehydration if not properly treated. The good news is there are some simple, sensible precautions that can be taken to avoid such happenings. The Food Standards Agency (FSA) recommends the four 'C's:

- cleaning;

- cooking;

- chilling;

- cross-contamination (avoiding it).

They also recommend that you stick to a food's 'use by' date and the storage instructions on the packet.

For detailed information on prevention of food poisoning, see NHS Choices website: **www.nhs.uk/Conditions/Food-poisoning/Pages/Prevention.aspx**.

In summary, their suggestions include:

- *Cleaning* – The spread of harmful bacteria and viruses can be minimized by maintaining good personal hygiene standards and keeping work surfaces and utensils clean. Regularly wash hands with soap and warm water before preparing food, after handling raw food and after touching bins or pets. If you are ill with stomach problems do not handle food.

- *Cooking* – In order to kill any harmful bacteria that might be present, it is important to cook food thoroughly, particularly meat and most types of seafood. Food that is cooked thoroughly should be steaming hot in the middle. When re-heating food, make sure it is steaming hot all the way through, and do not re-heat food more than once.

- *Chilling* – Certain foods need to be kept at the correct temperature to prevent harmful bacteria from growing and multiplying. Your fridge should be set to 0–5 degrees Celsius (32–41 degrees Farenheit). Cooked leftovers should be cooled quickly and then put in the fridge or freezer.

- *Cross-contamination* – This occurs when bacteria are transferred from raw foods to other foods. To prevent cross-contamination always wash your hands after handling raw food. Raw meat should be stored in sealable containers at the bottom of the fridge so it cannot drip on to other foods. Chopping boards, knives and other utensils should be thoroughly washed after using them with raw food. Do not wash raw meat or poultry – any harmful bacteria will be killed by thorough cooking, and washing may splash harmful bacteria around the kitchen.

(*Source*: NHS)

# Drink

If unwinding at the end of the day with a glass of wine is something you have been used to, there is no reason to give up this pleasure. However, the more you drink the greater the risk to your health. If you want to check how many units of alcohol you are drinking each week it is simple to do using the NHS Change4Life drinks checker on: **www.nhs.uk/change4life/**.

Should you think it sensible to cut down a bit, the benefits in doing so include: feeling better in the mornings, having more energy and feeling less tired in the day, saving money and reducing your calorie intake. If you drink every day, you could try having two days a week when you don't drink alcohol.

For people who suspect they may have a drinking problem, the first point of contact should be their GP. There are organizations to help those in need of support, such as:

- Al-Anon Family Groups UK and Eire: **www.al-anonuk.org.uk**;

- Alcohol Concern: **www.alcoholconcern.org.uk**;

- Alcoholics Anonymous: **www.alcoholics-anonymous.org.uk**.

# Smoking

It's no secret, smoking is bad for your health; quitting makes life better, according to the NHS website: **www.nhs.uk/Livewell/smoking**. The benefits of stopping smoking include slower facial ageing, healthier teeth and gums, improved lung capacity and longer life. There's a lot of help for those thinking of giving up the habit, and many websites to check. The following five have good advice:

1 NCSCT (National Centre for Smoking Cessation and Training): **www.ncsct.co.uk**;

2 Quit: **www.quit.org.uk**;

3 Smokefree: **www.nhs.uk/smokefree**;

4 Smokeline (Scotland only): **www.canstopsmoking.com**;

5 Stop Smoking UK: **www.stopsmokinguk.org**.

# Accident prevention

The prevention of accidents – particularly those likely to occur in the home – is something we should all be aware of. There is a section in Chapter 5 – Your home, which deals with this in detail. There is further advice on safety issues to be found in Chapter 10 – Taking care of elderly parents. For anyone who feels at risk of accidents, the best advice is to consult your GP. He/she will be able to assess whether any medical problems you suffer from could make you more vulnerable, such as sleep disorders, diabetes or epilepsy. There is some good general advice to be found on this website: **www.patient.co.uk/doctor/accidents-and-their-prevention**. RoSPA (Royal Society for the Prevention of Accidents) also has some excellent advice on this subject: **www.rospa.com/home safety**.

Should you be unlucky enough to be injured in an accident, whether in the street or elsewhere, the National Accident Helpline, may be able to help with claiming compensation: **www.national-accident-helpline.co.uk**.

# Aches, pains and other abnormalities

Recognizing signs of illness, at whatever age, is difficult. We are warned that it can take up to three weeks to actually see our GP, yet we are told not to clog up the nearest hospital's A&E department with minor complaints. Many people do not recognize warning signs when things are wrong as these can vary hugely from person to person. For example, chest pain is the most common symptom of a heart attack in both men and women, yet some people will not experience chest pain at all. Heartburn can be so severe it may be mistaken for a heart attack. Knowing the signs and what to look out for is essential. Use the NHS 111 service for non-emergency calls. Trained advisers, supported by healthcare professionals, will ask you questions to assess your symptoms and immediately direct you to the best medical care for you. NHS 111 is available 24 hours a day, 365 days a year. Calls are free from landlines and mobile phones. For less-urgent health needs, contact your GP or local pharmacist for advice.

The following symptoms should always be investigated by a doctor:

- any pain that lasts more than a few days;
- lumps, however small;
- dizziness or fainting;
- chest pains, shortness of breath or palpitations;
- persistent cough or hoarseness;
- unusual bleeding from anywhere;
- frequent indigestion;
- unexplained weight loss.

# Health insurance

The UK is one of the few places in the world that has a universal free health service, so why would anyone choose to pay for medical care? The main reasons (according to Bupa) are avoidance of long waiting lists and fear of superbugs and hospital cleanliness. Private medical insurance (PMI) allows you to avoid long queues for treatment, receive fast-track consultations, and be treated privately in an NHS or private hospital.

PMI is not essential, but if you have disposable income and your finances are in order, it can buy you peace of mind. Not every eventuality is covered by PMI so it is important to check your policy details. The following are some of the best known organizations that provide PMI cover:

- Aviva: **www.aviva.co.uk**;
- AXA PPP Healthcare: **www.axappphealthcare.co.uk**;
- Bupa: **www.bupa.co.uk**;
- Exeter Family Friendly Society: **www.exeterfamily.co.uk**;
- Prudential: **www.pruhealth.co.uk**;
- Saga: **www.saga.co.uk**;
- simplyhealth: **www.simplyhealth.co.uk**.

## Choosing a scheme

With so many plans on the market, seeking advice from a specialist insurance broker or intermediary is the best way to ensure you get the right health insurance policy for you. Here are two websites to investigate: Association of Medical Insurance Intermediaries (AMII): **www.amii.org.uk** and Private Healthcare UK: **www.privatehealth.co.uk**.

## Private patients – without insurance cover

If you do not have private medical insurance but want to go into hospital in the UK as a private patient, there is nothing to stop you, provided your doctor is willing and you are able to pay the bills from your savings. The choice if you opt for self-pay lies between the private wings of NHS hospitals or hospitals run by charitable or non-profit-making organizations, such as: BMI Healthcare: **www.bmihealthcare.co.uk** and Nuffield Health: **www.nuffieldhealth.com**.

## Medical tourism

The term 'medical tourism' refers to travellers who have chosen to have medical/dental/surgical treatment abroad. Cosmetic surgery, dental procedures and cardiac surgery are the most common procedures that medical tourists undertake.

Since the standards of medical treatments and available treatments vary widely across the world, anyone considering undertaking medical treatment abroad should carry out their own independent research. Further information and advice can be found here:

- **www.nhs.uk/NHSEngland/Healthcareabroad**;

- **www.themedicaltouristcompany.com**;

- **www.treatmentabroad.com**.

# Long-term care insurance (LTCI)

Paying for care in old age is a growing issue. Long-term care insurance provides the financial support you need if you have to pay for care assistance for yourself or a loved one. Although Government state benefits can provide some help, the level of support you receive will depend on where in the UK you live.

There are a number of different types of long-term care plans which makes it difficult to know what would be best. Future planning involves anticipating unknowns: who is most likely to need long-term care, and for how long. Before deciding what you need, it is essential to obtain good advice. SOLLA, The Society of Later Life Advisers can help (**www.societyoflaterlifeadvisers.co.uk**), or an IFA through APFA, the Association of Professional Financial Advisers (**www.apfa.net**). In addition, there are three main providers of care annuities:

- Partnership Assurance: **www.partnership.co.uk**;

- Just Retirement: **www.justretirement.com**;

- Friends Life: **www.friendslife.co.uk**.

A useful booklet, *A Brief Guide to Long-Term Care Insurance, Choosing the right option for you*, is available from Association of British Insurers (ABI): **www.abi.org.uk**.

A possible alternative to a conventional long-term care policy is critical illness insurance, which pays a lump sum if you are unfortunate enough to suffer from cancer or have a stroke.

## Hospital care cash plans

A healthcare cash plan is an insurance policy that lets you claim back the cost of treatments, such as eye tests, dental treatment and physiotherapy. You pay a monthly premium, sometimes as little as £5. When you receive the treatment you send the receipt to the insurer and it reimburses you, depending on the terms of your policy. More information available from British Health Care Association: **www.bhca.org.uk**.

# Income protection (IP)

Income protection insurance (IP) used to be known as Permanent Health Insurance (PHI). It is a replacement-of-earnings policy for people who are still in work. While highly recommended for the self-employed, many employees have some protection under an employer's policy. Either way, if you are close to retirement, IP is unlikely to feature on your priority list.

# Health screening

Personalized health assessments are a wise investment because they give an overview of your current general health and aim to identify any future health risks. Private health screening, outside the NHS, can give people peace of mind that they are not suffering from a serious health problem. There are a number of health assessment options depending on your personal needs, covering key lifestyle and health risks. For more information see:

- **www.bmihealthcare.co.uk**;
- **www.bupa.co.uk**;
- **www.privatehealth.co.uk**.

# National Health Service

## Choosing a GP

If you need to choose a new GP for whatever reason, it is important to find a good one. There was a great article in *The Oldie* magazine

(December 2014) by Dr Tom Stuttaford entitled 'How to spot a bad physician'. The essential quality of a good GP, according to him is:

> ... one who is interested in individual patients, their minds as well as their bodies. They must enjoy meeting and talking with them, whatever their background, age, intellect, gender and supposed vices or beliefs. In short, an effective GP is one who cares enough to listen...

The best way to find such a paragon is to ask for recommendations. Otherwise following the advice given on the website: **www.nhs.uk/ choiceintheNHS/** is a good starting point. It will help you find a suitable practice, and give you the information you need before registering with your new doctor.

## Changing your GP

If you want to change your GP, you go about it in exactly the same way. If you know of a doctor whose list you would like to be on, you can simply turn up at his or her surgery and ask to be registered. You do not need to give a reason for wanting to change, and you do not need to ask anyone's permission.

## NHS 111 service

The 111 service is the NHS's non-emergency number. It's fast, easy and free. When you call 111, you will speak to an adviser, supported by healthcare professionals, who will ask a number of questions to assess symptoms and direct you to the best medical care available. NHS111 is available 24 hours a day, 365 days a week. Calls are free from landlines and mobile phones. For further information see: **www.nhs.uk**.

## Help with NHS costs

Although treatment on the NHS is free, there may be some additional costs, such as your journey to hospital. The NHS Low Income Scheme (LIS) or Universal Credit may be able to help you. There is more information to be found on: **www.nhs.uk/NHSEngland/Healthcosts**. If you live in Scotland, see: **www.scotland.gov.uk/healthcosts**.

## Prescriptions

The current prescription charge is £8.20 but both men and women aged 60 and over are entitled to free NHS prescriptions. Certain other groups are also entitled to free prescriptions, including those on low income. Leaflet HC12 NHS 'Help with Healthcosts' gives full information. There are also PPCs (Prescription prepayment certificates) which can save you money if you require a lot of medication on a regular basis. See **www.nhs.uk/nhsengland/healthcosts** or, if you live in Scotland, **www.scotland.gov.uk/healthcosts**.

## Going into hospital

Going into hospital can cause people a lot of anxiety. Many patients are unaware that they can ask their GP to refer them to a consultant at a different NHS trust or even, in certain cases, help make arrangements for them to be treated overseas. Before you can become a patient at another hospital, your GP will need to agree to your being referred. Those likely to need help on leaving hospital should speak to the hospital social worker, who will help make any necessary arrangements. Help is sometimes available to assist patients with their travel costs to and from hospital.

If you go into hospital you will continue to receive your pension as normal. Your pension – as well as Employment and Support Allowance, Severe Disablement Allowance, Income Support and Pension Credit Guarantee Credit – will continue to be paid in full, without any reductions, for the duration of your stay. For full information see **www.nhs.uk**. You can access NHS Northern Ireland, NHS Scotland and NHS Wales websites and information from this site.

## Complaints

If you want to make a complaint about any aspect of NHS treatment you have received or been refused, go to the practice or the hospital concerned and ask for a copy of their complaints procedure. This is the same for GPs, opticians, dentists, hospitals and any care given in the NHS. Full details of how to do this can be found on NHS Choices: **www.nhs.uk/choiceinthenhs/rightsandpledges/complaints**.

You can take the matter to the Health Services Ombudsman should you be dissatisfied after an independent review has been carried out. For further details see:

- Parliamentary and Health Service Ombudsman for England: **www.ombudsman.org.uk**;
- Public Services Ombudsman for Wales: **www.ombudsman-wales.org.uk**;
- Scottish Public Services Ombudsman: **www.spso.org.uk**.

An alternative would be to get in touch with your local PALS (Patient Advice and Liaison Service) office in the event of a problem with the health service which can be found via the NHS Choices website: **www.nhs.uk/choiceinthenhs**.

# Complementary and alternative medicine

Complementary and alternative medicines are treatments that fall outside mainstream healthcare. Although 'complementary and alternative' medicines (CAMs) are often used as a single category, there are distinct differences between them. Complementary medicine is a complementary treatment that is used alongside conventional medicine, whereas alternative medicine is a treatment used in place of conventional medicine. The best known of these practices are Homoeopathy, Reflexology, Osteopathy, Chiropractic, Aromatherapy, Herbal remedies and Hypnosis.

For further information and fuller descriptions see the NHS Choices website: **www.nhs.uk/Livewell/complementary-alternative-medicine/Pages/**.

Information on the most popular forms can be found on the following websites:

- Association of Reflexologists: **www.aor.org.uk**;
- British Acupuncture Council (BacC): **www.acupuncture.org.uk**;
- British Chiropractic Association: **www.chiropractic-uk.co.uk**;
- British Homoeopathic Association: **www.britishhomeopathic.org**;
- British Hypnotherapy Association: **www.hypnotherapy-association.org**;
- General Osteopathic Council: **www.osteopathy.org.uk**;
- International Nature Cure Society: **www.naturecuresociety.org**;
- National Institute of Medical Herbalists: **www.nimh.org.uk**.

# Eyes

Did you know that eyes rarely hurt when there's a problem? Like most other parts of the body, it pays not to neglect them, and regular eye tests are a sensible precaution as we get older. You will find out a lot more than whether or not you need new glasses, your sight test is an important eye health check. Some of the most common eye problems include: difficulty reading, floaters, cataracts, glaucoma, macular degeneration. Some people on low incomes can get help with costs of eye tests, people with mobility problems can request an eye test in their own home. People who are registered blind are entitled to a special tax allowance: for 2015/16 it is £2,290.

For more information on matters relating to sight, see:

- Royal National Institute of Blind People (RNIB): **www.rnib.org.uk**;
- International Glaucoma Association: **www.glaucoma-association.com**;
- Partially Sighted Society: **www.partsight.org.uk**;
- BT: **www.bt.com/includingyou**;
- British Wireless for the Blind: **www.blind.org.uk**;
- Calibre Audio Library: **www.calibre.org.uk**;
- Talking News Federation: **www.tnf.org.uk**.

# Feet

You only get one pair of feet so it's essential to take good care of them. Looking after your feet is one of the most important aspects of personal health care whatever your age, as unhappy feet can cause mobility problems. Foot health is particularly significant for people with diabetes. To make sure your feet stay fit you need to keep them clean, warm and well supported. Many of us will develop some foot problems with age, simply as a result of wear and tear. Most common problems can be treated successfully by a chiropodist or podiatrist. You can find some good advice for 'fitter feet' on the Age UK website: **www.ageuk.org.uk**.

The professional association for registered chiropodists and podiatrists has a list of over 10,000 private practitioners. Society of Chiropodists and Podiatrists: **www.scpod.org**.

# Hearing

Hearing is 'invisible', so when changes occur to this sense, it is not immediately apparent to ourselves or others. If you're concerned about hearing loss, early tests are advisable as deafness can adversely affect relationships and your quality of life. Deafness can be socially isolating and four million people in the UK have undiagnosed hearing loss, according to the UK charity Action on Hearing Loss. Hearing aids have been viewed negatively by people but there are now many recent advances in technology and design of these, as well as a number of helpful gadgets. If you think you are losing your hearing, take a free hearing test. Your GP can then refer you, if necessary, for further tests and advice.

Here are some of the specialist organizations that can help on hearing aids and other matters:

- Action on Hearing Loss: **www.actiononhearingloss.org.uk**;
- British Deaf Association (BDA): **www.bda.org.uk**;
- British Tinnitus Association (BTA): **www.tinnitus.org.uk**;
- Hearing Link: **www.hearinglink.org**.

# Sleep/insomnia

A good night's sleep is restorative and refreshing. Did you know that sleep accounts for approximately one third of our lives? Yet over 60 per cent of the population get less adequate sleep than required, 35 per cent are affected in their daily activities due to drowsiness. Most people need on average about seven hours sleep a night. But it is difficult to define what 'normal' sleep is, because everyone is different. Sleeping problems tend to increase with age, and women are more likely to be affected than men. Some tips to help you get a good night's sleep include: don't eat too close to your bedtime; avoid stimulants (alcohol, caffeine, TV and computer) if you have trouble getting to sleep, drink water before you go to sleep and on waking; open the bedroom window to get fresh air; sleep when you are actually tired rather than at a particular time; and make sure your bedroom is silent and in total darkness.

If you have difficulties sleeping, it is important to speak to your GP. There is some good advice to be found on the NHS website: **www.nhs.uk/ Livewell/insomnia**.

# Teeth

Oral health is important because it can affect our general health. Did you know that recent research reveals that infections in the mouth can cause problems in other parts of the body? Exercise, eating a healthy diet, and keeping a normal body weight will help you to maintain healthy teeth. Should you experience any of the following: inflammation of the gums, unpleasant taste in the mouth, bad breath, loose teeth, regular mouth infections, visit your dentist or hygienist to have a check up. Dentistry is one of the treatments for which you have to pay under the NHS, unless you are on a very low income. This also applies to the hygienist, should you need to see one. To find a dentist in your area, search NHS Choices: **www.nhs.uk**.

Prevention is always better than cure. If you want free, independent and impartial advice on all aspects of oral health, and free literature on a wide range of topics, including patients' rights, finding a dentist and dental care for older people, see British Dental Health Foundation: **www.dentalhealth.org**.

For those who like to be able to budget ahead for any dental bills, the best advice is to take out a dental health plan. One of the UK's leading dental payment plan specialists has over 6,500 member dentists and approximately 1.8 million patients across the UK – Denplan: **www.denplan.co.uk**.

# Personal relationships

Reaching retirement age is something many people look forward to, but remember, it brings with it a significant lifestyle change. The first few months of retirement can be both exciting and a challenge for people. Personal relationships can be affected and a little preparation can ensure that any difficulties are minimized. The key to keeping personal relationships harmonious depends on your ability to share, compromise and be flexible. Personal relationships are a key factor in determining how happy our retirement years will be, according to Relate. In a March 2013 survey, it was found that 91 per cent of people aged over 50 in the UK said that a close personal relationship is as important as good health and financial security. This emphasizes that as we grow older, strong and healthy personal relationships do matter. Should the need arise, the following organizations can offer help and advice:

- Marriage Care: **www.marriagecare.org.uk**;
- The Spark (formerly Scottish Marriage Care): **www.thespark.org.uk**;
- Relate: **www.relate.org.uk**;
- Relationships Scotland: **www.relationships-scotland.org.uk**.

# Help for grandparents

Grandparenting is a hugely important role: being responsible but not 'in charge' requires both delicacy and tact. More and more couples are now relying on grandparents for money, time, wisdom and support to help bring up the children. Mutually reliant relationships where each side has power and vulnerability can take a while to settle down, but in most cases the advantages outweigh the disadvantages. Should this extended relationship be impossible to maintain, for whatever reason, grandparents may need support. There are a number of organizations that can offer practical help and support when difficulties occur:

- Grandparents' Association: **www.grandparents-association.org.uk**;
- Grandparents Plus: **www.grandparentsplus.org.uk**;
- Grannynet: **www.grannynet.co.uk**.

# Depression

According to the Royal College of Psychiatrists:

> ... everyone feels sad sometimes, but later life can give you more reasons to feel down. Dealing with stopping work, having less money, health problems, death of parents, partner or friends, can all contribute to depression.
> Yet most older people cope well in spite of these difficulties...
>
> (**www.rcpsych.ac.uk/healthadvice/problemsdisorders/
> depressioninolderad.aspx**)

One helpful antidote to depression, for which there is increasing evidence, is laughter. It really is one of the best (free) medicines you can give your body. When you start to laugh, it doesn't just help to cheer you up, but it actually brings about physical changes in your body that can have real benefit. There are also long-term benefits: happy positive thoughts help fight stress and other potential illnesses.

However, depression is not a laughing matter, so if you think someone is depressed, they may not enjoy things as they used to; may lose their appetite and weight; feel irritable and be sleeping badly. In such cases encourage them to get help from their GP. Depression is not a sign of weakness and there are numerous treatments available. More information is available from these websites:

- Depression Alliance: **www.depressionalliance.org;**
- Mind: **www.mind.org.uk;**
- Samaritans: **www.samaritans.org;**
- Sane: **www.sane.org.uk.**

# Some common disorders

The rest of this chapter deals with some of the more common disorders such as back pain and heart disease. If you are unfortunate enough to be affected, or have a member of your family who is, here are some organizations that provide information and support.

## *Aphasia*

Aphasia is an impairment of language, affecting the production or comprehension of speech and the ability to read or write. It is due to an injury to the brain, most commonly from a stroke, particularly in older people. This condition affects a person's ability to *communicate*, but not their intelligence. The national charity that can help is: Speakability: **www.speakability.org.uk.**

## *Arthritis*

There are about 200 different musculoskeletal conditions. Arthritis is a term used by doctors to describe inflammation within a joint, while rheumatism is a more general term that's used to describe aches and pains in or around the joints. The two most common forms are *osteo-arthritis* and *rheumatoid arthritis*. Osteoarthritis is characterized by gradually worsening symptoms, including sore or stiff joints, stiffness after resting (which improves with movement), and pain that worsens after activity or towards the end of the day. Rheumatoid arthritis is caused by the body attacking its own tissues, producing symptoms that vary but often involving pain, fatigue, and warm, swollen, inflamed-looking joints. Although arthritis is often thought of as an older person's complaint, it accounts for the loss of an estimated 70 million working days per year in Britain, and 10 million people suffer from it. You don't have to put up with the pain of arthritis, however, as there are a number of organizations that can help:

- Arthritic Association: **www.arthriticassociation.org.uk**;
- Arthritis Care: **www.arthritiscare.org.uk**;
- Arthritis Research UK: **www.arthritisresearchuk.org**.

## Asthma

Asthma is a common long-term condition that can cause coughing, wheezing, chest tightness and breathlessness. The severity of these symptoms varies from person to person. Asthma can be controlled well in most people most of the time. Occasionally asthma symptoms can get gradually or suddenly worse, this is known as an 'asthma attack'. Asthma is caused by inflammation of the small tubes, called bronchi, which carry air in and out of the lungs. Common asthma triggers include: house dust mites, animal fur, pollen, cigarette smoke, exercise and viral infections. Asthma can develop at any age. Full details of this condition can be found on the NHS website: **www.nhs.uk/conditions/asthma/Pages/Introduction.aspx**.

For more information and advice see Asthma UK's website: **www.asthma.org.uk**.

## Back pain

Back pain is a common problem that affects most people at some stage of their lives. It may be triggered by bad posture while sitting or standing, bending awkwardly or lifting incorrectly. In most cases back pain will improve within a few weeks or months, although some people experience long-term pain which keeps recurring. Regular exercise such as walking or swimming, or activities such as yoga or pilates are an excellent way of improving flexibility and strengthening back muscles. There is good advice to be found at **www.nhs.uk/Conditions/Back-pain** and more information is available from BackCare: **www.backcare.org.uk**.

## Blood pressure

As we get older, we need to watch our blood pressure. The higher our blood pressure becomes the higher the risk of (at some stage) a heart attack or a stroke. But the good news is that if you have high blood pressure, healthy lifestyle changes will help to bring it down. The only way to find out the level of your blood pressure is to have it measured. Recommendations for keeping blood pressure low include: reduce salt intake, eat more fruit and vegetables, keep to a healthy weight, reduce alcohol and keep active. A lot of information and advice can be found on the website for Blood Pressure UK: **www.bloodpressureuk.org**.

## Cancer

Cancer has become so common today that one in 30 people living in the UK either has cancer or is in remission. By 2030 it is estimated that three million people in England will have had some form of cancer. (**www.bbc.co.uk/news/health-21667065**). Survival rates are improving and have doubled in the last 40 years. More men are surviving prostate and bowel cancer, and women with breast cancer have a better outlook than ever before. But the UK still lags behind other European countries in terms of cancer survival. Cancer Research UK says that part of the problem is unhealthy lifestyles. It is estimated that about a third of cancers are caused by smoking, diet, alcohol and obesity. Early diagnosis is paramount, so it goes without saying that anyone with a lump or swelling, or unexplained tiredness or weight loss, should have it investigated by their doctor.

There are now over 300 cancer charities in existence, each researching or focusing on a particular variant of the disease. Here are a few, but to find a list of all of them consult: **www.charitychoice.co.uk**:

- Beating Bowel Cancer: **www.beatingbowelcancer.org**;
- Bowel Cancer UK: **www.bowelcanceruk.org.uk**;

- Breast Cancer Care: **www.breastcancercare.org.uk**;
- Cancer Research UK: **www.cancerresearch.org**;
- Macmillan Cancer Support: **www.macmillan.org.uk**;
- Marie Curie Cancer Care: **www.mariecurie.org.uk**.

## Chest and heart diseases

Coronary heart disease (CHD) is responsible for over 73,000 deaths in the UK each year. It can't be cured but treatment can help manage the symptoms and reduce the chances of problems such as heart attacks. Keeping your heart healthy, whatever your age, is the most important thing you can do to help prevent and manage heart disease. The earlier sections on smoking, diet, drink and exercise list some of the most pertinent 'dos and don'ts' that can help. The following charity plays a leading role in the fight against diseases of the heart and circulation: British Heart Foundation: **www.bhf.org.uk**.

## Diabetes

Diabetes is a common lifelong condition that causes a person's blood sugar level to become too high. There are 3.2 million people diagnosed with diabetes in the UK and an estimated 850,000 who have the condition but don't know it. It can sometimes be treated by diet alone; sometimes pills or insulin may also be needed. There are two main types of diabetes: type 1 and type 2. It can be diagnosed at any age, although it is common in the elderly and especially among individuals who are overweight. The main symptoms of diabetes are: feeling very thirsty; urinating more frequently than usual; feeling tired; weight loss and loss of muscle bulk; cuts or wounds that heal slowly; blurred vision. For further information see: Diabetes UK: **www.diabetes.org.uk** and Independent Diabetes Trust: **www.iddt.org**.

## Migraine

This is a chronic health condition that affects over 10 million people in the UK. It can involve severe head pains, nausea, vomiting, visual disturbances and in some cases temporary paralysis. Most of the time migraines are not a threat to your overall health but they can interfere considerably with your day-to-day quality of life. Migraines are more common in women but often become less severe and less frequent with age. The leading UK charity that funds and promotes research, holds international symposia and runs an extensive support service is: Migraine Trust: **www.migrainetrust.org**.

## Osteoporosis and menopause problems

Bone is a living tissue that reacts to increases in loads and forces by growing stronger. Maximum bone density and strength are achieved around the age of 30. They change throughout our lifetime, with new bone constantly replacing old bone. From the age of 35 our bones begin to weaken gradually as most of us become less active. For women, bone loss is usually most rapid during the first few years after menopause, during which time women's levels of the hormone oestrogen naturally decrease. This can lead to osteoporosis: a condition in which bones become so fragile that they can break very easily. The most common injuries from falls affect the spine, hip and wrist. One in two women (and one in five men) suffers from osteoporosis.

Age UK compiled a list of ways to boost bone health:

- Weight-bearing exercise is important to help keep your bones strong. Walking, tennis, aerobics and dancing strengthen your bones.

- Enjoy a balanced diet. Milk, cheese, yoghurt, baked beans, lentils and dried apricots are great sources of calcium.

- Taking a stroll in the summer sun (just 10 minutes will help) is a great way of absorbing vitamin D, which keeps bones healthy.

- Avoid smoking. Smokers lose bone density at a faster rate than non smokers.

- Drink moderately.

The following websites may be useful:

- Menopause Exchange: **www.menopause-exchange.co.uk**;

- National Osteoporosis Society: **www.nos.org.uk**;

- Women's Health Concern: **www.womens-health-concern.org**.

## *Stroke*

A stroke is a serious, life-threatening medical condition that occurs when the blood supply to part of the brain is cut off. Strokes are a medical emergency and urgent treatment is essential because the sooner the person receives treatment for a stroke, the less damage is likely to happen. Every year over 150,000 people in England alone suffer a stroke. People over 65 are most at risk and it has recently been discovered that iron deficiency may lead to an increased risk of suffering a stroke. Prevention is similar to the avoidance of heart disease. A stroke has a greater disability impact than any other medical condition. Most people experience a faster period of recovery just after a stroke; this is followed by a longer period of slower rehabilitation.

If you come across someone who may be having a stroke, remember the word 'FAST'. This stands for face – arms – speech – time. Look out for:

- *Face* – if the face droops on one side, or cannot smile evenly.
- *Arms* – if the person cannot lift one or both arms and keep them up because of weakness or numbness.
- *Speech* – if speech becomes slurred or garbled, or if the person finds it difficult to talk.
- *Time* – if you see any of these symptoms and suspect a stroke, dial 999 immediately. A stroke is a medical emergency that requires immediate professional attention.

(*Source*: **www.nhs.uk/conditions/stroke/**)

The Stroke Association is the only UK-wide charity solely concerned with combating stroke in people of all ages. See:

Stroke Association: **www.stroke.org.uk**.

# Disability

Disability is covered in Chapter 10, 'Taking care of elderly parents'. If you or someone in your family has a problem not mentioned here, you may look there to find the answer you need.

# Chapter Seven
# Starting your own business

 *'Screw it – let's do it!'*

SIR RICHARD BRANSON

The number of small businesses now account for over 15 per cent of occupations. More and more people are setting up their own business and becoming their own boss. Whether it is earning £2,000 to supplement a pension, or building a business that can keep you earning and occupied for years to come beyond your intended retirement date, this is the chapter for you. While financially rewarding, this is not the only reason people want to start a business, as social and emotional benefits also feature. It may even be a route to providing more freedom than that available in corporate structures where endless meetings start to lose their appeal for the 50-plus age group. It may even rekindle a passion for work and a can-do attitude (that broadcaster Liz Barclay comments on in this chapter). Importantly, you will not be alone and this chapter will signpost you to plenty of help and support – and most of it is free (it is just a matter of knowing where to look!).

## All you need to know about this chapter and what it contains

This chapter will give you the confidence to get started and has plenty of straightforward advice. The key issues covered are:

- Starting a small business in just one page.

- Understanding the differences between starting a small business and employment, especially if both options are still open to you.

- Do I need to bother with a business plan?

- Getting off to a good start – practical and emotional tips and buying your first equipment.

- Administration, finance and tax – keep on top of the paperwork or it will keep on top of you!

- Filling the diary with work, and some clever tips for marketing that will make a difference.

- The trading format – should you set up your own limited liability company, work as a sole trader or maybe go into partnership?

- Other ways of getting started and operational issues.

- Where you can go for further help – remember you are not alone and these are enterprising times in the UK.

- A summary checklist to help you tick off the key issues once you decide to get started in business.

# Start a small business – in one page

This one page will get you on the way to starting a small business – just follow this step-by-step guide:

- Find something you enjoy doing and/or goods or services that you can sell (advisory businesses sell 'services' at an hourly or daily rate).

- Register as self-employed with Her Majesty's Revenue and Customs (HMRC) on 0300 200 3504, or for customers who are deaf or hard of hearing on 0845 915 3296 (textphone) and say you're calling to register as self-employed. Or register via **www.gov.uk** (then go to 'Set up as a sole trader').

- You will then have to complete a self-assessment each year and declare your taxable income from your business every year. Check out HMRC's website (**www.hmrc.gov.uk**) for guidance on the basics of income tax – and keep a list of your income and costs.

- Acquire some files and keep all your business records to prove your business and its transactions – sales invoices, purchases receipts, bank statements, cash books. If it 'proves' your business transactions you must keep it for six years after the end of the tax year.

- The big lesson: HMRC don't like people evading tax (it is illegal!) and have taken on lots of new investigators in the last few years. If you have acted honestly, kept your records and help HMRC with their questions you will have little to worry about. But if you can't prove your transactions then you will be charged the tax that HMRC believe they were due, plus a penalty of up to an extra 100 per cent plus interest. They can go back six years without much fuss and even longer if they believe your errors were deliberate.

- If you are self-employed you don't actually need an accountant to prepare the year-end accounts and self-assessment tax return – many people can do this themselves. In time your business may generate enough to pay an accountant or a bookkeeper for some assistance.

- To help your business grow (the vital bit!), jump to the marketing section and case studies of this chapter. The tips should take you to the next level and, in time, you may benefit from delving into even more of this chapter and our hints and tips.

# Yes, you can!

Broadcaster Liz Barclay and Maree Atkinson of the Federation of Small Businesses share their insights into starting a business and offer some tips, which reveal that 'Yes, you can!'

Liz Barclay is one of the most recognized voices on British radio today with her common-sense approach to money and finance on BBC London. She presented *You and Yours* for more than 10 years and presents *Pick of the Week* on Radio 4. As well as writing on personal finance and small business issues Liz advises businesses on customer service, employee engagement and internal and external communications. She shares her experience and tips below:

First, forget about the salary spiral where you will only consider taking a job that offers you as much as or more than you have earned in the past. Do your calculations carefully and work out how much you need to make to pay your bills and enjoy life. That shift in thinking alone opens up all sorts of possibilities. You can do work that pays less but that you enjoy more, choose your own working hours and when to take breaks, and mix work with rest, play, retraining, learning and even unpaid voluntary work. The world is your oyster.

Many of the people I talk to who are moving out of full-time employment are thinking of retraining or brushing up long-disused skills at a further education college, or about how they can turn a hobby into an income-generating venture. Self-employment or starting a small business after a lifetime of being an employee can be daunting, but it can be done and this chapter will help you on the way. The people I know who are most successful are those who are doing something they love. They're passionate about their businesses and willing to give them the time and TLC they need to make them flourish. Hard work doesn't seem like a chore so they're less likely to give up when the going gets tough, as it will.

The section within this chapter on 'Marketing tips to fill your diary' will assist you with your marketing and research. On generating business ideas Liz adds:

There are ideas everywhere. You don't have to come up with something new. You might do what you did before as an employee but on a consultancy basis with new customers. The more important thing is research. Be sure there are enough people who will pay you for what you do and that they have easy access to your products or services. Just because two tanning salons on the high street are buzzing doesn't mean there are enough customers to support a third. Many businesses that I saw fail had not done enough market research before spending money. Ask your customers what they like about your business and what they don't. Listen, act and add value – like the butcher in Glasgow who has long queues because he gives his customers recipes for the meat they buy. Talk to your employees who often know the business and customers better than you do. Keep building those relationships so that you spot the trends and stay ahead of the competition.

Liz's concluding advice is:

Success comes with having a positive and optimistic attitude to your business. This is a must – yes, you can. The glass is always half full! Be passionate about your business. Do not just turn up to work, but enjoy what you do. Put your life and soul into achieving a good day's work.

Maree Atkinson runs her own business and sees hundreds of small businesses start up in her role as an award-winning membership adviser for the Federation of Small Businesses (FSB). The FSB has around 200,000 members and promotes and protects the interests of the self-employed and owners of small firms. For Maree, the watchwords are 'Yes, you can', but she advises that you take special care over your marketing:

> Certainly starting a business later in life may be daunting – I can personally vouch for that. But one big advantage for mature entrepreneurs is the wealth of experience and contacts gathered in work and general life over many years. The more successful start-ups that I see have a real passion to succeed and normally a willingness to adapt. I would agree with Liz Barclay about the importance of market research and really getting to know your customers and the competition you face. This is also a key part of planning and I definitely agree with Allan that the first draft of your business plan does not need to run on for pages and pages. Indeed some business plan 'templates' that I have seen put people off the whole planning process.
>
> I would encourage you to start the planning process by getting something down in writing to show you have researched and understood your business idea and your target customers. Where are they? What is their profile and what might they need (could you change your proposition)? What price are they prepared to pay? How will you get your product or service to them? These are all good starting questions and you can then build things from there by investigating the competition. With further help from your advice network your plan will start to take shape. Remember that there is a lot of help out there and you are definitely not alone.
> I see lots of idea sharing, hints and tips and introductions at the various members' networking and social events we run at the FSB: this is one of the vital needs in the first year of starting a business – knowing where to find the *right* answers.

Maree goes on to advise:

> One challenge that I see is new business owners becoming overwhelmed by the many hats they have to wear. People underestimate the time it takes to do even the simplest of tasks. Perhaps this is because they came from larger organizations with in-house functions for marketing, legal, accounts and health and safety. Unless you bring in specialists to deal with these areas you are left with a choice: deal with the issues or they will simply get left

behind. So manage your time and make lists to make sure all the 'must-dos' are tackled first. If you find your precious family time is being spent on disliked jobs, think about hiring in help if you can afford it. Check out trade and professional associations (including the Federation of Small Businesses, which I represent) as these can provide contacts to assist you.

Maree's concluding advice is:

I must have seen over 4,000 people start up in business over the past 12 years. Those who have taken time to research their product or service, sought input from others, understood the financial requirements and developed the plans needed to launch and continue have a much better prospect of success.

Some further marketing tips from Maree feature in the 'Marketing tips to fill your diary' section of this chapter.

# Some of the differences between starting a small business and employment

In some cases where there is an opportunity to start a small business there could be a similar opportunity to take a full- or part-time employed position. Which route is right for you?

Here are some of the reasons for starting a small business:

- focus on what you are best at or enjoy;
- be your own boss;
- provide a legacy for your children;
- flexibility (around other interests/responsibilities);
- freedom to organize things your way;
- no commuting;
- less involvement in internal politics and no more pointless meetings;
- enjoy working on your own;
- try something new/an experiment;
- getting paid for overtime.

On the other hand, here are some of the reasons for seeking a part- or full-time employed position:

- a local employer with known travel requirements;
- security of income;
- benefits of holiday pay, pension, paid sick leave, and perhaps private health and life cover;
- bonuses and perhaps a car;
- team aspect and friendship of colleagues;
- no personal liability if things go badly wrong;
- staff discounts or other perks.

# Why bother with a plan?

There are thousands of success stories about those who took the plunge nearing or post-retirement to build a business that provided involvement, fun and income, plus a legacy for their children. However, for every three success stories there is a business that does not work out and your money could disappear fast if you set up in the wrong way or overstretch yourself. Worst of all you could lose your home if things go really badly wrong, so the reasons below and tips throughout this chapter should help you understand and deal with the risks.

## Why businesses fail – learning the lessons

Businesses can fail for many reasons. Learn from the mistakes of others and you will be doing yourself a favour. The number one reason why businesses fail is that *the market moves on and you are left behind*. Take time out to think and keep abreast of what your customers really want (have you tried asking them recently?). Where are your competitors and what are they doing to keep on top of or ahead of the market and, overall, how is the market moving?

A second reason (and one that will increase in 2016 as HMRC increases its resources on tackling tax evasion and avoidance) is the *failure to deal with tax affairs properly*. The implications of penalties and interest levied by HMRC (Her Majesty's Revenue and Customs) are often ignored and only hit home when it is too late. Keep your books properly and retain all records for seven years after the year end – in brief, if you can't prove it, you may lose the tax benefit and pay additional tax, penalties and interest. If there is a problem, HMRC can go back and inspect previous years' accounts (for up to six years or even longer). If you fail to pay your tax fully when it is due, HMRC will pursue you vigorously and you are giving them a reason to have a closer look at you and your business. On the other hand, if you have genuine cash flow difficulties and cannot pay your tax on the due date, talk to HMRC and you may find their attitude refreshing (especially if it is the first time you have stumbled).

*Other reasons include a failure to plan and also bad debts* (where the customer goes bust and cannot pay your invoices), as this will come off your bottom-line profit and can really hurt. There are a few simple steps that you can take to reduce the potential of taking such a hit. What are your credit terms and have you encouraged all customers to pay electronically? Do you contact them as soon as your invoices become overdue? Do you require cash on delivery or prepayment? (PayPal and mobile credit card machines are transforming the payment services.) In some cases it is worth remembering that a bad customer is sometimes worse than no customer at all.

So 'why bother' when it comes to planning? The answer should now be evident from the above – you are improving your chances of succeeding and may even do rather better than you first thought.

## What goes into a plan?

'*I have always found that plans are useless but planning is indispensable*': this is a quote from General Eisenhower and is about planning for battle. We can draw a couple of lessons from this but the starting point is to make a promise that you will put your plan in writing. Too many people run a mile when the subject of a plan comes up, especially the notion of a grand-sounding business plan. Some new businesses – perhaps armed with confidence gained from a book on setting up a business, business banking literature, or even after attending a setting-up-in-business course – start a plan but never get it finished.

The reason for this is twofold: first, fear of the planning process and, second, intimidation by daunting plan templates and spreadsheets seen in books or banking literature. The prescription is a three-stage plan that will get you started and then, with experience, you can tweak it and make it that bit slicker.

## Stage 1 of the plan: objectives

What, financially, do you need to set as objectives to bring you in that £2,000 or £20,000 or £60,000? This takes a bit of thinking through but you should be able to come up with two or three simple objectives based on income, gross profit (if you sell stock) and overheads.

For someone who sells advice based services and who does not sell stock there could be just two objectives. *Objective 1*: I aim to invoice £30,000 in my first year of trading based on working at least 100 days at an average billing rate of £300 per day. I will review my billing rates quarterly and my performance monthly. *Objective 2*: I will aim to keep my overheads (after expenses recharged to clients) in my first year to £5,000.

Then, for the more complicated businesses which is one that trades in buying and selling stock you will need a further objective based around the difference between sales price and purchase price. *Objective 3* will be something like: I will aim to achieve the following gross profit percentages:

Product line A: 30 per cent;
Product line B: 40 per cent;
Product line C: 50 per cent.
Gross profit percentages are calculated using:
(Sales price less cost of materials/product sold ÷ sales price) × 100

The key point with objectives is that less gives more: you don't want a long list of objectives.

## Stage 2 of the plan: your market research

The next page of your plan should be all about your marketing effort: this is a topic that is often misunderstood and mistaken for advertising. Think about approaching this section under the following three headings: products, customers and competitors.

## Products

Start with your main product or service and think about the features and benefits of what you are selling. Understanding these and discussing them with your trusted advisers will allow you to start thinking about other related services or goods that you could offer.

## Customers

For each main product area ask lots of questions to tease out your research. Who are my customers? Where are they based? When do they tend to buy? How and where do they tend to buy and at what price? How should I contact them? Keep asking those important questions of who, what, why, where, when and how – as they tease out all sorts of gems.

## Competitors

Again, ask yourself who, what, why, where, when and how? This should lead to a series of activities that you can do to help secure new quality work and customers (note that the marketing section later on in this chapter has further tips). If you end up with a jumble of unfocused ideas try ranking each idea on the basis of priority, impact and cost (free is good!).

## Stage 3 of the plan: your income and expenditure forecast

This is your income and expenditure forecast for the year and this third page is the tricky one. It is your map for the year ahead financially and will allow you to monitor your actual performance against the plan. You can then do something about it when you are off target. You should be able to do this yourself but if it becomes a struggle, ask your accountant to help.

## Is there more?

Once you have completed your first plan keep it alive and keep reviewing how you are doing against it; even if the plan is useless you will find, as Eisenhower did, that the planning process itself teases out things that will make things that little bit better – guaranteed!

# Practical and emotional tips

Your partner's attitude is crucial. Even if not directly involved, he or she will have to accept (at least initially) the loss of some space in the house to give you an office. Do you have space available to work from home initially or would you need/prefer to rent accommodation? There will be the added distractions of out-of-hours phone calls and, perhaps, suddenly cancelled social engagements. Can your family/partner cope with having you and your business in the house? Can you cope without the resources/back-up provided by an employer (IT/HR/training/administrative support) – as you will have to do it yourself or buy it in.

# Keep on top of the paperwork

Generally, this one topic causes the most groans! But simple bookkeeping, if done properly, is just a by-product of your business and flows naturally from raising sales invoices and paying for purchases. As a bonus, you will never miss an unpaid invoice if you are on top of your bookkeeping.

An even more compelling reason for doing your own bookkeeping is that HMRC has a 'prove it or lose it' view if enquiring into an aspect of your tax return. Under the system of self-assessment, HMRC relies on you completing your tax returns. In the case of an enquiry, HMRC tells you precisely what part of your tax return is under investigation and you are expected to be able to validate sample payments. If you are unable to prove the expenditure, you lose it as far as HMRC is concerned, resulting in fewer purchases being accepted as a deduction from your profits and more tax to pay. There will be penalties and interest to pay and the scope of HMRC's enquiries will be widened.

## Basic bookkeeping

All incoming and outgoing payments need to be recorded throughout the year. Records of outgoings need to be categorized according to type; examples of some categories you might need to consider are: stock, subscriptions/meeting fees, office equipment, office supplies, post and courier costs; travel fares, parking and subsistence; telephone and internet; sundry; accountancy and professional fees; and insurance.

Many small business owners opt to do their own bookkeeping, with or without the help of a computer software package. If you opt for a software package choose one that your accountant understands as their fees should then be less. For many small businesses your accountant should be able to provide some Excel spreadsheets that will do the job, together with a bookkeeping guide to help get you started.

If you are really averse to bookkeeping yourself, consider hiring a bookkeeper. Bookkeepers currently charge between about £16 and £23 per hour, depending on geographical location and experience, and can be found by recommendation from your accountant or business network contacts.

## Accountants

Depending on qualifications and experience, accountants assisting new small start-up businesses could charge from £35 to about £120 per hour to assist you in setting up in business and to prepare your accounts and tax. Anyone can call themselves an accountant so it can be a bit hit and miss with very variable quality when things go wrong at the lower end of the spectrum (and sometimes even with seemingly respectable firms claiming to have thousands of clients). Unreturned calls and not dealing factually with enquiries and questions, vague verbal assurances and not dealing with formal complaints are all part of the 'deal' when you end up with a lower-end accountant. If there are mistakes in your accounts and tax you will also find that you are very much on your own when it comes to dealing with HMRC enquiries. Lower-end accountants may neither be regulated by a professional body nor have professional indemnity insurance. What should you look for? The letters ACA or FCA after the accountant's name mean that you can be assured that you are dealing with a Chartered Accountant.

Some accountancy firms offer a combination of bookkeeping, accountancy and tax services and, if so, you can expect to pay a premium on the bookkeeping hourly rates quoted above. Ask your trusted family members or friends if they can recommend an accountant. Then ensure you get clarity on three things: 1) confirmation of the accountant's qualifications (the type of qualification); 2) the professional body you would complain to if there is ever a problem; and 3) check that they hold professional indemnity insurance. These three points would usually be clarified by an accountant; if you have to actually ask for them it probably tells you a lot. It is advisable to meet at least two accountants and see how you feel about rapport and the availability of proactive hints and tips. Make sure you believe you can get on with the accountant you select as it is likely to be a long and mutually beneficial relationship. Will the person you meet be the person who does your accounts and tax and provides proactive advice? Get written confirmation of hourly rates plus an estimate of fees for the year, and get clarity on what happens if you decide to change accountants halfway through the year if fees are paid up front or monthly. Most accountants would be used to providing clients with a 'retainer', clarifying the above and what you and the accountant will do and by when. A good accountant who knows your industry area will be able to help with general guidance and offer input to your plan on marketing and pricing, drawing on experience beyond accounting and tax.

Finally, there is sometimes some confusion over the term 'audit of accounts'. Many years ago, smallish companies in the UK had to have an audit of their accounts. The turnover threshold (one of three thresholds) for being required to have an audit has been increased and currently stands at £6.5 million, so the vast majority of start-ups need not concern themselves with audited accounts.

# Paying tax and National Insurance

## *Sole traders*

Self-employed individuals running their own businesses are usually called 'sole traders'. All new businesses that trade as sole traders need to register as self-employed with HMRC on 0300 200 3504, or for customers who are deaf or hard of hearing on 0845 915 3296 (textphone) and say you're calling to register as self-employed. Or register via **www.gov.uk** (then go to 'Set up as a sole trader').

While tax can be daunting, some sole traders with relatively straight-forward billing and overheads do their own tax returns and pay income tax on their profits. With income tax, you first have a personal allow-ance, which gives you a tax-free amount, and then any excess income (including your profits) is taxed at 20 per cent, then over a certain limit at 40 per cent and then 45 per cent. The precise yearly limits are available from the HMRC website or your accountant. In very broad terms, if you are under 65, you currently (summer 2015) have a tax-free allowance of £10,600 which will rise to £11,000 in April 2016 and rise again to £11,200 in April 2017. You are then taxed on the *next* £31,785 at 20 per cent (rising to £32,000 in April 2016 and then £32,400 in April 2017) and then 40 per cent tax applies to further taxable income up to £150,000. Anything above £150,000 gets taxed at 45 per cent. Many sole traders choose to run their bookkeeping for the year to 5 April to coincide with the tax year end (or 31 March, which HMRC effectively accepts as equivalent to 5 April).

If you are past the state retirement age there will be no National Insurance contributions (NICs) to pay. Subject to this, sole traders are liable for Class 2 NICs (currently a nominal amount of £2.80 per week). You are also liable for the much more significant Class 4 NICs that are assessed and collected by HMRC at the same time as assessing your income tax on profits. Currently (Summer 2015) these are at 9 per cent on profits between £8,060 and £42,385 and this reduces to just 2 per cent on profits over £42,385 (rising to £43,000 in April 2016 and then to £43,600 in April 2017).

The payment of sole-trader income tax is reasonably straightforward but there is a twist in your first year of trading. Assuming that you have a year end of 5 April 2017, the first payment will be due by 31 January 2018 so you have a long period of (effectively) interest-free credit, as some of the profits on which the tax is due may have been earned as long ago as May 2016. With the first payment, however, you get a 'double whammy' as you also have to pay on 31 January 2018 a payment on account of your second year's trading. Then on 31 July 2018 you have to make a second on-account payment of the second year's trading. Both on-account payments are set by default on the basis of your year 1 profits. You can 'claim' a reduction if year 2 is proving to have lower profits than year 1; your accountant will help you with this if it is appropriate.

After this initial tax famine, followed by double payment of tax, you will thereafter receive a tax demand twice a year. Payments need to be made by 31 January (during the tax year) and then by 31 July after the end of that tax year, with any overpayment or underpayment sorted out by the following 31 January. Many sole-trader businesses set up a reserve bank account in addition to their current account, and place a percentage of their income aside, which is earning interest each month (albeit not amounting to much in the current climate). This tactic should help you resist the temptation to raid money that is not for spending – and ensure you can pay your tax on time.

Additionally, as a self-employed person you are allowed certain other reliefs. Ask your accountant, but the following expenses and allowances are usually tax deductible:

- *Business expenses.* These must be incurred 'wholly and exclusively' for the purposes of the trade. Office supplies that you buy will probably qualify; however, any business entertaining will not.
- *Partially allowable expenses.* These mainly apply if you are working from home. They include such items as the part of your rent, heating, lighting and telephone usage that you devote to business purposes, and also possibly some of the running expenses on your car, if you use your car for your business.
- *Spouse's wages.* If you employ your partner in the business, his or her pay (provided this is reasonable) qualifies as a legitimate expense, in the same way as any other employee's, but must be accounted for through a PAYE system.
- *Pension contributions.* Tax relief is generally available for pension contributions at the higher of £3,600 (gross) or 100 per cent of relevant earnings up to a maximum of £40,000 (this is subject to a tapered reduction from April 2016 for taxpayers with 'adjusted income' in excess of £150,000).
- *Capital allowances.* This is a tax break for expenditure on equipment.

## Partnerships

Partnership tax is broadly similar to the process described above for a sole trader, with the exception of some more paperwork. In addition to submitting each partner's individual personal self-assessment tax return a composite partnership tax return must also be submitted.

## Limited company

Companies pay corporation tax on their profits (currently 20 per cent and reducing to 19 per cent in April 2017 and then 17 per cent in April

2020). Your company accounts need to be finalized and any corporation tax paid nine months after your year end.

The key point with a company is that the money coming in is not your money – it is the company's money – so how do you extract your money? The first option is salary and this means running a 'pay-as-you-earn' (PAYE) system: another form of tax with a rigorous calculation regime and payments that have to be made to HMRC. PAYE carries the income tax rates as featured for the sole trader, but NICs (National Insurance contributions) are much higher as these are a composite of employee *and* employer NICs (as the company is an employer). Currently these are 12 per cent employee NICs on £8,060 to £42,380, reducing to 2 per cent for amounts above £42,380 and then an additional 13.8 per cent employer NICs on everything above £8,112. Salary and employer's NICs are deductible when calculating corporation tax.

The second option for extracting funds is dividends, but these are not deductible when calculating your corporation tax. The big selling point for dividends is that, at face value, they are not subject to NICs but, from April 2016, there will be significant change to the dividend tax regime. The change is designed to reduce what the government perceives to be an incentive for companies to extract profits through a dividend due to (until now) lower overall rates of tax. The proposal (at Summer 2015) is that:

- There will be a new annual dividend allowance of £5,000 that is tax-free.

- The 1/9 tax credit will disappear.

- The new rates of tax on dividend will then be 7.5 per cent if the dividend falls in the basic rate tax band, 32.5 per cent if it falls in the higher-rate tax band (£42,785 to £150,000) and 38.1 per cent if it falls in the additional rate tax band (£150,000 plus).

There is a further possible 'tax trap' for the unwary known as HMRC regulation number 35 (IR35) that came into force in April 2000.

HMRC is particularly interested in ex-employees setting up service companies that work exclusively for their former employer or for just a few clients (sometimes called 'personal service companies' to use an HMRC term) – sometimes called 'freelancers'. This is an extremely wide-ranging and difficult subject but, in very simplified terms, IR35 is to be avoided if at all possible and it only applies to companies (not sole traders).

There are many hints and tips and some urban myths about IR35 all of which are outside the scope of this guide. It is a big issue and one that you have first got to recognize and then do something about. One of the key players in helping freelancers guide themselves through the minefield of IR35 is the Association of Independent Professionals and the Self Employed (IPSE) at **www.ipse.co.uk**. This organization, working in conjunction with a chartered accountant who understands IR35, is probably your next step if you are concerned. Briefly, if you fall foul of IR35, the tax inspector will seek to set aside the dividends you have paid and treat the dividend payment as if it were subject to PAYE and NICs (including employer NICs) and the tax advantage you thought you may have had will disappear.

## Registering for VAT

Value added tax (VAT) was introduced in 1973 and it seems that many people have lost sight of the name of this tax and especially the word 'added'. You are, in effect, adding a tax and are an unpaid tax collector.

If your taxable turnover is likely to be more than £82,000 in a 12-month period or less, you must register for VAT unless your supplies/services are outside the scope of VAT. Any expenses that you recharge to clients need to be included in the calculation of taxable turnover.

UK business clients are invariably registered for VAT so are not concerned about having it added to your invoice, and for that reason some businesses register for VAT before reaching the £82,000 compulsory registration limit so that they can claim VAT on their purchases. Before voluntarily applying consider whether registration will really be of benefit to you, that is, whether reclaiming the VAT paid on items needed for your business (such as office equipment) is worth the trouble of sending in mandatory, quarterly VAT returns and keeping separate VAT records for possible inspection by visiting VAT officers.

You can claim back VAT on pre-start/pre-registration expenditure involved in setting up the business. If you elect for 'Cash Accounting' status, this means that VAT only becomes payable or reclaimable when invoices are actually paid. It avoids having to pay the VAT on your own invoices before slow-paying clients pay you, which can create cash-flow problems. One final positive if you do register for VAT is that it seems to give you added credibility with clients.

## VAT flat-rate scheme

HMRC introduced the flat-rate scheme in 2004, with the aim of simplifying record keeping for small businesses. This allows you to charge VAT to your clients at the standard rate of 20 per cent and to pay VAT as a percentage of your VAT-inclusive turnover (instead of having to work out the VAT payable on your sales less purchases). You can apply to join the scheme if your taxable turnover (excluding VAT) will not be more than £150,000 in the next 12 months.

HMRC publishes a list of business categories from which you need to decide which best describes your business. A further bonus is that you can deduct 1 per cent from the flat rate that you use for your first year of VAT registration. As a tip, do not do anything without checking it out with your accountant as there are a few twists and turns that could make the VAT flat-rate scheme unsuitable. But, at face value, it seems to have been beneficial to many small businesses.

# Marketing tips to fill your diary

It is a sad fact that many new business owners believe that marketing simply means placing an advert in some well-known directory. This will achieve only a fraction of the sales of any comparable business with a decent grasp of marketing. So how can you generate sales for a new business? The following nine tips should start to help you along.

1 *Your own website and/or social media.* Business and the public now rely so heavily on the internet that a presence seems almost vital either through a website and/or harnessing social media. Is there a vital domain name (website unique address) that you need to secure and register? If this one question alone fills you with fear the solutions are nearer than you think – just try asking friends and don't ignore help that is right in front of your nose: young friends or relatives may know more than you.

   It is also worth checking out websites run by trade or professional associations that may allow you to register and set up a profile. You can set up profiles on various social media 'networking websites' such as LinkedIn. Depending on your business, Facebook and Twitter can provide the benefits of building your online contacts and allow you to showcase your expertise in a certain area. Social media (very like networking, below) is not about sell, sell, sell. It is more about building relationships and trust with an ever-increasing contact list.

**2** *Personal contacts and networking.* Once you decide to set up your own business, your personal contacts, ex-colleagues or other small business owners are a potential source of work. Too many small businesses forget that behind every contact there is another layer of potential contacts, who are just one introduction away; so ignore this multiplier effect at your peril. In your first year you should be re-educating your contacts to think of you not as 'Jane who used to work at IBM' but 'Jane who now runs her own business advising small businesses on their IT needs'. Do not be afraid to pick up the phone or send business cards explaining your new business and what you can offer. Joining the best trade or professional association you can find will be a great way of networking, with the added bonus of research facilities, information and other fringe benefits.

**3** *Discounts and offers.* These can be used to great effect during seasonal dips, introducing a new service or clearing old stock. Whether it is 20 per cent off, a buy-one-get-one-free offer or the numerous variations of this basic approach, there are three golden rules:

- Always state the original or usual price (to show the value in the offer).

- Always specify an expiry date.

- Always explain that the offer is subject to availability.

**4** *Flyers and business cards.* Generally speaking, a response rate of 1 per cent to a flyer is considered fairly good. With some clever thinking you can increase the response rate. Have you targeted the flyer? A good example would be a wedding gown designer who neatly persuades a sought-after wedding location hotel to keep a flyer dispenser in their foyer. Are you able to include your professional or trade association logo on your flyer and business cards? Have you asked if this is possible? There are two sides to a flyer and business card – have you thought about putting information on the blank reverse side? Could this contain some useful tips or, perhaps, a special offer or discount? Anything that ensures the card or flyer is kept rather than dumped will help your business to edge ahead.

5 *Testimonials.* People generally buy on trust, and testimonials show prospective customers that you have done a good job and can be relied upon. Positive testimonials can be powerful and should never be underestimated.

6 *Agencies.* Agencies will be especially important for prospective consultants or contractors as many recruitment agencies also place full- and part-time contracts (as opposed to employed positions). The contract market is growing and offers dynamic and fast-moving industries the opportunity to hire (and fire) swiftly. When marketing yourself through an agency the same rules apply as when marketing yourself to a potential employer. Good personal and written presentation will help the agency to sell you on to its clients – and it is in their interest to find you work, given the fee they receive for placing you.

7 *Advertising.* There are many options for advertising yourself and your business such as website banners, free and paid-for directory listings. Another approach could be 'free' advertising through a press release that you forward to local or trade press with an interesting story. A clever variant is advertising yourself and your skills by writing articles in professional or trade journals – what do you have that is news or novel or leading edge?

   Another subset of advertising is sponsorship. The driving instructor who sponsored the playing shirts on the local under-17s football team is a great example of cost-effective and rather clever sponsorship.

8 *Awards.* Business awards can offer new businesses an opportunity to make a splash in the local area, introduce you to other vibrant businesses, and there may even be a category for mature business owners newly starting up. These are often sponsored by local press and the Federation of Small Businesses (**www.fsb.org.uk/**) where more information can be found.

## Learn when to say 'no'

This is one of the hardest lessons to learn and comes with experience. The fear of losing a sale to a competitor, or the uncertainty of where the next piece of work or sale will come from if you reject this one, may induce you to overstretch or undercut yourself. If you continually face this dilemma the resulting stress means you may not survive in business for long. So learning how to say 'no' in a way that does not burn bridges is important.

Maree Atkinson of the Federation of Small Businesses (see 'Yes, you can!' above) has some tips to help you say 'no' and advises:

- *Be wary of the promises of business.* You will want to help customers and will want to secure those early sales. You may even find yourself bending over backwards to help. But have you given away your ideas and spent hours of your time with no prospect of the work? A very talented garden designer was asked to redesign a large garden. Excited by the project he prepared some initial plans and the client made a number of changes, which he incorporated. The client did go ahead with the work but used the plans with another contractor. I guess it is a balance between 'marketing time' and showing your wares but not going too far – all of which you will learn in time!

- *Marketing to the wrong people.* In the early days of starting a small business you will receive invitations for a meeting from possible business partners or joint ventures, who want to 'see if there's a way we could do some work together'. Networking is vital to many businesses, but don't network with random people just because you think you're supposed to network. Do some research about the offer and listen to your 'gut feeling' before you say 'yes'. In time, work out what sort of networking is best for you and what offers to explore further.

Maree's advice reminds me of Lord Alan Sugar's words on what makes an entrepreneur, in his book *The Way I See It: Rants, revelations and rules for life,* published by Pan Macmillan (2011, website: **www.panmacmillan.com**): 'If you have partners, they have to bring something to the party.'

# Trading formats

## *Sole trader*

A self-employed person is someone who works for him/herself, instead of an employer, and draws an income from their personally run business. If the profits from the work are accounted for on one person's tax return, that person is known as a sole trader. If the profits are shared between two or more people, it is a partnership (see below).

There is no clear definition of self-employment. Defining an employee, on the other hand, is slightly easier as it can generally be assumed that if income tax and NICs are deducted from an individual's salary before they are paid, then that individual is an employee.

Importantly, the business has no separate existence from the owner and, therefore, all debts of the business are debts of the owner who is personally liable for all amounts owed by the business. This strikes fear into the hearts of many business owners. You only need to think of the number of business owners who go bust every time a recession comes around and lose their house. Should this be a worry?

First and foremost, you must consider the risk to you in any work that you do. Could it go wrong and could you be sued? Is that a realistic prospect or so remote that it does not even warrant thinking about? Or is it somewhere in the middle? Can insurance help? (On this, see the relevant section later in this chapter.) Remember that such insurance is only as good as the disclosures you make and the levels of cover provided. At the end of the day you know your business, your customers and the work that you do, so the risk assessment can only be done by you.

### How to start up as a sole trader

- You can start trading immediately.

- You can trade under virtually any name, subject to some restrictions that are mostly common sense, such as not suggesting something you are not (connection to government, royalty or international pre-eminence). A B Jones trading as Super Lawns is fine.

- The full name and address of the owner and any trading name must be disclosed on letters, orders and invoices.

- A phone call to HMRC's helpline for the newly self-employed (0300 200 3504) and say you're calling to register as self employed. Or register via **www.gov.uk** (then go to 'Set up as a sole trader').

## Partnership

Two or more self-employed people who work together on a business and share the profits are trading in partnership. The profits from the work are accounted for on a partnership tax return and extracts from that partnership tax return are then copied into the partners' individual tax returns.

The business has no separate existence from the partners and, therefore, all debts of the business are debts of the partners, so they are personally liable for all amounts owed by the business. In addition, partners are jointly and severally liable for the debts of the business or, put more simply, the last person standing pays the lot. There is a saying that you need to trust your business partner better than your husband/wife/civil partner.

As with sole traders, the first consideration is the potential for business risk, since your personal wealth is backing the debts of the business. First and foremost you must consider the risk to you in any work that you do and, given the 'joint and several liability' point explained above, the trust and faith you have in your business partner. As mentioned above, could it go wrong and could you be sued? Is that a realistic prospect or so remote that it does not even warrant thinking about? Or is it somewhere in the middle? Can insurance help? Again, remember that such insurance is only as good as the disclosures you make and the levels of cover provided. At the end of the day you know your business, your business partner, your customers and the work that you do, so the risk assessment can only be done by you.

### How to start up as a partnership

- You can start trading immediately.
- You can trade under virtually any name, subject to some restrictions that are mostly common sense, such as not suggesting something you are not (connection to government, royalty or international pre-eminence). A B Jones and A B Smith trading as J & S Super Lawns is fine.

- You will need to consult a solicitor to assist with the preparation and signing of a partnership deed. The partnership deed is for your protection and is essential because it sets out the rules of the partnership including, for example, the profit or loss split between partners, what happens if one partner wishes to leave or you wish to admit a new partner.

- The full name and address of the partners and any trading name must be disclosed on letters, orders and invoices.

- A phone call to HMRC's helpline for the newly self-employed (0300 200 3504) explaining that you are starting a partnership or visit the website via **www.gov.uk** (then go to 'Running a business partnership').

## *Limited company*

A limited liability company (often the shorthand of 'limited company' is used to describe this trading format) is a company whose liability is limited by shares and is the most common form of trading format. The company is owned by its shareholders. The company is run by directors who are appointed by the shareholders.

The shareholders are liable to contribute the amount remaining unpaid on the shares – usually zero as most shares are issued fully paid up. The shareholders therefore achieve limited liability.

### How to start up a limited company

- A company needs to be registered with Companies House and cannot trade until it is granted a Certificate of Incorporation. The registration process is a quick and inexpensive process using Companies House's web incorporation service (it currently costs £15 and is completed within 24 hours). Some people use a company formation agent (Google this term to find such an agent – there are plenty of them) and the process should cost less than £50.

- The company name needs to be approved by Companies House. No two companies can have the same name and approval is usually completed in a day. Names that suggest, for instance, an international aspect will require evidence to support the claim and certain names are prohibited unless there is a dispensation (for example 'Royal').

- You must appoint a director and this 'officer' of the company carries responsibilities that can incur penalties and/or a fine. The appointment of directors should therefore not be done lightly. The full range of responsibilities is set out in The Companies Act; further guidance is available from the Companies House website (**www.companieshouse.co.uk**). Some examples of the responsibilities include the duty to maintain the financial records of the company, to prepare accounts, to retain the paperwork and to avoid conflicts of interest. Small businesses no longer require a separate company secretary but it can be useful to have another office-holder signatory and the risks associated with this position are relatively light. In addition you will need to appoint a registered office, which is a designated address at which official notices and communications can be received. The company's main place of business is usually used as the registered office but you could also use the address of your accountant or solicitor (there may be a charge for this).

# Alternative ways of getting started

Rather than start a new business, you could buy into one that is already established, or consider franchising.

## Buying a business

Buying an established business can be an attractive route to becoming your own boss, as it eliminates many of the problems of start-up. The enterprise is likely to come equipped with stock, suppliers, an order book, premises and possibly employees. It is also likely to have debtors and creditors. Take professional advice before buying any business, even one from friends. In particular, you should consider why the business is being sold. It may be for perfectly respectable reasons – for instance, a change of circumstances such as retirement. But equally, it may be that the market is saturated, that the rent is about to go sky-high or that major competition has opened up nearby.

Before parting with your money, verify that the assets are owned by the business and get the stock professionally valued. You should also ensure that the debts are collectable and that the same credit terms will apply from existing suppliers. Get an accountant to look at the figures for the last three years and have a chartered surveyor check the premises. A solicitor should be engaged to vet any legal documents, including staff and other ongoing contracts.

The value of the company's assets will be reflected in its purchase price, as will the 'goodwill' (or reputation) that it has established. For more information, agents specializing in small business sales have useful guides (for instance see **www.christie.com**).

## *Franchising*

Franchising continues to be a popular form of business entry route with attractions for both franchisor and franchisee. The franchisor gains, as their 'brand' is able to expand quickly. The advantage to the franchisee is that there are normally fewer risks than starting a business from scratch.

A franchisee buys into an established business and builds up his or her own enterprise under its wing. In return for the investment, plus regular royalty payments, he or she acquires the right to sell the franchisor's products or services within a specified geographic area and enjoys the benefits of its reputation, buying power and marketing expertise. As a franchisee you are effectively your own boss. You finance the business, employ the staff and retain the profits after the franchisor has had its cut. You are usually expected to maintain certain standards and conform to the broad corporate approach of the organization. In return, the franchisor should train you in the business, provide management support and give you access to a wide range of backup services.

The amount of capital needed to buy a franchise varies enormously according to the type of business, and can be anywhere between a few hundred pounds and £500,000 or more. The franchisee is normally liable to pay an initial fee, covering both the entry cost and the initial support services provided by the franchisor, such as advice about location and market research.

The length of the agreement will depend both on the type of business involved and on the front-end fee. Agreements can run from 3 to 20 years and many franchisors include an option to renew the agreement, which should be treated as a valuable asset.

Many franchises have built up a good track record and raising money to invest in good franchises may not be too difficult. Most of the leading high-street banks operate specialist franchise loan sections. Franchisors may also be able to help in raising the money and can sometimes arrange more advantageous terms through their connections with financial institutions.

The British Franchise Association (BFA) represents 'the responsible face' of franchising, and its members have to conform to a code of practice. When considering opportunities a good franchisor will provide a great deal of invaluable help. However, some franchisors may be less helpful and this will usually tell its own story. Make careful enquiries before committing any money: as basic information, you should ask for a bank reference together with a copy of the previous year's accounts. Also check with the BFA whether the franchisor in question is a member, and visit some of the other franchisees to find out what their experience has been. Before signing, seek advice from an accountant or solicitor. For more information, see the British Franchise Association website: **www.thebfa.org**.

# Operational and other issues

## Inventions and intellectual property

If you have a clever idea that you would like to market, you should ensure that your intellectual property is protected. For information about patenting an invention, and much more, look at the UK Intellectual Property Office website: **www.gov.uk** (and go to 'Intellectual Property Office').

## Licences

Certain types of business require a licence or permit to trade; these include pubs, off-licences, nursing agencies, pet shops, kennels, minicabs or buses, driving instructors, betting shops, auction sale rooms, cinemas, street traders and, in some cases, travel agents and tour operators. You will also require a licence to import certain goods. Your local authority planning office will advise you whether you require a licence, and in many cases your council will be the licensing authority.

## Permissions

Depending on the nature of your business, other permissions may need to be obtained, including those of the police, the environmental health department, licensing authorities and the fire prevention officer. In particular, there are special requirements concerning the sale of food, and safety measures for hotels and guest houses. Your local authority will advise you on what is necessary.

## Employing staff

Should you consider employing staff, you will immediately increase the complexity of your business. As well as paying salaries, you will have to account for PAYE, keep National Insurance records and conform to the multiple requirements of employment legislation. If you are worried or don't want the bother of doing the paperwork yourself, your accountant is likely to be able to introduce you to a payroll service, which will cost you money but will take some of the burden off your shoulders. Keeping personnel records will bring you into the scope of data protection; see **www.ico.gov.uk**.

### Employment legislation

As an employer, you have certain legal obligations in respect of your staff. The most important of these cover such issues as health and safety at work, terms and conditions of employment, and the provision of employee rights including, for example, parental leave, trade union activity and protection against unfair dismissal. Very small firms are exempt from some of the more onerous requirements, and the government is taking steps to reduce more of the red tape. However, it is important that you understand in general terms what legislation could affect you. You will usually find free support on this subject via membership of a trade association or organization such as the Federation of Small Businesses (**www.fsb.org.uk**). The Health and Safety Executive has a useful website: **www.hse.gov.uk**.

An employer, however small the business, may not discriminate against someone on the grounds of sex, race, disability, religion, marital status, sexual orientation or age. This applies to all aspects of employment, including training, promotion, recruitment, company benefits and facilities. More information at: **www.equalityhumanrights.com**.

## Disputes

If you find yourself with a potential dispute on your hands, it is sensible to approach the Advisory, Conciliation and Arbitration Service (ACAS), which operates an effective information and advisory service for employers and employees on a variety of workplace problems, including employment legislation and employment relations. It also has a wide range of useful publications, giving practical guidance on employment matters. See website: **www.acas.org.uk**.

# Insurance

Insurance is more than just a wise precaution. It is essential if you employ staff, have business premises or use your car regularly for commercial purposes. Many insurance companies now offer 'package insurance' for small businesses, which covers most of the main contingencies in a single policy. This usually works out cheaper than buying a collection of individual policies. An insurance broker should be able to guide you through the risks and insurance products available:

- *Employers' liability* – this is compulsory if you employ staff. It provides indemnity against liability for death or bodily injury to employees and subcontractors arising in connection with the business.

- *Product and public liability* – this insures the business and its products against claims by customers or the public.

- *Professional indemnity* – this is essential if a client could suffer a mishap, loss or other damage in consequence of advice or services received.

- *House insurance* – if you operate your business from home, check that you have notified your house insurer of this fact.

- *Motor risks* – check that you have notified your insurer if you use your motor vehicle for your business.

- *Life assurance* – this ensures that funds are available to pay off any debts or to enable the business to continue in the event of your death.

- *Permanent health insurance* – otherwise known as 'income protection', it provides insurance against long-term loss of income as a result of severe illness or disability.

- *Key person insurance* – this applies to the loss of a key person through prolonged illness as well as death. In small companies where the success or failure of the business is dependent upon the skills of one or two key executives, key person insurance may be demanded by lenders.

You should discuss these points with your insurance company or a broker. To find an insurance broker, see the British Insurance Brokers' Association website: **www.biba.org.uk**, or the Association of British Insurers website: **www.abi.org.uk**.

## Property investment

A frequent avenue that some people explore when nearing retirement is property investment, either in the UK or abroad. Since they may be armed with spare funds and perhaps have the advantage of more time available and perhaps even some maintenance skills, you can understand why this happens. Up until 2007 people thought they had it made in property investment with the magic mix of good capital growth and decent returns on their investment through rental income. The capital growth bubble burst in the summer of 2007 and some people have been nervous about this sector ever since. It is beyond the scope of this section to comment on whether or not the tide is turning but it can alert you to some of the key issues and potential sources of further help. Some of the issues are around minimizing your property tax bill, deciding whether to use a letting agent or not, complying with all the red tape and avoiding 'tenants from hell'.

Remember that there are many players in this market – including mortgage lenders, mortgage brokers, developers, property syndicates and letting agents – and that most will know more than you and all will want some of your money. Some even pay for your flights and travel expenses to visit property abroad and then play on this in a subsequent high-pressure sales environment. You are strongly advised to consider carefully before signing up – there will always, of course, be another day, another deal. For anyone thinking about property investment you would be wise to invest in David Lawrenson's bestselling property book *Successful Property Letting: How to make money in buy-to-let* (published by Constable & Robinson, website: **www.littlebrown.co.uk**) and review his website, **www.lettingfocus.com**. This will open your eyes to some of the issues touched upon here and will give you straightforward and clear advice and information on this market. For instance, one of David's candid tips is: 'You must like property. So, if houses bore you stiff, you're probably better off doing something else.'

Armed with this and advice from friends and relatives who have invested in property, you might then be ready to put your toe in the water and start to explore this area.

# Further help, advice and training

Small businesses are well served when it comes to general help and training. Some of the best available feature below.

## *Organizations providing free or subsidized help*

### Government resources

The government website (**www.gov.uk**) contains the government's online resource for businesses.

Regional or country-specific support is also available at:

- Northern Ireland – **www.nibusinessinfo.co.uk**;
- Scotland – **www.business.scotland.gov.uk**;
- Wales – **www.business.wales.gov.uk**.

### Business is great

Business Is Great has been set up by the government to help you with support, advice and inspiration for growing your business including advice on imports and exports, finance, employment, intellectual property and regulation. It includes a 'business support tool' and after answering a few questions you get a report of resources and schemes to start to support your business. Further information is available from: **www.greatbusiness.gov.uk**.

## Start-up Britain

Start-up Britain has been set up by the government to help you find information about starting a business and contains offers and discounts available to new business start-ups. Further information is available from: **www.startupbritain.org**.

## Adult education centres

Short courses in specific business skills are run by business schools and colleges of higher and further education. Further information is available from **www.learndirect.co.uk** and the Workers Education Association, website: **www.wea.org.uk**.

## PRIME

PRIME (The Prince's Initiative for Mature Enterprise) helps people over the age of 50 to set up in business and offers free information and business-networking events. See website: **www.prime.org.uk**.

## Other useful organizations

- Many solicitors offer a free initial consultation and advice can be sought on a range of issues. To find solicitors in your local area use the 'find a solicitor' section at the website: **www.lawsociety.org**.

- The Federation of Small Businesses (**www.fsb.org.uk**). The networking opportunities and benefits of FSB make it a 'must have' for most new small businesses.

- Association of Independent Professionals and the Self Employed (IPSE). The IPSE's 'Guide to Freelancing' is free and can be downloaded from its website, **www.ipse.co.uk**. IPSE's knowledge of and guidance on IR35 for freelancers and contractors are second to none.

- Business start-up websites. These are packed with free hints and tips and a useful one is **www.bstartup.com**; their exhibitions are free, well attended and have some excellent free workshops and guest speakers.

# Useful reading

An extensive list of books for small and start-up businesses is published by Kogan Page, website: **www.koganpage.com**, including *Start Up and Run Your Own Business* and *Working for Yourself: An entrepreneur's guide*, both by Jonathan Reuvid; *Soul Trader: Putting the heart back into your business*, by Rasheed Ogunlaru; *The Rebel Entrepreneur: Rewriting the business rulebook*, by Jonathan Moules.

# Starting and running a business – checklist

When starting or running a business you will encounter a vast range of information and this can lead to you feeling swamped. This checklist has been developed to help you on the journey. Try annotating each item – N: not applicable; W: work on now; A: review with accountant; C: complete:

- If you want to travel somewhere you use a map. In business it's just the same except you get yourself a *plan*. Commit it to writing and don't expect to get it right first time (no one does!). A few pages are fine to start with based on objectives, a profit-and-loss forecast and your marketing research and action plan. Review it with your accountant and a trusted friend, then build it up.

- Choose your *trading format*, ie company (usually signified by 'limited') or sole trader or partnership or limited liability partnership. This is an important step and one to talk through with your accountant or a business adviser. You can set up a company for £15 at Companies House (**www.companieshouse.gov.uk**) 'web incorporation service'. Understand the personal liability risks of sole trader/partnership and, indeed, joint and several liability if trading in partnership ('last person standing pays the lot'!). If things go badly wrong your personal wealth could be at risk – but perhaps insurance could help (see below).

- Choose your *accountant* – there are many accountancy organizations; chartered accountants can be found at **www.icaew.co.uk** (England and Wales); **www.icas.org.uk** (Scotland) and **www.charteredaccountants.ie** (Ireland). Accountants are usually prepared to see you for an initial 'no obligation' meeting. Be clear about who your regular contact will be, and their qualifications and knowledge of your industry, their hourly rates and check they have professional indemnity insurance.

- Make sure you have a source of *legal help*. Could your local solicitor help? Alternatively, your trade association may offer a free legal helpline that may suffice initially. An early legal question that will usually arise is about your terms and conditions of trade or contracts.

- There is some *free government help* that you will find at **www.gov.uk**, which contains the government's online resource for businesses.

  You should also check out the government-backed initiative **www.startupbritain.org** and **www.greatbusiness.gov.uk** for inspiration and ideas. Regional or country-specific support is also available at:

  - Northern Ireland: at **www.nibusinessinfo.co.uk**;

  - Scotland: at **www.business.scotland.gov.uk**;

  - Wales: at **www.business.wales.gov.uk**;

  - For the over-50s try: **www.prime.org.uk**.

- Join the best *trade or professional association* that you can identify and consider the extra benefits each provides in the areas of research information, networking events, helplines, tax investigation help and insurance offerings.

- Choose and, if appropriate, protect your *business name*. There is some useful free help available on intellectual property (patents, brands, etc) at the Intellectual Property Office at **www.ipo.gov.uk**.

- Choose a *business bank account*. Shop around for the best deal that suits your business (often a trade-off between the convenience of a local 'bricks and mortar' branch accompanied by internet banking versus free or reduced charges for internet-only accounts).

- Assess your *pension* needs. See **www.unbiased.co.uk** for finding an independent financial adviser (IFA).

- Sort out your *tax and record keeping* (documents need to be kept for seven years and you need to become a receipt/invoice hoarder with a logical 'system for filing'), as the taxman might say, 'Prove it or lose it.' Check with your accountant that your proposed bookkeeping and record-keeping systems are acceptable before you buy them.

- Understand the implications of failing to deal with your *tax* affairs properly. This can be penalties ranging from 30 per cent to 100 per cent plus interest. Some trade associations include 'free' tax investigation cover – a very useful benefit.

- Understand your key *tax obligations* and deadlines. For companies you are obliged to file your annual accounts at Companies House nine months after your year end and your *annual return* on the anniversary of setting up a company each year. There is good-quality free help at Companies House, **www.companieshouse.gov.uk**.

- Understand your obligations on *VAT*. The current (Summer 2015) registration threshold for compulsory registration is £82,000. Consider VAT schemes especially the VAT flat-rate scheme for small businesses.

- Set up your *premises* so that you can work effectively. If you work from home, manage your family's and neighbours' expectations – suddenly the phrase 'Time is money' takes on a new meaning.

- Set up your *suppliers* (set up contracts and bills in the company or business name) and, if appropriate, set up stock control and delivery systems.

- Consider *insurance* policies for identified business risks (professional indemnity, public liability, product liability, etc). An insurance broker can advise on this and you should also consider policies available via trade associations as these can provide increased cover at less cost.

- Consider protecting the income you take from your business (especially if you have dependents) in the event of long-term *illness* or of *death* (**www.unbiased.co.uk** for finding an independent financial adviser).

- If running your *business at home* you must tell your insurer that you run a business from home.

- *Marketing and selling* will be massively important to your success. If you are not from a selling/marketing background, talk to trusted friends who run their own business and your accountant/ adviser or mentor about your market research and marketing plan. Understand your customers and what they need.

- Do not underestimate the importance of networking.

- Plan the *pricing* strategies for your product or service. A different package means a different price. How have you benchmarked your price and how have you differentiated your offering (features and benefits) to allow you to charge that little bit more? Conversely, what features and benefits have you stripped out to allow you to offer a headline price that comes in beneath the competition?

- Plan your *marketing promotion strategy*. Remember that 'folk are different' and that it is a bit like fishing – you use different hooks depending on what you are trying to catch.

- Get paid promptly for your sale. What are your *payment terms* (terms and conditions)? Follow up on outstanding debts. If you sell stock have you included a reservation of title clause to help you retrieve unpaid stock if your client goes bust?

- Set up your *IT system* and support and have a system to back up your data securely. Check whether you need to notify the Information Commissioner under the *data protection* laws (**www.ico.gov.uk**).

- Consider other *red tape*, especially if your area is a specialized sector (food, health and safety, etc). Investigate and apply for the licences and permits that your business may need.

- Review and update your business plan in the light of experience and keep it a living document.

# Chapter Eight
# Working for others – volunteering and paid work

*'I have nothing against work, particularly when performed, quietly and unobtrusively, by someone else.'*

**BARBARA EHRENREICH**

The good news? We are living longer. The challenge? With most of us retiring at the same sort of age, we'll be spending two or more decades in retirement, but doing what? Encouraging and enabling those who want to work longer is happening, along with recognizing the potential of older workers. Statistics show that the over-50s are a major resource, who can boost output, employment and living standards now and in the future.

One of the most noticeable changes in lifestyle, as shown by a recent Saga survey, is that since 2010 the number of people over 65 still in work has risen by around 36 per cent. The end of the default retirement age is largely responsible, as employees may continue working if they wish. The primary reason for many continuing to work beyond 65 is to augment their disappointing pensions. However, many of us wish to continue working as it provides a boost to our self-esteem, a social life and much-appreciated mental stimulation. Wanting to have something to do to avoid boredom, and a desire to feel useful are the key reasons many people continue working (paid or unpaid). And why not? If they enjoy it, feel they are too young to stop, or want to try their hand at becoming 'grand-trepreneurs' – adults of state-pension age who are choosing to use their new-found freedom to set up or invest in businesses

– (Chapter 7 covers all of this in detail), they should be encouraged to do so.

Maybe it's time to rethink your later life working plans, and look for purpose, structure and fulfilment by doing something different. It is not correct to think of work as just a source of income, it also gives us a goal, identity, social connections and (for many) dignity. Whether you are considering working for yourself (see Chapter 7), volunteering or looking for paid employment, working beyond our 50s gives us the opportunity to try new things, meet new people and keep our minds, bodies and spirits in good shape. This is an important consideration if we wish to age well.

## All you need to know about this chapter and what it contains

In this chapter we cover options available when working for others, either voluntarily or by taking paid employment. The advice contained here applies across the spectrum, whether you are thinking of working for just a few hours a week/month or longer. So, whether you are just idly considering working (again), or are actively searching for something gainful to do, this chapter is for you.

- The first section is all about volunteering opportunities (because so many early retirees enjoy working in the not-for-profit sector – we really are a generous bunch!) It is very important to choose the right type of work for you, so read this section carefully; it could save you hours of frustration.

- There is also a section on long-term volunteering and opportunities for volunteering overseas.

- If you are thinking of getting a job because you wish for paid employment, read the section on how to find a job, to give yourself some ideas on how to plan your job search. If you don't prepare, you could waste hours of your precious time, and end up wondering why you are bothering.

- There is also information and advice on training opportunities and other employment ideas. Once you start reading, you will be on the way to finding the ideal occupation for you.

# Volunteering opportunities

One of the many good things about retirement is the flexibility – it gives us the time to do what we want to do when we want to do it. If there is no need to work to earn more money, some people find volunteering brings heightened benefits simply because they are working without financial reward. The feeling of contributing to society in later life is enhanced because they do it for free. Before making a commitment to voluntary work we need to think carefully how much time we wish to devote to it. There are voluntary roles that allow more flexibility than others. Getting the balance between flexibility and commitment can sometimes be difficult, so it's important to think about where we want the balance and then choose an appropriate voluntary role that fits.

The range of jobs in the voluntary sector is enormous, from the predominantly physical, cerebral, sedentary or active, indoor or outdoors, interacting with other people, or working alone. You may not find your ideal role immediately but with patience and persistence you should discover the right one for you.

Someone who becomes a volunteer at the age of 60 could have two decades or more years of positive contribution to make. The most frequently cited reasons why people volunteer include:

- wanting to 'make a difference' to other people's lives;
- enjoying using their skills in new and valuable ways;
- feeling better both physically and mentally;
- supporting local activities and neighbourhood organizations;
- being a committed member of social and charitable projects;
- actively participating in democratic institutions – such as parish/community councils, boards of school governors, or neighbourhood watch;
- finding opportunities to help in education, sport, culture, leisure, conservation and the environment.

There are so many types of work available to volunteers, depending on what you enjoy doing and what skills you have, you should be able to find something to suit. It is entirely dependent on you what you choose – from the large international or national charities to much smaller organizations. Always play to your strengths: if you are a keen gardener, helping the elderly with their gardens in your neighbourhood would be one suggestion. DIY or home decorating, are popular and sought-after skills particularly with those who can no longer do such things themselves. There are probably many clubs and organizations in your local community who will eagerly accept voluntary help. Types of work could include:

- *Administrative* – Any active group is likely to need clerical help, from stuffing and labelling envelopes to organizing committees. This may involve a day or so a week or occasional assistance at peak times. Many smaller charities are desperate for help from individuals with IT expertise and accountancy experience.

- *Committee work* – This can cover anything from very occasional help to a virtually full-time commitment as chair, treasurer or secretary. People with business skills or financial or legal backgrounds are likely to be especially valuable, and those whose skills include minute-taking are always in demand.

- *Direct work* – Driving, delivering 'meals on wheels', counselling, visiting the housebound, working in a charity shop, helping with a playgroup, respite care for carers – the list is endless and the value of the work incalculable. There are many interesting and useful jobs for those without special training. As regards time commitment, do as much as you feel comfortable with. Whether one morning per month or a certain number of hours per week, it is far better to be reliable than to over-promise and have to cancel or let people down.

- *Fundraising* – Every voluntary organization needs money, and when donations are static or falling, more creativity and ingenuity are required to help bring in funds. Events are many and varied, but anyone with energy and experience of organizing fundraising events would be welcomed with open arms as a volunteer.

- *Overseas* – Many more people in later life are now combining volunteering with travel. There are many in their 50s and 60s who are seizing this opportunity as they may have missed their 'gap year' when they were young. Further information on voluntary work overseas will be found later in this chapter.

If you are serious about volunteering, as with paid work, do your research. Before you start, think carefully about what volunteering jobs would suit you and what would fit in best with your family and other commitments; there are a variety of openings as described above.

Then you will need to ask questions of the organization such as: who you will be working with; what is expected; when you will be needed; if expenses are paid – and if so, what for and how much. Once you have all this mapped out you will find that volunteering can be very rewarding. As it is a big commitment, finding the right role is essential, otherwise you may be less than enthusiastic about it. Voluntary work is not only rewarding in its own right but also allows you to make a real contribution to the community.

Should you consider working with vulnerable people (young or old) you will need to have a full Disclosure and Barring Service (DBS) (formerly Criminal Records Bureau, or CRB) check. For further information about this see the government website: **www.gov.uk** – Employing people (select the 'Recruiting and hiring' link).

## Choosing the right voluntary work

Once you've decided that you might take on some volunteering, doing the research to see what is available in this huge sector is essential. You could ask friends who are experienced volunteers for their advice and recommendations. Locally there are a number of options: the local council should have someone who liaises with the voluntary sector; the library; local newspaper; church and shop noticeboards.

The organization REACH is:

> ... the skilled volunteering charity and has been connecting charities and skilled professionals for over thirty years. Reach's services boost the resources of the voluntary sector, working with over 10,000 organizations across the UK. Each year Reach volunteers contribute £31 million of expertise to the organizations they assist...

For more information see: **www.reachskills.org.uk**.

The following UK-wide general websites will give you lots of help and information:

- Volunteering Matters: **www.volunteeringmatters.org.uk**;
- Volunteering England: **www.volunteering.org.uk**;

- Volunteer Scotland: **www.volunteerscotland.net**;
- Volunteering Wales: **www.volunteering-wales.net**;
- Volunteer Now (Northern Ireland): **www.volunteernow.co.uk**.

Also:

- Business in the Community: **www.bitc.org.uk**;
- Citizens Advice: **www.citizensadvice.org.uk**;
- Do-it Trust: **www.doittrust.org**;
- Lions Clubs International – British Isles and Ireland: **www.lionsclubs.co**;
- RVS: **www.royalvoluntaryservice.org.uk**;
- The Media Trust: **www.mediatrust.org**;
- TimeBank: **www.timebank.org.uk**.

The following are just a few specialist areas for which you could consider volunteering. There are no descriptions given because they are self-explanatory. The websites listed are the more well-known ones for each category, though there are many, many smaller charities you could research via such sites as: **www.charitychoice.co.uk**.

# Animals

- Blue Cross: **www.bluecross.org.uk**;
- Cats Protection: **www.cats.org.uk**;
- Cinnamon Trust: **www.cinnamon.org.uk**;
- Dogs Trust: **www.dogstrust.org.uk**;
- Horse Trust: **www.horsetrust.org.uk**;
- PDSA: **www.pdsa.org.uk**;
- Pets As Therapy (PAT): **www.petsastherapy.org**;
- RSPCA: **www.rspca.org.uk**;
- Royal Society for the Protection of Birds (RSPB): **www.rspb.org.uk**;
- Wildfowl & Wetlands Trust (WWT): **www.wwt.org.uk**;
- World Wildlife Fund UK: **www.wwf.org.uk**.

# The elderly

- Age UK: **www.ageuk.org.uk;**
- Carers Trust: **www.carers.org;**
- Carers UK: **www.carersuk.org;**
- Contact the Elderly: **www.contact-the-elderly.org.uk;**
- Independent Age: **www.independentage.org.uk.**

# Armed and ex-services

- ABF The Soldiers' Charity: **www.soldierscharity.org;**
- Blind Veterans UK: **www.blindveterans.org.uk;**
- Combat Stress: **www.combatstress.org.uk;**
- Help for Heroes: **www.helpforheroes.org.uk;**
- Royal Air Force Benevolent Fund: **www.rafbf.org;**
- Royal British Legion: **www.britishlegion.org.uk;**
- Royal Marines Charitable Trust Fund: **www.rmctf.org.uk;**
- Seafarers UK: **www.seafarers-uk.org;**
- SSAFA: **www.ssafa.org.uk.**

# Bereavement

- Cruse Bereavement Care: **www.cruse.org.uk;**
- Grief Encounter: **www.griefencounter.org.uk;**
- Winston's Wish: **www.winstonswish.org.uk.**

# Children and young people

- Action for Children: **www.actionforchildren.org;**
- Barnardo's: **www.barnardos.org.uk;**
- Children's Society: **www.childrenssociety.org.uk;**

- Children's Trust: **www.thechildrenstrust.org.uk**;
- Girl Guiding: **www.girlguiding.org.uk**;
- Marine Society and Sea Cadets: **www.ms-sc.org**;
- NSPCC: **www.nspcc.org.uk**;
- Save the Children: **www.savethechildren.org**;
- Scout Association: **www.scouts.org.uk**;
- UNICEF: **www.unicef.org.uk**.

## Conservation

- Architectural Heritage Society of Scotland: **www.ahss.org.uk**;
- Campaign to Protect Rural England (CPRE): **www.cpre.org.uk**;
- Churches Conservation Trust (CCT): **www.visitchurches.org.uk**;
- Friends of the Earth: **www.foe.co.uk**;
- Greenpeace: **www.greenpeace.org.uk**;
- Ramblers: **www.ramblers.org.uk**;
- The Conservation Volunteers (TCV): **www.tcv.org.uk**.

## Family

- British Association for Adoption and Fostering (BAAF): **www.baaf.org.uk**;
- Family Action: **www.family-action.org.uk**;
- Marriage Care: **www.marriagecare.org.uk**;
- Relate: **www.relate.org.uk**.

## Health and disability

- British Deaf Association: **www.bda.org.uk**;
- British Heart Foundation (BHF): **www.bhf.org.uk**;
- Cancer Research UK: **www.cancerresearchuk.org**;

- Diabetes UK: **www.diabetes.org.uk;**
- Guide Dogs: **www.guidedogs.org.uk;**
- Leonard Cheshire Disability: **www.leonardcheshire.org;**
- Marie Curie Cancer Care: **www.mariecurie.org.uk;**
- Mind: **www.mind.org.uk;**
- Parkinson's UK: **www.parkinsons.org.uk;**
- RDA (Riding for the Disabled Association): **www.rda.org.uk;**
- RNIB (Royal National Institute of Blind People): **www.rnib.org.uk;**
- St John Ambulance: **www.sja.org.uk.**

# Heritage

- Ancient Monuments Society: **www.ancientmonumentssociety.org.uk;**
- Architectural Heritage Fund: **www.ahfund.org.uk;**
- Archaeology for All: **www.new.archaeologyuk.org;**
- English Heritage: **www.english-heritage.org.uk;**
- National Trust: **www.nationaltrust.org.uk;**
- SPAB (Society for the Protection of Ancient Buildings): **www.spab.org.uk.**

# Politics

- Conservative Party: **www.conservatives.com;**
- Green Party: **www.greenparty.org.uk;**
- Labour Party: **www.labour.org.uk;**
- Liberal Democrats: **www.libdems.org.uk;**
- Plaid Cymru: **www.plaidcymru.org;**
- Scottish National Party: **www.snp.org;**
- UKIP: **www.ukip.org.uk;**
- Ulster Unionist Party: **www.uup.org.**

# Social welfare

- British Red Cross: **www.redcross.org.uk**;
- Elizabeth Finn Care: **www.elizabethfinncare.org.uk**;
- Oxfam: **www.oxfam.org.uk**;
- Salvation Army: **www.salvationarmy.org.uk**;
- Samaritans: **www.samaritans.org**;
- Shelter: **www.shelter.org.uk**.

# Long-term and overseas volunteering

Volunteering in the long term requires a different sort of commitment and there are organizations that require long-term volunteers both in the UK or abroad. With a wide range of projects, some require specialist skills such as engineering or medicine; while others essentially need people with practical qualities, common sense and enthusiasm. Each organization has a minimum period of service. General conditions are similar for all of them; travel is paid, plus a living allowance or salary that is based on local levels rather than on expatriate rates. Couples without dependent children are welcome, as long as both have the necessary skills. National Insurance contributions are provided, and a resettlement grant is paid on completion of the tour. If you are up to the challenge, it can be immensely rewarding. See:

- AidCamps International: **www.aidcamps.org**;
- Helpx: **www.helpx.net**;
- Progressio ICS: **www.progressio.org.uk**;
- TCV The Conservation Volunteers: **www.tcv.org.uk**;
- Skillshare International: **www.skillshare.org**;
- VSO (Voluntary Service Overseas): **www.vso.org.uk**;
- Workaway.info: **www.workaway.info**;
- World Wide Opportunities on Organic Farms: **www.wwoof.net**.

# Searching for paid employment

If the need for some extra money in your retirement pot is the incentive for continuing to work, one of the top tips advisers give is, quite simply, not to leave your job early if you have that choice. Although the opportunities are increasing, some people in their 50s and 60s find it difficult to get back into work once they have left the workplace – be that because of redundancy or voluntarily. So, if you currently have a job which you enjoy, hang on to it. The longer people are out of work the harder it is to get back into it. If this is a situation someone is facing, the previous section on Volunteering is particularly relevant, as showing that someone has worked as a volunteer rather than remaining unemployed, effectively and efficiently fills a gap in a CV. Indeed, volunteering roles can, on occasion, lead to paid jobs within the organization.

It might be a good idea to think about whether you wish to redefine what you do. You will be negotiating with your current employer from a position of strength when discussing a change of role, or the number of days or hours you wish to work. If you cut your working down to four or three days per week, this could represent a saving of 20 per cent, or 40 per cent, of your salary to your employer. Should this appeal to you, you can then use your free time to take up other activities that you have not previously had the time to do. A win-win situation?

It also goes without saying, that if you wish to remain in the workplace, never turn down the chance of any sort of training. Opportunities to refresh skills or add new ones will make you a valuable resource in whatever job you take. You may not realize how many skills you have attained over your working life. Spend some time considering what these are, as a number of them will be transferable and useful in a whole host of jobs.

Should a change of direction (and employer) appeal to you, you will need to start your research. There is a lot of useful information on how to obtain work available via the Laterlife website: **www.laterlife.com/jobs-and-work**. If you are seeking work while coping with redundancy, you will find some excellent independent advice on Redundancy Help's website: **www.redundancyhelp.co.uk**. Another couple of organizations that specialize in helping the over-50s find work are:

- Retired 4 Hire: **www.Retired4Hire.co.uk**;
- Skilled People: **www.skilledpeople.com**;
- The Age and Employment Network: **www.taen.org.uk**.

## Top tips for preparing your job search campaign

- *Do the sums.* This is particularly important if you are currently out of work, you must work out how long you can manage financially without getting into difficulties. With regard to salary, what is your acceptable and your minimum level?

- *Get organized.* Planning your job-hunting campaign is vital. Unless you are a firm believer in serendipity, you will not achieve what you want without a plan. Set aside a study area in your home, and devote a number of hours each day to job searching.

- *Assess yourself.* Knowing what you have to offer to a potential employer makes sense. List things you have done throughout your career, including your outside interests. In addition to work skills, what are your personal strengths?

- *CV writing.* Presentation is key, your CV should not be longer than two pages of A4 and contain the following sections: personal and contact information; education and qualifications; work history and/or experience; relevant skills to the job in question; personal interests, achievements and hobbies, and referees. Use assertive, positive language, emphasizing the skills you have gained from past work. Referees are important: one should be a previous employer, the other someone who can vouch for you personally.

- *Make your network work for you.* More older people get back into work through people they know than any other method. Essentially the people in your network are people you know who may be able to help with advice, information or eventually a potential job lead. Decide what the best means of approach will be for each one – personal contact, email, telephone or letter.

Don't forget to regularly review the results: how much progress you make each week, how many contacts on your network you have made, and what results these have yielded.

## *Training opportunities*

Knowing what you want to do is one thing, but before starting a new job you may want to brush up existing skills or possibly acquire new ones. Most professional bodies have a full programme of training events, ranging from one-day seminars to courses lasting a week or longer. Additionally, adult education institutes run a vast range of courses or, if you are still in your present job, a more practical solution might be to investigate open and flexible learning, which you can do from home.

# Open and flexible learning

There are a number of vocational education and training opportunities for individuals of all ages. You are more likely to be successful if you learn at a time, place and pace best suited to their own particular circumstances. The following organizations offer advice and an excellent range of courses:

- Adult Education Finder: **www.adulteducationfinder.co.uk**;
- Home Learning College: **www.homelearningcollege.com**;
- Learn Direct: **www.learndirect.co.uk**;
- National Extension College: **www.nec.ac.uk**;
- Open and Distance Learning Quality Council (ODLQC): **www.odlqc.org.uk**;
- Open University (OU): **www.open.ac.uk**.

IT skills are essential, so make sure your skills are current. These websites could help:

- Computeach: **www.computeach.co.uk**; and
- Home and Learn: **www.homeandlearn.co.uk**.

# Employment ideas

## *Consultancy*

If the idea of hiring yourself back to your former employer as a consultant appeals to you, you may be able to build up a steady stream of assignments and be recommended to other companies who could use your skills. Consultancy by definition is not limited to a single client. Small firms especially often buy in expertise as and when required. The following websites are worth checking:

- Consultancy UK: **www.consultancy.uk**;
- Institute of Consulting: **www.iconsulting.org.uk**;
- Mindbench: **www.mindbench.com**.

## Interim management

Interim management is the temporary provision of management resources and skills. It is a short-term assignment of a proven heavyweight interim executive manager to manage a period of transition, crisis or change within an organization. Assignments could be full time or involve just one or two days per week. For more information:

- Executives Online: **www.executivesonline.co.uk**;
- Interim Management Association (IMA): **www.interimmanagement.uk.com**;
- Interim Partners: **www.interimpartners.com**;
- Odgers Interim: **www.odgersinterim.com**.

## Non-executive directorships

Senior management experience would suggest the route of non-executive director. A NED is a non-working director of a firm who does not participate in the day-to-day management of the organization. Instead, they are expected to monitor and challenge the performance of the executive directors and the management. Such appointments carry heavy responsibilities made more onerous by recent legislation. See the following:

- Executives Online: **www.executivesonline.co.uk**;
- First Flight: **www.nonexecdirector.co.uk**;
- Non Executive Directors: **www.nonexecutivedirectors.com**.

## Public appointments

A public appointment is typically the appointment of a chair or non-executive director for a board of a public body or for a member of an advisory committee. Public appointments vacancies at local, regional and national levels across the UK can be found on the Cabinet Office website: **www.publicappointments.cabinetoffice.gov.uk**.

## Market research

Market research provides relevant data to help solve marketing challenges that a business will most likely face, enabling that business to maintain competitiveness over its competitors. The work involves the capture and analysis of consumer, competitor and market trend data. See websites:

- Market Research Society: **www.mrs.org.uk**;
- National Centre for Social Research: **www.natcen.ac.uk**;
- Research Job Finder: **www.researchjobfinder.com**.

## Paid work for charities

If you are thinking of working (for money) in the third sector, it might be helpful to work as a volunteer before seeking a paid appointment. Anyone thinking of applying for a job with a charity must be sympathetic to its aims and style. The following organizations may help:

- CF Appointments: **www.cfappointments.com**;
- Charity Job: **www.charityjob.co.uk**;
- Charity People: **www.charitypeople.co.uk**;
- Harris Hill: **www.harrishill.co.uk**;
- ProspectUs: **www.prospect-us.co.uk**;
- TPP not-for-profit: **www.tpp.co.uk**.

# Jobs with travel

If you have stamina, enjoy meeting people and like travelling, working in the tourism sector could be interesting. It requires an academic mind and involves a certain amount of study. Tour guides need an interest in history and culture, and in many cases an aptitude for languages. Some people with specialist knowledge sign on as a lecturer with one of the travel companies offering special interest holidays, others specialize in tourist attractions nearer to home. Air courier jobs are also good for people who like travelling abroad. See the following websites:

- Guild of Registered Tourist Guides: **www.britainsbestguides.org**;
- Travel Job Search: **www.traveljobsearch.com**;
- Travel Weekly: **www.jobs.travelweekly.co.uk**;
- Overseas Experience: **www.overseas-experience.com**.

## Teaching and tutoring

If you have experience of teaching, there are a number of possibilities open to you, both in the UK and abroad. With examinations becoming more competitive many parents require private tutors to help their children prepare for public examinations. There is always a demand for people to teach English to foreign students at the many language schools. Most UK universities offer language courses during the summer. For more information, see:

- Gabbitas Education Consultants: **www.gabbitas.co.uk**;
- Home Tutors: **www.hometutors.org.uk**;
- British Council: **www.britishcouncil.org**;
- Intensive Tefl Courses: **www.tefl.co.uk**.

## House-sitting

Taking care of someone else's home (and pets) while they are away on holiday or business trips, is something mature, responsible people can do. Agencies prefer car owners, non-smokers, with no children or pets of their own. It can be rather like a paid holiday. Some companies who specialize in this kind of work include:

- Homesitters Ltd: **www.homesitters.co.uk**;
- Rest Assured House Sitters: **www.restassuredhousesitters.co.uk**.

## Caring for others

If you are able to care for other people, there are a number of opportunities for paid work in this field. You may be required to have a full DBS (Disclosure and Barring Service) check if you are considering working with vulnerable people (young and old). For further information about DBS checks, see: **www.gov.uk** – Employing people. *The Lady* magazine, published every Wednesday, has classified advertisements for domestic help. A number of agencies specialize in finding temporary or permanent companions and housekeepers for elderly and disabled people, or for those who are convalescing. Some of these include:

- Consultus Care and Nursing Agency: **www.consultuscare.com**;
- Country Cousins: **www.country-cousins.co.uk**;
- Universal Aunts Ltd: **www.universalaunts.co.uk**.

# Chapter Nine
# Hobbies and holidays

*'There is no nation in the world which has so little capacity for doing nothing gracefully, and enjoying it, as the English.'*

**A C BENSON**

You've worked hard for years and you've planned well for your retirement. This could, according to recent statistics, last for about thirty years, so all that remains is to fill your new-found leisure with activities, hobbies and holidays. Sounds ideal, doesn't it?

**Everything you need on hobbies and holidays – could this be the chapter for you?**

- Joining a book club or planning a parachute jump – or even more? The array of hobbies and interests in the UK is second to none and the friendship and enjoyment is an added bonus that can propel you down all sorts of new and interesting avenues. Many of these keep you active, so what's not to like?

- If you take no other action from this book, except for taking up a new hobby or interest, this book will have more than covered its purchase price. As a well known branded sports firm says 'Just do it' and you might even surprise yourself at a hidden talent that has lain dormant until now.

- Other nuggets of information in this chapter include how to access free 'big name' entertainment through signposts to accessing TV audience tickets – and we all like quality and free (and those two words do not often go hand in hand).

- Holidays are, for some people, the oasis in an otherwise unremarkable calendar. The range of holidays for the disabled, singles or those wishing to learn is often untapped and our book will help you navigate the options and direct you to some great further help.

- The flip side is that our perfect 'oasis' can be spoilt by others and there is good help around for dealing with bust holiday companies, cancelled flights etc. Our tips about paying by credit card and always carrying the Consumer Council's 'Plane Facts' in your hand luggage could just help get you out of a pickle.

If this is the chapter for you... read on (and enjoy).

According to *Mature Times*, some of the most popular pastimes people enjoy in retirement include: cooking and baking; researching your family tree; going to the gym; joining a book club; visiting antique fairs; knitting; golf; yoga; and playing poker or bridge.

You may already be delighting in these and other leisure pursuits, however, some such activities could seem rather tame. It was recently revealed that British pensioners actually have rather a wild side, considering the goals on their Bucket List. They are refusing to spend their autumn years sitting quietly, instead they are travelling the world, writing a novel, mountain-climbing and even planning a parachute jump. (Source: **www. express.co.uk/news/uk/514400/UK-pensioners-top-20-bucket-list**). When recently surveyed by Centra Pulse (part of the not-for-profit group Circle Housing, which helps 125,000 people to live independently with the aid of technology), more than 2,000 people aged over 65 planned on filling their retirement by visiting new countries – most popular destinations being Australia, New Zealand, The United States, Canada and China. Many wanted to see their family settled and others were determined to live to the grand old age of 100. Also included on the list were flying a helicopter, seeing the Northern Lights, going to University and falling in love – for some people, perhaps, it's never too late.

The list of top 20 goals are:

**1** travelling the world;

**2** seeing family settled;

**3** living to 100;

 **4** winning the lottery;

 **5** buying a house;

 **6** learning a language;

 **7** becoming financially secure;

 **8** becoming a grandparent;

 **9** watching favourite sport team play one more time;

 **10** providing for the family;

 **11** learning to fly;

 **12** buying a classic car;

 **13** learning to play a musical instrument;

 **14** seeing the Northern Lights;

 **15** going on a world cruise;

 **16** losing weight;

 **17** taking up charity work;

 **18** skydiving or parachute jumping;

 **19** getting a hole-in-one;

 **20** creating the ultimate garden.

Age, far from being an excuse not to be adventurous, is in fact for many of us a spur to drive us on, to see what we can achieve. *Saga* magazine (January 2015) featured some extraordinary athletes, all of whom are over 50, whose achievements are inspirational. This list included Vivien Guthrie, 64, a retired dentist from the Wirral, who is a Grand Master Bowman, the highest achievement in the world of longbows. Fauja Singh, 103, holds the title of the world's oldest marathon runner – a sport he took up at the age of 89. Charlie Pitcher, 52, a former professional yachtsman from Essex, competed in the America's Cup and in 2013 broke the world record for rowing solo across the Atlantic. Jane Leslie, 65, from Bristol was crowned champion at the 2014 World Triathlon Grand Final (swimming 1,500 metres, cycling 40 kilometres and running 10 kilometres) in Canada. Brian East, 70, a former aviation worker from Surrey, was the oldest contender in the 2012 Tour de Force, which covers the route of the (3,500 kilometres) Tour de France. So, as the article said, what are you waiting for?

Doing something – being active and involved – is beneficial to mental and physical health. This chapter deals with hobbies and holidays. It is brimming with ideas for activities – some you can do without leaving home, and alternatives where a special interest can include a vacation and opportunities for learning and exploring new places. Here we go...

# Arts and culture

Arts and culture enrich our lives, whether we participate or appreciate the performance of others. There is one umbrella organization, The Arts Council, that champions, develops and invests in artistic and cultural experiences that enhance people's lives. For more information see: **www.artscouncil.org.uk**.

## Arts and crafts

The following organizations offer residential arts and crafts holidays:

- Field Studies Council: **www.field-studies-council.org**;
- Marlborough College Summer School: **www.mcsummerschool.org.uk**;
- Missenden Abbey: **www.missendenabbey-al.co.uk**;
- West Dean College: **www.westdean.org.uk**.

## Creative arts

To study creative arts, the Open College of Arts (OCA) is an educational charity whose purpose is to widen participation in arts education. For further information see: **www.oca.ac.uk**.

## Cultural holidays

One of the best ways to enjoy luxurious travel with the opportunity to explore beautiful places. If you choose a cultural holiday it offers a combination of visits to places of artistic, historic, musical and architectural interest, with lectures given by professional academics, writers and curators. They are carefully researched and provide high standards of customer service, including comfortable hotels and authentic restaurants. Here are a few to consider:

- Abercrombie & Kent: **www.abercrombiekent.co.uk**;
- Ace Cultural Tours: **www.aceculturaltours.co.uk**;
- Andante Travels: **www.andantetravels.com**;
- Cox and Kings: **www.coxandkings.co.uk**;
- Kirker Holidays: **www.kirkerholidays.com**;
- Martin Randall Travel: **www.martinrandall.com**;
- Opera Tours Italy: **www.operatoursitaly.com**;
- Peter Sommer Travels: **www.petersommer.com**;
- Specialtours: **www.specialtours.co.uk**;
- Travel for the Arts: **www.travelforthearts.co.uk**.

## Festivals

There are a huge number of annual festivals to experience, if you wish to feast on music, drama, literature and the arts. This is not confined to the UK and Europe, festivals are to be found all over the world. When going on holiday many people plan their trips around a festival – be it folk music in the mountains in Bulgaria, or a horse fair in Portugal. Depending on your purse, you can arrange your trip as a budget break, or a more comfortable holiday. There are literally hundreds of festivals across Britain and many of them are free. From music festivals like The Three Choirs which started in 1715 and is the oldest continuous music festival in Europe, flower festivals in many of the beautiful ancient cathedrals, literary and poetry festivals to things like Cheese Rolling and Black Pudding Throwing. To find out what is going on where, in your local area or any other part of the UK, contact the Arts Council or your regional Arts Council office. There are simply too many to list here, but the booklet *Go Away Great Britain – The Oldie's Guide to Britain through its Festivals* provides a comprehensive list: **www.theoldie.co.uk**.

## Film

Cinema is a hugely popular art form, and the choices include your local community cinema, local film society or visiting the National Film Theatre.

See the following websites:

- British Federation of Film Societies (BFFS): **www.bffs.org.uk**;
- British Film Institute (BFI): **www.bfi.org.uk**;
- Damaris Film Club: **www.damaris.org/filmclubs**.

## Museums

If you enjoy lectures and guided tours on collections and special exhibitions, one of the best ways to absorb culture is by visiting museums and galleries. You can join as a Friend, and benefit from certain advantages, such as private views, visits to places of interest, receptions and other activities. Apart from the famous national museums, there are many smaller ones around the country, depending on your area of interest. Here are a few well known ones to consider:

- British Association of Friends of Museums (BAFM): **www.bafm.org.uk**;
- Ashmolean Museum of Art and Archaeology: **www.ashmolean.org**;
- British Museum: **www.britishmuseum.org**;
- Fitzwilliam Museum: **www.fitzmuseum.cam.ac.uk**;
- National Museums of Scotland: **www.nms.ac.uk**;
- Natural History Museum: **www.nhm.ac.uk**;
- Royal Museums Greenwich: **www.rmg.co.uk**;
- Science Museum: **www.sciencemuseum.org.uk**;
- V&A (Victoria and Albert Museum): **www.vam.ac.uk**.

## Opera, ballet and concerts

Classical music, ballet or opera can be enjoyed by anyone at any age. There are venues throughout the country, as well as the more obvious ones listed here:

- Covent Garden: **www.roh.org.uk**;
- English National Opera (ENO): **www.eno.org**;
- Royal Albert Hall: **www.royalalberthall.com**;

- Sadler's Wells: **www.sadlerswells.com**;
- Scottish National Opera: **www.scottishopera.org.uk**;
- Southbank Centre: **www.southbankcentre.co.uk**;
- Welsh National Opera: **www.wno.org.uk**.

## TV and radio audiences

Participating as members of studio audiences and contributions to programmes may be for you. If so, here are a couple of websites to look at:

- Applause Store: **www.applausestore.com**;
- BBC Shows: **www.bbc.co.uk/showsandtours/tickets**.

## Theatre

Keeping up with current and forthcoming productions for national and regional theatres, as well as reviews, is easily researched on the internet. The following websites are useful for all keen theatregoers:

- ATG Tickets: **www.atgtickets.com**;
- Barbican: **www.barbican.org.uk**;
- Donmar Warehouse: **www.donmarwarehouse.com**;
- National Theatre: **www.nationaltheatre.org.uk**;
- National Theatre Wales: **www.nationaltheatrewales.org**;
- Official London Theatre: **www.officiallondontheatre.co.uk**;
- Theatre Network: **www.uktheatre.net**;
- The Old Vic: **www.oldvictheatre.com**;
- TKTS: **www.tkts.co.uk**.

# Coach and rail holidays

Exploring can be done easily and comfortably if you allow others to take the strain. Whether you prefer travelling by road or rail, coach tours and train journeys can offer a huge variety of destinations for fat or slim purses. You can choose from hundreds of coach and rail holidays and short breaks to many popular destinations across Britain, Europe and further afield. To start your research, you could look at:

Find A Coach Holiday: **www.findacoachholiday.com** and National Express: **www.nationalexpress.com**.

Websites that offer good choices of coach holidays include:

- **www.grandukholidays.com**;
- **www.nationalholidays.com**;
- **www.shearings.com**.

Taking the train is often cheaper than flying, and can even be cheaper than travelling by bus – particularly if you invest in a Global Interrail pass for seniors. This offers major savings on long journeys plus flexibility. For more information visit: **www.voyages-sncf.com**.

Top tips for rail travellers include:

- *Book seats in advance to enjoy a window seat on scenic routes.*
- *Travel light – overhead luggage racks can be awkward.*
- *Be aware of pickpockets – keep your documents and wallet secure at all times.*
- *Information desks at stations are helpful and usually speak excellent English.*

(*Source: Mature Times* – November 2014)

Should you fancy a holiday by rail, but without the hassle of poring over timetables and transfers, one of the following tour operators or agents may be able to help:

- Danube Express: **www.danube-express.com**;
- Erail: **www.erail.co.uk**;
- Ffestiniog Travel: **www.ffestiniogtravel.com**;
- French Travel Service: **www.f-t-s.co.uk**;
- Golden Eagle Luxury Trains: **www.gwtravel.co.uk**;
- Great Rail Journeys: **www.greatrail.com**;
- Holidays By Rail: **www.holidaysbyrail.com**;
- PTG Tours: **www.ptg.co.uk**;
- Planet Rail: **www.planetrail.co.uk**;
- Rail Trail: **www.railtrail.co.uk**;

- Railway Holidays: **www.railwayholidays.com**;
- The Venice Simplon-Orient-Express: **www.orient-express.com**;
- The Man in Seat 61: **www.seat61.com**;
- Trainbreaks.com: **www.trainbreaks.com**.

# Cruising

Do you enjoy the occasional gin and tonic? If so, maybe you've been on a *Saga* cruise? According to their magazine, last year more than 241,500 gin and tonics were served on board their cruise ships, amounting to over 9,296 gallons! The average age nationally of cruisers in 2015 was 55, down from 60 years old in 2004. Some 2 million people in the UK take a cruise holiday every year – and that figure is rising. The reasons that so many people enjoy them includes the good value; seeing multiple destinations but unpacking only once; the wide choice as cruise ships come in all shapes and sizes. Cruise vacations are easy to plan, it's social and there are continuous activities and entertainments galore. Finding a cruise to suit you has never been easier. If you are interested, visit the following: Cruise Critic: **www.cruisecritic.co.uk** and The Cruise Show: **www.cruisingshow.com**.

Here are some top tips for cruising:

- *Avoid an inside cabin*: it will be cheaper because there is no natural light, but it plays havoc with your body clock.
- *Don't pay the brochure price*: protect yourself by booking your cruise through an ABTA agent.
- *Remember that prices usually include extras*: if you think the cost is high, remember that food and non-alcoholic drinks are included.
- *Watch out for on-board credit offers*: cruise lines tempt customers with on-board credit that can only be spent on the ship.

From among the many companies offering cruise travel advice and tours, here are just a few websites to look at:

- Alastair MacKenzie's Travel Lists: **www.travel-lists.co.uk**;
- Avalon Waterways: **www.avaloncruises.co.uk**;

- Blue Water Holidays: **www.cruisingholidays.co.uk**;
- Celebrity Cruises: **www.celebritycruises.co.uk**;
- Cunard: **www.cunard.co.uk**;
- Fred.Olsen Cruise Lines: **www.fredolsencruises.com**;
- Hebridean Island Cruises: **www.hebridean.co.uk**;
- Hurtigruten Norwegian Cruises: **www.hurtigruten.co.uk**;
- NCL (Norwegian Cruise Line): **www.ncl.co.uk**;
- Noble Caledonia: **www.noble-caledonia.co.uk**;
- P&O Cruises: **www.pocruises.com**;
- Princess Cruises: **www.princess.com**;
- Regent Seven Seas Cruises: **www.rssc.com**;
- Royal Caribbean International: **www.royalcaribbean.co.uk**;
- SeaDream Yacht Club: **www.seadream.com**;
- Silversea: **www.silversea.com**;
- Six Star Cruises: **www.sixstarcruises.co.uk**;
- Titan: **www.titantravel.co.uk**;
- Viking River Cruises: **www.vikingrivercruises.co.uk**;
- Voyages of Discovery: **www.voyagesofdiscovery.co.uk**;
- Voyages to Antiquity: **www.cruisedirect.co.uk**;
- Windstar Cruises: **www.windstarcruises.com**.

## Cargo ship cruises

Seeing the world by cargo ship doesn't offer the trappings of a conventional cruise, but being aboard a freight ship as a paying passenger is like being in another world. Many carry up to 12 non-crew members on routes from a week to months long. Securing a berth can be complicated, and periods in port tend to be brief, but life on board is uneventful – perfect for reading and writing. Price, accommodation and facilities (gyms and pools) vary according to the size and type of vessel. See:

- Cargo Ship Voyages: **www.cargoshipvoyages.com**;
- Strand Voyages: **www.strandtravelltd.co.uk**;
- The Cruise People: **www.cruisepeople.co.uk**.

### *And one more...*

Why not discover one of the most remote places on earth, by visiting St Helena? Isolated in the South Atlantic, 1,200 miles from Angola and more than 2,000 miles from Brazil, St Helena remains a distant monument to Britain's imperial past. Until the new airport opens later this year (2016), the only way is by ship on the *RMS* St Helena from Cape Town, which calls at various islands along the way. It's the world's best-kept travel secret. See website: **www.rms-st-helena.com**. Currently, three companies offer tours to St Helena:

- Halcyon Travel Collections: **www.halcyon-collections.com**;
- Island Holidays: **www.islandholidays.co.uk**;
- Voyages Jules Verne: **www.vjv.com**.

## Education and learning holidays

A bit of cerebral stimulation is good for everyone, and it's never too late to learn. Your local library should have information on classes and courses available close to home. If you look on line you will be presented with a myriad of choices. Whether it's a simple occasional class or something more ambitious such as a degree course, you should be able to find what suits you. Here are just a few suggestions to whet your appetite:

- Adult Education Finder: **www.adulteducationfinder.co.uk**;
- Birkbeck, University of London: **www.bbk.ac.uk**;
- Home Learning College: **www.homelearningcollege.com**;
- National Extension College (NEC): **www.nec.ac.uk**;
- Open University (OU): **www.open.ac.uk**;
- University of the Third Age (U3A): **www.u3a.org.uk**.

For those who enjoy absorbing knowledge and enlarging the mind while enjoying a break, the choice is enormous. There is nothing you cannot accomplish if you are prepared to do your research. The following (by no means exhaustive) is an eclectic mix to get you started:

- Arblaster & Clarke Wine Tours: **www.winetours.co.uk**;
- Centre for Alternative Technology: **www.cat.org.uk**;

- Dana Holidays: **www.danaholidays.com**;

- Denman College: **www.denmancollege.org.uk**;

- Field Studies Council: **www.field-studies-council.org**;

- Forestry Commission: **www.forestry.gov.uk**;

- Go Learn To: **www.golearnto.com**;

- Grape Escapes: **www.grapescapes.net**;

- HF Holidays: **www.hfholidays.co.uk**;

- Inland Waterways Association: **www.waterways.org.uk**;

- National Association of Flower Arrangement Societies (NAFAS): **www.nafas.org.uk**;

- National Trust Working Holidays: **www.nationaltrust.org.uk**;

- Painting and Cooking in Italy: **www.paintinginitaly.com**;

- Responsible Travel: **www.responsibletravel.com**;

- Smooth Red: **www.smoothred.co.uk**;

- SwimTreck: **www.swimtreck.com**;

- TCV The Conservation Volunteers: **www.tcv.org.uk**;

- Truffle Hunters Dog School: **www.trufflehuntersdogschool.com**;

- Winetasting France: **www.winetastingfrance.com**.

# Gardens and gardening

Visiting beautiful and historic gardens has always been a popular pastime, with so many people being enthusiastic about horticulture. If it's a hobby you would like to take up, whether you enjoy watching gardening programmes on TV in the comfort of an armchair, have acres of garden yourself, or simply yearn to have an allotment of your own, there is a vast amount to choose from on the horticultural landscape. You can take courses, visit historic homes and gardens, attend shows and learn about garden charities. The following organizations have information for you:

- English Gardening School: **www.englishgardeningschool.co.uk**;

- Garden Organic: **www.gardenorganic.org.uk**;

- Gardening for Disabled Trust: **www.gardeningfordisabledtrust.org.uk**;

- Garden History Society: **www.gardenhistorysociety.org**;
- National Gardens Scheme: **www.ngs.org.uk**;
- National Society of Allotment and Leisure Gardeners Ltd: **www.nsalg.org.uk**;
- Perennial: **www.perennial.org.uk**;
- Royal Horticultural Society: **www.rhs.org.uk**;
- Scotland's Gardens: **www.scotlandsgardens.org**;
- Thrive: **www.thrive.org.uk**;
- Welsh Historic Gardens Trust (WHGT): **www.whgt.org.uk**.

# History and historical holidays

Are you a keen amateur historian? You may enjoy reading, researching, watching excellent TV programmes, exploring historic monuments, studying genealogy or be an expert on your local history. Whether you want to enjoy history as a gentle hobby, take a course or go on a special interest holiday to a historic destination, you should find all the information you need on the following sites:

- Age Exchange: **www.age-exchange.org.uk**;
- Architectural Heritage Society of Scotland: **www.ahss.org.uk**;
- Battlefield Tours: **www.battlefieldtours.co.uk**;
- British Association for Local History: **www.balh.co.uk**;
- Churches Conservation Trust: **www.visitchurches.org.uk**;
- Commonwealth War Graves Commission: **www.cwgc.org**;
- English Heritage: **www.english-heritage.org.uk**;
- Federation of Family History Societies: **www.ffhs.org.uk**;
- Georgian Group: **www.georgiangroup.org.uk**;
- Historic Houses Association (HHA): **www.hha.org.uk**;
- Historical Association: **www.history.org.uk**;
- Holts Tours – Battlefields and History: **www.holts.co.uk**;
- Military History Tours: **www.militaryhistorytours.co.uk**;
- Monumental Brass Society: **www.mbs-brasses.co.uk**;

- National Trust: **www.nationaltrust.org.uk**;
- National Trust for Scotland: **www.nts.org.uk**;
- Northern Ireland Tourist Board:
  **www.discovernorthernireland.com**;
- Oral History Society: **www.ohs.org.uk**;
- Remembrance Travel (formerly Poppy Travel):
  **www.remembrancetravel.org.uk**;
- Society of Genealogists: **www.sog.org.uk**;
- The Cultural Experience: **www.theculturalexperience.com**;
- Victorian Society: **www.victorian-society.org.uk**.

# Sport

Taking exercise, as we all know, gets more important as we become older. Retirement presents the ideal opportunity to start (or spend more time enjoying) a sporting hobby. To find out what is available near to your home, your local authority recreational department, or your nearest sports or leisure centre, are sure to have details. If you want to combine a favourite sport with a holiday, you can research holidays with on-site or nearby sporting facilities quite easily. The list that follows (by no means all-embracing) gives suggestions for popular sports, and includes organizations that can advise you about courses and facilities near you, and others which offer special interest holidays.

## *Boats and boating*

Should you wish to find out whether you like the water, you can do so without a huge financial commitment. Your nearest sailing club may be able to arrange a trial sail, or you could try a water-sports holiday. For further information see: New to Sailing: **www.newtosailing.com**.

The beauty of life aboard a boat is that you're not on a set holiday itinerary. There's no rushing to the next destination, unless you want to. Whether you choose to holiday abroad or in Britain, there's loads of choice. If you're new to boating, it's akin to travelling in a cosy floating villa, with all the comforts of home – and each day you wake up in a beautiful new destination. See the following websites:

- Barge Cruises France: **www.bargedirect.com**;
- Beautiful Boating Holidays: **www.leboat.co.uk**;
- Blakes: **www.blakes.co.uk**;
- Hoseasons Boating Holidays: **www.hoseasons.co.uk**;
- Narrowboat Holidays Wales: **www.castlenarrowboats.co.uk**;
- Royal Yachting Association (RYA): **www.rya.org.uk**;
- Waterways Holidays: **www.waterwaysholidays.com**.

## *Cycling*

Cycling is the third most popular recreational activity in the UK. An estimated 3.1 million people ride a bicycle each month. Cycling is one of the easiest ways to fit exercise into your daily routine because it's also a form of transport. For older people it is a non-impact sport, so doesn't put strain on the joints. It saves you money, gets you fit and is good for the environment. Whatever your level of experience, there are plenty of ways to get into the sport:

- British Cycling: **www.britishcycling.org.uk**;
- CTC (Cyclists' Touring Club): **www.ctc.org.uk**;
- Road Cycling UK (RCUK): **www.roadcyclinguk.com**;
- UK Cycling Events: **www.ukcyclingevents.co.uk**.

Should you fancy a cycling holiday, there is an enormous choice. Depending on age, health and fitness, it is sensible to choose the terrain carefully. But you will be able to enjoy stunning views and scenery on two wheels. Here are some options:

- CTC Cycling Holidays: **www.cyclingholidays.org**;
- Cycle Active: **www.cycleactive.com**;
- Cycle Breaks: **www.cyclebreaks.com**;
- Cycling for Softies: **www.cycling-for-softies.co.uk**;
- Explore: **www.explore.co.uk**;
- Hooked on Cycling: **www.hookedoncycling.co.uk**;
- Saddle Skedaddle: **www.skedaddle.co.uk**;
- The Bike Bus: **www.bikebusuk.com**.

# Fishing

Fishing as a hobby is a good choice for both novice and expert. For example, it gives you time outside in the fresh air which benefits your health. It's relaxing, you can do other things at the same time, such as reading, listening to music and thinking. There are many varieties of the sport: local rivers and lakes, deep-sea fishing, fly-fishing and much more. For more information about the sport and angling holiday providers, see:

- Angling Trust: **www.anglingtrust.net**;
- Anglers Paradise: **www.anglers-paradise.co.uk**;
- Fly Fishing Holidays: **www.flyfishingholidays.co.uk**;
- Go Fishing Worldwide: **www.gofishingworldwide.co.uk**.

# Golf

Golfing enthusiasts are well aware of why this sport enjoys such popularity. It is seen by many as a social game, a way to get healthy as it is an effective exercise programme. It is also an excellent way to relax, and can be enjoyed as a family sport. For those who enjoy participating in tournaments, some of the places where these are held gives an opportunity to travel and experience a different culture and exotic scenery. If you want to go no further than your local course, there are municipal courses and private clubs. For further information:

- England Golf: **www.www.englandgolf.org**;
- Golf Union of Wales: **www.golfunionwales**;
- Golfing Union of Ireland: **www.gui.ie**;
- Scottish Golf Union: **www.scottishgolf.org**.

For those with a yen to travel and enjoy their hobby at the same time, there are some amazing holiday destinations for golfers. Whether it is a short break with friends, a trip in the sun with some courses nearby, or a full golf club tournament, there is a destination or vacation to suit you. Just a few websites, among the myriad choice available, to consider:

- Glencor Golf: **www.glencorgolf.com**;
- Golf Breaks UK: **www.golfbreaks.com**;

- Golf Escapes: **www.golf-escapes.com**;
- Golf Par Excellence: **www.golfparexcellence.com**;
- Your Golf Travel: **www.yourgolftravel.com**.

## Rambling and walking holidays

Walking is an excellent form of exercise that is accessible to almost everyone. It costs nothing, doesn't require expensive equipment and is the best form of natural exercise as it can keep you healthy, prolong your life and improve your mental health. The positive things that walking can do for your health include:

- helping your heart and lungs work better;
- lowering your blood pressure;
- keeping weight down;
- lightening mood;
- keeping joints, muscles and bones strong.

A good way to start, if you are thinking of taking up walking and rambling as a hobby, is to join a small group. See the following websites for more information: Ramblers' Charity: **www.ramblers.org.uk** and Walking for Health: **www.walkingforhealth.org.uk**.

The choice of walking and rambling holidays is extensive. It can be a very affordable holiday, if you stay in the UK or more exotic (and expensive) should you travel abroad. There are loads of companies offering a wide range of trips, and here are a just a few to help you decide what is right for you.

- ATG Oxford: **www.atg-oxford.co.uk**;
- Exodus: **www.exodus.co.uk**;
- HF Holidays: **www.hfholidays.co.uk**;
- National Trails: **www.nationaltrail.co.uk**;
- Rambling Tours: **www.ramblingtours.co.uk**;
- Ramblers Holidays: **www.ramblersholidays.co.uk**;
- Secret Hills Walking: **www.secrethillswalking.co.uk**;
- Walks Worldwide: **www.walksworldwide.com**.

## Skiing

Skiing has been described as 'the best fun you can have as an adult without taking your clothes off'. Perhaps that is why it is such a popular sporting hobby. It is good for you, there's plenty of fresh air and it is very social, particularly when you indulge in the 'après'. Skiing and snowboarding is now accessible for everyone: whatever your level of ability, there are lots of organizations, tour operators and destinations to choose from. Here are a few:

- Classic Ski: **www.classicski.co.uk**;
- Crystal Ski Holidays: **www.crystalski.co.uk**;
- Disability Snowsport UK: **www.disabilitysnowsport.org.uk**;
- Powder White: **www.powderwhite.com**;
- Ski Club Great Britain: **www.skiclub.co.uk**;
- Ski Collection: **www.skicollection.co.uk**;
- Ski Solutions: **www.skisolutions.com**;
- Snow Trex: **www.snowtrex.co.uk**;
- VIP Ski: **www.vip-chalets.com**.

## Swimming

An obvious reason why it is important to be able to swim is that it gives us the ability to survive in water. We are often near or in water, and if it is deeper than your height, knowing how to swim could save your life. Swimming is also one of the best forms of exercise, it builds strength and endurance and is beneficial for your metabolism and cardiovascular system. Swimming as a hobby, whether you are a beginner or seasoned swimmer, is a great way to relax and get fit. For more information see: British Swimming: **www.swimming.org**.

You could, if you wish, take a swimming holiday. Often referred to as 'wild swimming', swimming in open water is increasingly popular. There are many seas, rivers and lakes which attract adventurous people, and the following organizations can help you to find the perfect wild swimming experience for you.

- Outdoor Swimming Society: **www.outdoorswimmingsociety.com**;
- Rivers and Lakes Swimming Association: **www.wild-swimming.org**;

- Strel Swimming Association: **www.strel-swimming.com**;
- Swim Quest: **www.swimquest.uk.com**;
- Swim Treck: **www.swimtreck.com**;
- The Big Blue: **www.thebigblueswim.com**;
- Wild Swimming: **www.wildswimming.com**.

## Tennis

Tennis in some form or other has been played for thousands of years: monks, nobles and kings were avid fans of the game. The tennis court built at Hampton Court in 1625 survives to this day. According to the Tennis Industry Association some of the reasons for its popularity are because it is social, the whole family can participate, it is good for personal fitness, and it can be played all your life. Whether you want to take up tennis (or continue with it) as a hobby, or would like to enjoy playing tennis when you are on holiday, the choices are enormous. As a spectator sport it also is enormously popular, see:

- International Tennis Federation: **www.itftennis.com**;
- Lawn Tennis Association: **www.lta.org.uk**;
- Seniors' Lawn Tennis Club of Great Britain: **www.sltcofgb.org.uk**.

The key ingredients of a good tennis holiday are: good weather, a great tennis venue and exceptional accommodation. There are a number of companies who offer tennis holidays to suit your needs, whether you are a single traveller, a family or a group of friends.

- Active Away: **www.activeaway.com**;
- Annabel Croft Tennis Holidays: **www.annabelcrofttennis.com**;
- Discovery Tennis: **www.discoverytennistours.com**;
- Jonathon Markson Tennis: **www.marksontennis.com**;
- Lawn Tennis Association (LTA): **www.lta.org.uk**;
- Roger Walker Travel: **www.tennisholidays.co.uk**.

# Hobbies and holidays for people with disabilities

Facilities for the disabled have improved enormously over recent years, and there are some sporting organizations who cater specifically for the disabled. If you look at the England Athletics website (**www.englandathletics.org/disability-athletics**) you will find a complete list of NDSOS (National Disability Sports Organizations) as well as lots more useful information.

If it is a holiday, rather than a sporting hobby, you are looking for, there is more good news. Affordable, accessible and enjoyable holidays for the disabled are on the increase. Airlines, hotels and resorts are providing people with disabilities or mobility issues the opportunities to travel, enjoy holidays and see the world. Specially designed self-catering units are more plentiful and of a higher standard. Also, an increasing number of trains and coaches are installing accessible loos. An elderly or disabled person seeking a holiday must explain clearly what their care needs are, not only in terms of getting to and from but also with regard to accommodation requirements. Some people take companions/carers with them. Organizations that can help you include:

- Age UK: **www.ageuk.org.uk**;
- Able Community Care: **www.uk-care.com**;
- Accessible Travel and Leisure: **www.accessibletravel.co.uk**;
- Choice Care Assisted Holidays: **www.choicecareservices.co.uk**;
- Disabled Access Holidays: **www.disabledaccessholidays.com**;
- Enable Holidays: **www.enableholidays.com**;
- Holidays for the Disabled: **www.holidaysforthedisabled.com**;
- Tourism for All: **www.tourismforall.org.uk**;
- Vitalise: **www.vitalise.org.uk**.

# Hobbies and holidays for singles

Being single is not everyone's choice. Whether you are on your own, widowed, divorced or simply having to create a life outside the home because your partner cannot accompany you, you will feel the benefit if you make the effort. All the organizations listed earlier in this chapter will help you to make new friends and enjoy companionship while taking up a new leisure pursuit. Friendships will be forged while partaking in mutually enjoyable recreational activities, so it's well worth making the attempt. You should find it rewarding.

When it comes to travelling on your own, this can be a tough decision whatever your age. Many people travel solo, some may be single, others not. There are tour holidays, exploring holidays and relaxing escape holidays. Travelling alone need not be expensive, because with single-traveller specialist firms there is no supplement to pay. There are a few websites that can help you find the perfect travelling companion, if you would rather not be part of an organized group. Here are a couple of them: Travellers Connected: **www.travellersconnected.com** and Companions 2 Travel: **www.companions2travel.co.uk**.

Travel companies specializing in solo travel include:

- Friendship Travel: **www.friendshiptravel.com**;
- Just You: **www.justyou.co.uk**;
- One Traveller: **www.onetraveller.co.uk**;
- Solitair: **www.solitairhols.co.uk**;
- Solos: **www.solosholidays.co.uk**;
- Travel One: **www.travelone.co.uk**.

# And some other ideas ...

## *3G holidays*

Have you heard about 3G holidays and do you know what they are? Apparently nearly one in five people have been on a '3G holiday' in the past year, according to Sainsbury's Bank. By definition it is simply a family holiday where at least three generations travel together. Reasons for taking such a trip can vary from a special occasion to helping with holiday expenses. Whatever your taste, you can always find a great location for a multi-generational holiday. If grandparents find themselves being invited to join their children and grandchildren on holiday, be prepared to pitch in. It is an excellent way to spend good quality time with family members who do not get enough moments together due to pressures of work. For more information on where to find suitable 3G holiday ideas and destinations, see:

- Grandkid Getaways: **www.carrier.co.uk**;
- Uniworld Family Friendly: **www.uniworldrivercruises.co.uk**;
- The Family Adventure Company:
  **www.familyadventurecompany.co.uk**.

## Home-swapping holidays

House swapping is becoming increasingly popular, because it saves the expense of hotel or villa accommodation. A bonus for those who dare to do this includes the experience of living life as a local, not a tourist. Holiday swap internet sites are on the increase, but do pay attention to the rules and conditions: some are more stringent than others. Most home swapping sites require payment of an annual subscription, and if this idea appeals to those adventurous among you, have a look at:

- HomeLink: **www.homelink.org.uk**;
- Intervac: **www.Gb.intervac-homeexchange.com**;
- Love Home Swap: **www.lovehomeswap.com**;
- Simply Home Exchange: **www.simplyhomeexchange.com**.

## Travel insurance

As we age we are far more likely to have a pre-existing medical condition that needs to be declared and covered on our travel insurance. The main reason travel insurance costs more for older people is that we are more likely to claim for health problems whilst on holiday than younger travellers. Medical claims are much more costly than most other types of claim. Travel insurance is an essential safety net should anything go wrong. It is one case where the cheapest option could be false economy.

Top tips (courtesy of *Mature Times*)when purchasing travel insurance are:

- *Make sure you have adequate personal liability cover; a minimum of around £1 million is advisable.*

- *Make sure your policy has appropriate cancellation and curtailment cover in case you fall ill or cut your holiday short.*
- *Don't leave arranging cover until just before you depart in case anything happens between booking and departure.*
  (*Source: Mature Times:* **www.maturetravelinsurance.co.uk**)

For travel insurance options, here are some other websites:

- Age UK: **www.ageuk.org.uk**;
- American Express: **www.americanexpress.com**;
- Avanti Travel Insurance: **www.avantitravelinsurance.co.uk**;
- Insurance Choice: **www.insurancechoice.co.uk**;
- Laterlife Travel Insurance: **www.laterlife.com**;
- Onestop4:Insurance: **www.onestop4.co.uk**;
- Saga: **www.saga.co.uk**;
- Staysure: **www.staysure.co.uk**.

A cost-effective idea may be to extend any existing medical insurance you have to cover you while abroad. Then take out a separate policy (without medical insurance) to cover you for the rest of your travel needs. Two websites that provide good advice regarding the amount of cover you should be looking for in your travel insurance policy are: The Association of British Insurers: **www.abi.org.uk** and The Association of British Travel Agents (ABTA): **www.abta.com**.

Another useful website to look at is Fit For Travel: travel health information for people travelling abroad from the UK – **www.fitfortravel.nhs.uk**.

## Help – when things go wrong

For complaints and assistance when things go wrong, and for the framing of a complaint, see Chapter 4: Protection from scams, help from professional advisers and how to complain.

One really important thing to remember is to make sure that when travelling you have a copy of the Consumer Council's 'Plane Facts' guide in your hand luggage before leaving. Here is the link:

**http://www.consumercouncil.org.uk/filestore/documents/Plane_Facts_Nov_2014.pdf**.

## Compensation for lost baggage

If the airline on which you are travelling loses or damages your baggage, you should be able to claim compensation up to a maximum value of about £850. (The figure may vary slightly up or down, depending on currency fluctuations.)

## How to complain to an airline

If you have reason to complain about an airline and are not getting satisfaction, don't give up. Contact the Civil Aviation Authority (CAA) with full details of your complaint. The CAA can help in these circumstances.

## Cancelled or overbooked flights

Denied Boarding, Cancellation and Delay Regulation sets out a number of rules on the level and nature of compensation and assistance to be provided to passengers in the event of their being adversely affected by overbooking, flight cancellation or long delay. The regulation applies to all flights operated within the European Economic Area (EEA), flights departing from airports in the EEA and flights arriving in the EEA from non-member states operated by Community carriers.

For full details and information on this subject, see: Air Travel Advisory Bureau (ATAB): **www.atab.org.uk** or Aviation Consumer Advocacy Panel: **www.caa.co.uk**.

# General information

## Airlines

Several of the airlines offer attractive discounts to older travellers. The terms and conditions vary, with some carriers offering across-the-board savings and others limiting them to selected destinations. Likewise, in some cases the qualifying age is 60; in others, it is a couple of years older. A particular bonus is that concessions are often extended to include a companion travelling at the same time. Ask your travel agent or the airline at the time of booking what special discounts, if any, are offered.

## Overseas

Many countries offer travel and other reductions to retired holiday-makers including, for example, discounts for entry to museums and galleries, day excursions, sporting events and other entertainment. As in Britain, provisions are liable to change, and for up-to-date information probably the best source to contact is the national tourist office of the country to which you are travelling. All EEA countries – as well as most lines in Switzerland – give 25 per cent reductions on international rail fares. These are available to holders of a RailPlus Card who are purchasing international rail travel tickets, and are applicable to both first- and second-class travel.

## Airport meet-and-greet services

With the number of 'meet-and-greet' parking services at UK airports on the increase, it can be hard to make a confident choice. While your vehicle is left at an airport at your own risk, the British Parking Association provides a few handy hints to follow when selecting a service:

- Is the member of staff that greets you wearing a uniform – and carrying an ID badge? If so, check the badge – does it match up with the company you think you're dealing with, in the location you're at?

- Are you doing business in a designated location – such as a stand at the airport or a kiosk in the vicinity of the airport? Not having premises is a sure-fire indication that something might not be right.

- Check where the company will be storing your car. Can they point out their storage facility? If it is off-site, which they usually are, can they tell you where it is, or show you a picture? Does the company own the storage facility?

- Ask whether the car park in which your car will be stored has the 'Park Mark'. The Park Mark® is given to car-parking facilities that have undergone an annual police assessment.

See the following websites:

- British Parking Association: **www.britishparking.co.uk**; and
- Park Mark Safer Parking: **www.parkmark.co.uk**.

Tips for overseas travelling:

- Most important – for everyone – when organizing travel, *always pay by credit card*. (Increased protection offered when things go wrong or a contract is broken.)

- *Insurance – always check the small print*. Going for the cheapest option can come back to haunt you under the 'what-you pay-is-what-you-get' rule of life.

- *Make sure that your carrier / travel company is ATOL-registered*. (Air Travel Organizer's Licence). Also ABTA have an arbitration scheme which is about as good as it gets in the absence of a travel ombudsman (lobbying point – maybe we say there should be one!). For further information, here is the link: **http://abta.com/go-travel/travel-clinic/arbitration-and-mediation**.

- Don't forget – you should *pack any regular medicines* you require, even familiar branded products can be difficult to obtain in some countries. In addition, take a mini first-aid kit with you. If you are going to any developing country, consult your doctor as to what pills (and any special precautions) you should take.

- *An overdose of sun can be painful*. In some countries it really burns, so take it easy, wear a hat and apply plenty of protective lotion.

- *Be careful of the water you drink*. Beware the water, ice, salads, seafood, ice cream and any fruit that you do not peel yourself. Always wash your hands before eating or handling food, particularly if you are camping or caravanning.

- *Have any inoculations or vaccinations well in advance of your departure date*. When flying, wear loose clothes and above all comfortable shoes, as feet and ankles tend to swell in the air.

- *To avoid risk of deep vein thrombosis*, which can be fatal, medical advice is to do foot exercises and walk around the plane from time to time. For long-haul travel especially, wear compression stockings and, another tip, unless advised otherwise by your doctor, take an aspirin before flying.

For more information and advice, see Safe Travel: **www.safetravel.co.uk**.

# Chapter Ten
# Taking care of elderly parents

*'Middle age is that time in life when children and parents cause equal amounts of worry.'*

**ROMY HALLIWELL**

According to an article in *Mature Times* (**www.maturetimes.co.uk**) a 100th birthday telegram from the Queen once was a rare occurrence. This is no longer the case. If proof were needed, apparently the Department for Work and Pensions (DWP) has increased its 'centenarian staff' from a single person, to a team of seven, to ensure all the congratulations cards and letters are mailed on time. There were 13,780 centenarians in 2013, and more than half a million people aged 90 and over. Our ageing society should be a cause for celebration and with over 300,000 people still living who were born between 1914 and 1920, it looks as if the staff at the DWP in Newcastle will continue to be busy in future.

Old age is a great gift; it wasn't many decades ago that white hair was rare. More and more people now live a long time in a healthy and happy way, with lots of entertainment, friends, trips to foreign parts and the company of family and loved ones. The elderly fare better when they live in the present as much as they can, not the past. As pensioners ourselves we become more generous with age, so looking after our parents is something we should regard as a privilege, as we wouldn't be here if it weren't for the care they gave to us.

## All you need to know about this chapter and what it contains

- Age UK, the national charity which campaigns for making life better for elderly people, has recently publicized its 'five key ambitions' where everyone in later life:
  - has the opportunities to enjoy life and feel well;
  - feels safe, comfortable and secure at home;
  - has enough money to live on;
  - can participate in society and be valued for their contribution;
  - has access to quality health and care services (**www.ageuk.org.uk**).

- This chapter is essential reading if you have elderly parents/loved ones who will (in time) need help. The first section is all about maintaining independence for as long as possible – the most highly prized ambition of older people. It covers the ways quality of life can be preserved, via help from local authority services, and healthcare and specialist services.

- There is a useful section on help with home repairs and adaptations, so that your loved ones can remain safely in their own home retaining their dignity and independence.

- If you don't already know the key voluntary organizations that help with the elderly, this chapter contains a list of these and how to get in touch with them. Knowledge is key here and it is better to do your research before it is needed rather than wait until a crisis occurs.

- Elderly people are just as entitled to travel around and enjoy holidays as the rest of us, so the section on getting around and holidays for the elderly (and disabled) has lots of useful information about this.

- On the legal side, you might want to read about LPAs (Lasting Power of Attorney) and when it is appropriate to draw these up. Having an LPA will safeguard your elderly relative once they cannot manage their own affairs.

- When the time comes for help, the section which covers practical help for carers is important reading. This goes on to give information on Benefits and Allowances and how to obtain financial assistance, if eligible.

- There is a huge amount of advice about special accommodation for the elderly, housing options and costs. This chapter covers this area and signposts where more information and research can be found.

- Finally, there is a section on some special problems that can afflict older people, and how to get help and assistance should this become necessary.

All of the information is intended to prepare those who are likely to become carers and show them what options and assistance is available and how to get it.

Now, did you know about Age UK's aim to end loneliness among the elderly? This is one of their latest campaigns, as their research reveals that around one million elderly people regularly go an entire month without speaking to anyone. They want to make Britain a great place to grow older by 2020 and they believe it can be achieved. Other campaigns to combat loneliness among older people include the Silver Sunday initiative, which is an annual day of fun and free activities for older people across the UK. Led by The Sir Simon Milton Foundation, it celebrates the value and knowledge older people contribute to our communities while combating loneliness and isolation. For more information see: **www.silversunday.org.uk**.

The most-often expressed wish by elderly people is that they remain independent and able to live in their own home for as long as possible. With assistance from friends, relatives or local care organizations, many should be able to do this. Should you become responsible for an elderly, frail or disabled relative, you are not alone. There are 6.5 million carers in the UK today (one in eight adults). You are doing valuable service too, as this unpaid care saves the state £119 billion a year (source: Carers UK: **www.carersuk.org**). One thing that is vital as people get older is attitude: remaining positive about their physical health, because it is good for their mental health as well. This chapter addresses some of the issues to be faced when elderly parents need to be cared for.

Some tips for healthy ageing, from Age UK:

- a cheerful outlook, good nutrition and healthy lifestyle;
- stay curious – be interested in others;

- socialize – loneliness causes stress and ill health;
- look after your eyes – good vision is essential to quality of life;
- keep as well as you can – have regular health checks.

# Maintaining independence

There is no question about it, being able to remain independent for as long as possible, living in their own home, is hugely important for the elderly. The time may come when a care home or nursing home becomes necessary. But until they are no longer safe living independently, your aged relatives will be happier if they can stay put. The Local Authority and your parents' doctor will be able to help in the first instance. If you can find out from where help and support is available, before you need it, you may be able to avoid emergency situations occurring where decisions have to be taken rapidly. Things to bear in mind for keeping older people safe include:

- *Home improvements* will help keep elderly loved ones safe all year round.
- *Front-door security*, such as fitting an extra lock and chain if security is something that worries them.
- *Fall prevention* – de-clutter walking areas and stairs and improve lighting.
- *Fire prevention* – fit smoke alarms, at least one on each floor of the house.

For more safety tips and other useful information, go to: **www.myageingparent.com**.

## *Local authority services*

Local authorities have a responsibility to help elderly people and provide services that vulnerable people and those with disabilities may need. Approaching the GP or the adult social services department is a first step. They will be able to advise what is essential and how to obtain the required help. Your elderly relatives should be assigned a social worker, who will be able to make the necessary arrangements or advise you on how to do this. Some of the services available include:

- practical help in the home, with the support of a home help;
- adaptations to the home, such as a ramp for a wheelchair;
- provision of day centres, clubs and similar;
- blue badge scheme for cars driven or used by people with a disability;
- advice about other transport services or concessions that may be available locally.

For full information on what services are available, see **www.nhs.uk/ Conditions/social-care-and-support**.

## Health care and specialist services

A number of specialist helpers, employed by local authorities are available to assist if required. The GP will help you by advising how they can be contacted.

*Social workers* are a first point of contact if your parents need a home help, have a housing difficulty or other query.

*Occupational therapists* have a wide knowledge of disability and can assist individuals via training, exercise or access to aids, equipment or adaptations to the home.

*Health visitors* are qualified nurses with a broad knowledge of health matters and specialized facilities that may be required.

*District nurses* are fully qualified nurses who will visit a patient in the home, change dressings, attend to other routine nursing matters, monitor progress and help with the arrangements if more specialized care is required.

*Physiotherapists* use exercise and massage to help improve mobility and strengthen muscles. They are normally available at both hospitals and health centres.

*Medical social workers* (MSWs) should be consulted if patients have any problems on leaving hospital. MSWs can advise on coping with a disablement, as well as such practical matters as transport, aftercare and other immediate arrangements. They work in hospitals, and an appointment should be made before the patient is discharged.

## Council tax

If an elderly relative has a disability, they may be able to claim a reduction on their council tax. If they have a blue badge on their car, they may get a rebate for a garage. They should apply to the housing benefits officer, but different councils employ different officers to deal with this; see website: **www.gov.uk** – Disabled people.

## Help with home repair and adaptations

**Disabled facilities grant:** your parents could get a grant from their local council if one of them is disabled and changes need to be made to their home. Such adaptations include widening doors and installing ramps, improving access to rooms and facilities including stair lifts or a downstairs bathroom, a suitable heating system, adjustment of heating or lighting controls. If eligible, the applicant could receive up to £30,000 in England, £25,000 in Northern Ireland and £36,000 in Wales. Disabled Facilities Grants are not available in Scotland. See website: **www.gov.uk** – Disabled people.

**Home improvement agencies** and handy person service providers are local organizations dedicated to helping older people with disabilities live in safety and dignity in their own homes. There are currently 200 home improvement agencies in England covering over 80 per cent of local authorities. Locally they may be known as Care and Repair or Staying Put Agencies. The websites that will give all the information you need are:

- Foundations: **www.foundations.uk.com**;
- Care and Repair Wales: **www.careandrepair.org.uk**;
- Care and Repair Scotland: **www.careandrepairscotland.co.uk**.

Other organizations that can help include:

- Age UK: **www.ageuk.org.uk**;
- British Red Cross: **www.redcross.org.uk**;
- Assist UK: **www.assist-uk.org**;
- CAE (Centre for Accessible Environments): **www.cae.org.uk**;
- DEMAND (Design and Manufacture for Disability): **www.demand.org.uk**;
- Disability Wales/Anabledd Cymru: **www.disabilitywales.org**;
- DLF (Disabled Living Foundation): **www.dlf.org.uk**;
- REMAP: **www.remap.org.uk**.

## Alarm systems

**Personal alarms** provide security for vulnerably elderly people as they know that help can be summoned quickly in the event of an emergency. Some alarm systems allow people living in their own homes to be linked to a central control, or have a telephone link, enabling personal contact to be made. Others simply signal that something is wrong. Sometimes a relative or friend who has been nominated will be alerted. For more information on what is available see:

- AgeUK: **www.ageuk.org.uk**;
- Callsafe: **www.callsafe.org**;
- Care Harmony Solutions: **www.careharmony.co.uk**;
- DLF (Disabled Living Foundation): **www.dlf.org.uk**;
- Saga: **www.saga.co.uk**.

**Community alarms:** These systems are also known as Lifeline, Careline, telecare or emergency monitoring services. They operate 24 hours a day, 365 days a year, giving elderly and vulnerable people the freedom to live life independently, knowing that assistance can be obtained when needed. They work via a special alarm unit connected to the telephone line, or can be activated via a pendant which is worn round the neck or on a wristband. For further information see:

- EAC (Elderly Accommodation Counsel) now combined with Housing Care and First Stop advice for elderly people) **www.housingcare.org**;
- Eldercare: **www.eldercare.co.uk**.

# Key voluntary organizations

In addition to the services provided by statutory health and social services for elderly people living at home, there are a number of voluntary organizations that can offer help, including:

- lunch clubs and day centres;
- holidays and short-term placements;
- aids such as wheelchairs;

- transport;
- odd jobs and decorating;
- gardening;
- good neighbour schemes;
- prescription collection;
- advice and information;
- family support schemes.

You will be able to find out more via the local Citizens Advice Bureau (**www.citizensadvice.org.uk**) but the key agencies are:

- Age UK: **www.ageuk.org.uk**;
- Age Scotland: **www.ageuk.org.uk/scotland**;
- Age Cymru: **www.ageuk.org.uk/cymru**;
- Age NI: **www.ageuk.org.uk/northern-ireland**;
- Disability Wales: **www.disabilitywales.org**;
- Independent Age: **www.independentage.org**;
- Update (Disability Information Scotland): **www.update.org.uk**;
- Care Information Scotland: **www.careinfoscotland.co.uk**;
- Centre for Individual Living, Northern Ireland: **www.cilbelfast.org**;
- Contact The Elderly: **www.contact-the-elderly.org**;
- British Red Cross: **www.redcross.org.uk**;
- St John Ambulance: **www.sja.org.uk**;
- Royal Voluntary Service: **www.royalvoluntaryservice.org.uk**.

Other sources of help and advice include:

- CSRF (Civil Service Retirement Fellowship): **www.csrf.org.uk**;
- Disability Rights UK: **www.disabilityrightsuk.org**;
- Jewish Care: **www.jewishcare.org**.

# Getting around

When mobility becomes an issue, quality of life is quickly diminished. For help with getting around, the facilities run by voluntary organizations just mentioned may be of assistance. Otherwise, look at these websites:

- Forum of Mobility Centres: **www.mobility-centres.org.uk**;
- London Taxicard: **www.londoncouncils.gov.uk/services/taxicard**;
- Motability: **www.motability.co.uk**.

Driving licence renewal at 70 is now compulsory. All drivers aged 70 are sent a licence renewal form to have their driving licence renewed – for free. The entitlement to drive will need to be renewed by the DVLA; the new licence will normally be valid for three years. See website: **www.gov.uk/renew-driving-licence-at-70**.

# Holidays

Old age may come with ailments, pains, health issues and disability, and in addition a lack of confidence about travelling away from home. But these considerations should not stop the elderly from enjoying a relaxing holiday. Perhaps all that is required for a pleasurable experience are a few helpful aids. There are a number of specialist organizations that provide holidays for people with special needs. (For the hale and hearty, see Chapter 9, Hobbies and holidays). Here are some websites giving advice and information for those needing special care:

- Accessible Travel and Leisure: **www.accessibletravel.co.uk**;
- Age UK: **www.ageuk.org.uk**;
- Can be Done: **www.canbedone.co.uk**;
- Disabled Holidays.com: **www.disabledholidaydirectory.com**;
- Enable Holidays: **www.enableholidays.com**;
- Holidays for All: **www.holidaysforall.org**;
- Holidays with Help: **www.holidayswithhelp.org.uk**;
- Revitalise: **www.revitalise.org.uk**;
- Richmond Retreats: **www.richmondretreats.co.uk**.

*The Disabled Travellers' Guide*, published by the AA, provides masses of information for the disabled traveller. Downloadable in pdf format, see: **www.theaa.com**.

# Lasting power of attorney

A lasting power of attorney (LPA) is a legal document that allows the donor (your elderly relative) to appoint people, known as attorneys, to make decisions on their behalf. It could be used when the donor becomes unable to make his/her own decisions. There are two types of LPA: health and welfare, and property and financial affairs. It is safest to have both types. To make an LPA, the person has to be over 18 and have mental capacity. It allows the donor to choose one or more people to make decisions for them in the event of their being unable to do so for themselves. A health and welfare LPA is legally binding and allows others to make decisions about the donor's day-to-day care, where they live and, if desired, their choice for end-of-life care. The property and financial affairs LPA covers paying bills, collecting benefits, selling property.

The right time to draw up an LPA is while the individual is in full command of his or her faculties, so that potential situations that would require decision making can be properly discussed and the donor's wishes made clear. If an elderly person you care about is considering setting up an LPA, it is important they consult both their GP and the family solicitor, as well as consulting with members of their family. When making an LPA make sure the attorneys your parent chooses have their best interests at heart. For further information see: **www.gov.uk/power-of-attorney**.

And another idea: When it comes to forward planning, many older people shrink from discussing their wishes with loved ones. But if their preferences are not known to nearest and dearest, it may be difficult when the time comes to do what is in their best interests. A helpful booklet which is available from Age UK is their LifeBook. This is a practical tool designed to help older people work through all the things they need, or wish, to put in order. The LifeBook will not only help an older person be more organized but it could also be invaluable to a family member or friend if they need to locate important information in an emergency. It is completely free and available from Age UK: see **www.ageuk.org.uk/lifebook**.

# When help becomes necessary

The time may come when elderly people are no longer able to cope with running their homes and caring for themselves without a bit of assistance. There are various options, some more expensive than others.

If approaching agencies, it is well worth asking friends and neighbours for personal recommendations, as this can give a lot of peace of mind. Some of the agencies listed below specialize in providing temporary help, rather than permanent staff. Others can offer a flexible service and nursing care, if appropriate. Fees are normally paid by private funding but depending on individual circumstances, public financial assistance may be available.

Charities such as Age UK and Carers Trust can provide home help and domestic assistance services. The Carers Trust supports carers by giving them a break from their caring responsibilities through home care services. There is a lot of information on the NHS website about care services in your home. **www.nhs.uk/Conditions/social-care-and-support**.

Some agencies that should be able to help include:

- Bunbury Care Agency: **www.bunburyagency.com**;
- Christies Care: **www.christiescare.com**;
- Consult Us: **www.consultuscare.com**;
- Country Cousins: **www.country-cousins.co.uk**;
- Cura Domi: **www.curadomi.co.uk**;
- Helping Hands: **www.helpinghandshomecare.co.uk**;
- Miracle Workers: **www.miracle-workers.co.uk**;
- The Care Agency: **www.thecareagencyco.uk**.

There are lots of advertisements in *The Lady* magazine (published weekly) which may be helpful. You could advertise in this if you are seeking help on a permanent basis. For some families these arrangements work well only for a while, in which case it may be necessary to consider the choice between residential care and inviting the elderly parent to live with you.

# Emergency care for pets

Older people love their pets, as they give companionship, fun and can be stimulating too if they require regular outdoor exercise. When an elderly parent becomes ill, incapacitated, hospitalized, or dies leaving a beloved pet, this can cause problems for relatives. To ensure the pet continues to receive care, should something unexpected happen, the following organizations will be able to help:

- Blue Cross: **www.bluecross.org.uk;**

- Cats Protection: **www.cats.org.uk;**

- Cinnamon Trust: **www.cinnamon.org.uk;**

- Dogs Trust: **www.dogstrust.org.uk;**

- National Animal Welfare Trust: **www.nawt.org.uk;**

- Pet Fostering Service Scotland: **www.pfss.org.uk.**

# Practical help for carers

The UK has 6.5 million carers. Carers Week is an annual campaign (usually taking place in June of each year) to raise awareness of caring, highlighting the challenges carers face and recognizing the contribution they make to families and communities throughout the UK. Carers Week is made up of nine charities, who have joined forces to promote the role of carers in our society. For more information and to see what support is available, see: **www.carersweek.org.**

While your elderly relative is reasonably active and independent – visiting friends, able to do his or her own shopping, enjoying hobbies and socializing – the strains of caring for them may be light. However, when this is not the case, far more intensive caring may be required. Make sure you find out what help is available and how to obtain it. Earlier sections of this chapter have given some information on this. The many services provided by local authorities and voluntary agencies apply as much to an elderly person living with a family as to someone living alone. If you cannot find a solution to a particular problem you have, one of these organizations may be able to help you:

- Age UK: **www.ageuk.org.uk;**

- British Red Cross: **www.redcross.org.uk;**

- Carers Trust: **www.carers.org;**

- Independent Age: **www.independentage.org;**

- Royal Voluntary Service: **www.royalvoluntaryservice.org.uk.**

**Respite care facilities** enable carers to take a break from their dependants from time to time. A particularly welcome aspect of respite care is that many schemes specially cater for, among others, elderly people with dementia.

Holiday breaks for carers – various schemes enable those with an elderly relative to go on holiday alone or simply enjoy a respite from caring. Some local authorities run fostering schemes, along similar lines to child fostering. There may be a charge, or the service may be run on a voluntary basis (or be paid for by the local authority). Some voluntary organizations arrange holidays for older people in order to give relatives a break. Different charities take responsibility according to the area where you live. The Citizens Advice Bureau, volunteer centre or social services department should know whom you can approach.

Another possible solution is a short-stay home, which is residential accommodation variously run by local authorities, voluntary organizations or private individuals, catering specifically for elderly people. The different types of home are described under the heading 'Special accommodation for the elderly' further on in this chapter. If, as opposed to general care, proper medical attention is necessary, you should consult your parent's GP. Many hospitals and nursing homes offer short-stay care arrangements as a means of relieving relatives. The doctor should be able to help organize this for you.

# Benefits and allowances

Should you have responsibility for the care of an elderly person, and/or to elderly people themselves, there are benefits and allowances available to help financially. The best place to look is on the government website, which has the latest and widest range of online public information. This is the gateway for government advice. There is a section for carers covering support services and assessments, carer's rights, working and caring, carer's allowance and much more. For full information details see: **www.gov.uk** – Disabled people.

There is other help to be found on the NHS website: **www.nhs.uk/ carersdirect/moneyandlegal/**.

## Entitlements for carers

### Home responsibilities protection

HRP was a scheme to help protect a person's State Pension. It was replaced with National Insurance credits for parents and carers in April

2010. You may still be able to apply for HRP if you were caring for a sick or disabled person for a complete tax year before April 2010. Any HRP credits you may have had before 6 April 2010 have been converted into National Insurance credits (up to a maximum of 22 years). You must have reached State Pension age on or after 6 April 2010 for these credits to go towards your State Pension. See: **www.gov.uk/home-responsibilities-protection/**.

## Carer's Allowance

This is paid to anyone who is caring for someone more than 35 hours per week, who is getting Attendance Allowance or the middle or highest rate of the Disability Living Allowance care component. You are not able to be paid carers' allowance if you are already getting the State Pension or are working and earn over £100 per week. For further information see: **www.gov.uk/carers-allowance**.

# Entitlements for elderly or disabled people

## Attendance Allowance

This is an allowance paid to people 65 and over to help with personal care if they are physically or mentally disabled. It is paid at two different rates and how much the elderly person receives is calculated on the level of care needed because of their frailty or disability. For full information see: **www.gov.uk/attendance-allowance**.

# Personal Independence Payment

This payment helps with some of the costs caused by long-term ill-health or a disability. It is gradually replacing the Disability Living Allowance for eligible people aged between 16 and 64. It is made up of two parts: a daily living component and a mobility component. There are two rates, standard and enhanced. For full information on the changes, and eligibility criteria, see: **www.gov.uk/pip**.

## Cold weather payment

If your elderly relative is in receipt of certain benefits, he/she may be eligible for a Cold weather payment. These are made when the local temperature is either recorded as, or forecast to be, an average of zero degrees Celsius or below, over seven consecutive days. The amount paid is £25. Those eligible should receive it without having to claim. See: **www.gov.uk/cold-weather-payment**.

## Winter fuel payment

This is a special tax-free payment of between £100 and £300 to help pay heating bills for all households with a resident aged 60 and over. See: **www.gov.uk/winter-fuel-payment**.

## Free off-peak bus travel

An older person's bus pass is available to people once they reach retirement age. Disabled people can also travel free on any bus service in the country. For full information on how to obtain a bus pass in England, Scotland, Wales and Northern Ireland, see: **www.gov.uk/apply-for-elderly-person-bus-pass**.

## Free TV licence

Once your elderly relative reaches 75, he/she may apply for a free TV licence. This licence will be renewed every three years, on provision of the individual's National Insurance number. For further details, see: **www.tvlicensing.co.uk**.

# Financial assistance

In cases of hardship, there are charities that give financial assistance to elderly people. For many people one of the main barriers to getting help is knowing which of the many thousands of charities to approach. There are free services that help older people in genuine financial need. When seeking financial assistance, have patience and be prepared to do a lot of research. Two helpful sites are: Charity Search: **www.charitysearch.org.uk** and Turn2Us: **www.turn2us.org.uk**.

Some organizations (amongst many others) who may be able to offer help are:

- Elizabeth Finn Care: **www.elizabethfinncare.org.uk**;
- Independent Age: **www.independentage.org**;
- RABI (Royal Agricultural Benevolent Institution): **www.rabi.org.uk**;

- SSAFA Military charity: **www.ssafa.org.uk**;
- The Professionals Aid Council (PAC): **www.pcac.org.uk**.

# Special accommodation for the elderly

The time to start looking for appropriate accommodation for elderly parents is before they need it. A lot of research will have to be done, and there will be a better (and happier) outcome for all concerned if this process is not rushed. Whether the search is prompted by a serious medical condition, or the desire for a lifestyle change, finding the right place to move to, when living independently at home is no longer an option, can be challenging and stressful for the whole family. The earlier you make an assessment of their needs, the more choices and control you all will have.

When deciding what senior housing option will be best for your relatives, the following factors need to be borne in mind: physical and medical needs; social and emotional needs and financial needs. The loss of some level of independence can be overwhelming for many older people, bringing with it, as it often does, feelings of shame, embarrassment, fear, confusion and anger. Brainstorm with family and trusted friends, and involve their medical team. Often the older person will listen more readily to their doctor or an impartial third party.

A good place to find information about options and funding, is FirstStop Advice, an independent, impartial and free service provided by the national charity Elderly Accommodation Counsel (EAC). This service is for older people, their families and carers. It aims to get elderly people the help and care they need to live independently and comfortably for as long as possible. See **www.firstopadvice.org.uk**.

## *Housing options*

The following is a very brief description of the different types of housing for elderly people:

### Living with family

This might seem the simplest option, but will they have friends, social amenities and what would happen if the family relationship broke down? It is advisable to take legal and financial advice before moving elderly relatives into your home, and have a written agreement about how to address disputes and how to end the arrangement should it become necessary.

## Sheltered or retirement housing

This type of housing is designed to meet the needs of older people. Most schemes have a manager, communal facilities, and there are many different types of sheltered/retirement housing both to rent and to buy. There is usually a minimum age for residents, 60 or sometimes 55.

## Housing with care

This is a newer form of specialist housing sometimes referred to as extra-care housing. Properties can be rented, owned or occasionally part-owned/part-rented. They are fully self-contained homes, usually with one or two bedrooms. If considering this option, if possible, take your parents to visit several schemes and speak to some of the current residents.

## Care homes

Deciding whether a care home is right for an elderly relative is a difficult decision which sometimes has to be made in a hurry. All care homes in England are registered and inspected by the Care Quality Commission (CQC) and must display their CQC rating throughout the home and on their website. In Wales, the inspectorate is called the Care Standards Inspectorate for Wales. In Scotland it is called the Scottish Commission for the Regulation of Care.

Some care homes provide personal care, some provide nursing care. Some older people with dementia may need a care home with an additional category of registration (DE).

Some very helpful advice is given in a clear and invaluable down-loadable document from First Stop Advice: Housing and Care Options for Older People, see **www.firststopcareadvice.org.uk/downloads/ kbase/3103.pfd**.

## Costs of retirement homes and care homes

### Retirement homes

If your elderly relatives are able to buy or rent a retirement property from their own private means, the choice is entirely theirs. Prices and types of property vary enormously, from small flats to luxurious homes on sites with every amenity. The majority of properties are sold on a long lease (typically 125 years). It is advisable to check that the management company is a member of The Association of Retirement Housing Managers (AHRM) and therefore bound by its Code of Practice. If looking to rent, retirement housing and housing-with-care is provided by local authorities, housing associations and some charitable and private sector providers. Some helpful websites include:

- RetirementHomesearch: **www.retirementhomesearch.co.uk**;
- Abbeyfield: **www.abbeyfield.com**;
- Anchor: **www.anchor.org.uk**;
- Girlings: **www.girlings.co.uk**;
- Hanover: **www.hanover.org.uk**;
- Jewish Community Housing Assocation: **www.jliving.org.uk**;
- Southern Housing Group: **www.shgroup.org.uk**.

There are charitable organizations that help particular groups of people in need. For example:

- Housing&Care21: **www.housingandcare21.co.uk**;
- Royal Alfred Seafarers' Society: **www.royalalfredseafarers.com**;
- Royal British Legion: **www.britishlegion.org.uk**;
- SSAFA Forces Help: **www.ssafa.org.uk**

## Care homes

There are currently about half a million older people living in residential and nursing homes in the UK. Care homes vary in cost, fees may range from £450 per week to more than £1,000 for a home providing nursing care. If your parents are paying their own fees in a home providing nursing care, the NHS will make a financial contribution towards the nursing care, subject to assessment.

The NHS should pay if the elderly person needs care primarily for a medical condition. Dementia is a medical condition, and so are the needs that come with it. If the elderly person is paying his/her own care home fees, they should be eligible for Attendance Allowance. Contact the Attendance Allowance helpline for a claim pack, or download a form from the Gov.uk website.

If the NHS will not pay, then your parents' income and capital will be assessed to see if they have to pay all or some of the fees themselves. Other rules apply regarding treatment of the elderly person's property. The funding aspect is complex. The starting point is to see what the local authority can provide. Beyond that, careful planning is required so that best use is made of your parents' income and assets. Further information and advice can be found at:

- Care Quality Commission: **www.cqc.org.uk**;
- Solicitors for the Elderly: **www.solicitorsfortheelderly.com**.

NHS continuing health care (NHS CHC) is a package of health and social care funded solely by the NHS when a patient's need for care is primarily due to their need for health care. This financial contribution is paid directly to the care home. There are a number of very useful downloadable fact sheets giving information relating to this and other relevant matters on the Age UK website: **www.ageuk.org.uk/publications**.

For information about care homes and nursing homes in the UK, and funding options, the following websites should be able to help:

- Citizens Advice Bureau: **www.citizensadvice.org.uk**;
- Elderly Accommodation Counsel: **www.eac.org.uk**;
- RNHA (Registered Nursing Home Association): **www.rnha.co.uk**;
- UKHCA (United Kingdom Home Care Association Ltd): **www.ukhca.co.uk**;
- Careways Trust: **www.carewaystrust.org.uk**;
- Friends of the Elderly: **www.fote.org.uk**;
- Independent Age: **www.independentage.org**;
- Jewish Care: **www.jewishcare.org**.

Two other sources of advice not previously listed are:

- Action on Elder Abuse: **www.elderabuse.org.uk**; and
- R&RA (Relatives and Residents Association): **www.relres.org**.

## Some special problems

Elderly people can suffer from special problems that cause great distress. Families do not like talking about these and they may be unaware of what services are available. Practical help and sometimes financial assistance may be obtainable, so it is worth doing some research.

## Hypothermia

Living in a cold home significantly increases the risk of death during the winter months. Approximately 24,000 more people die in England and Wales between December and March than at other times. Damp is another danger to health. In cold weather the risk of hypothermia is greater: those most at risk are people with dementia who may not be able to recognize the symptoms of hypothermia or recognize when they are cold.

Age UK produces a useful guide on how the elderly can keep warm in winter: 'Winter wrapped up'. See: **www.ageuk.org.uk/getinvolved/spread-the-warmth**.

Your parents should automatically be receiving the annual tax-free Winter Fuel payment (mentioned earlier in this chapter) to help with heating costs. See: **www.gov.uk – Winter Fuel Payment**.

## Incontinence

More than 3.2 million people over 65 in the UK suffer from urinary incontinence, and 6.5 million people of all ages are affected by some form of bowel problem. Many do not talk about this or seek help because of embarrassment and they often think nothing can be done. In the case of an elderly person, the doctor should always be consulted. Bladder and bowel problems can often be cured, or at least alleviated, by proper treatment. The Bladder and Bowel Foundation provides a range of resources for people with bladder and bowel problems. It runs a national helpline with a call-back service, offering confidential advice from a specialist nurse. For further information see: **www.bladderandbowelfoundation.org**.

## Dementia

It is predicted that there will be over one million people living with dementia in the UK within the next five years, according to Age UK. (Currently over 800,000 people are living with it.) It costs the national economy £26 billion per year. The most common type of dementia is Alzheimer's disease, and is the illness most feared by people over the age of 55, who are understandably concerned about losing their memory and identity. Despite the fact that this is a frightening and confusing illness, planning for the future will make life easier to bear and a positive attitude is vitally important.

The Alzheimer's Society suggests the following simple lifestyle tweaks to help reduce the risk of the disease:

- *Get active* – there's evidence that regular exercise will prevent dementia more than any other measure.

- *Eat Mediterranean style* – pile on the veg, fruit, fish, olive oil and nuts.

- *Keep up with the check-ups* – diabetes and high blood pressure increase the risk of dementia.

*(Source: Saga* magazine)

Should your elderly relative have been diagnosed with dementia there are some treatments available that can delay progression of some forms of the disease. Clinical signs are characterized by progressive cognitive degeneration, together with a decline in the ability to carry out common daily tasks and behavioural changes. The Alzheimer's Show, in association with the Alzheimer's Society, takes place each year in London. It is the UK's only dedicated exhibition and conference for families and professionals caring for someone with dementia. (**www.alzheimersshow.co.uk**). The Alzheimer's Society has masses of information and advice for carers and reminds us that people with dementia are still people. We should treat them with respect and dignity, be a good listener and communicator and remember that little things mean a lot. For more information, see Alzheimer's Scotland: **www.alzscot.org** and Alzheimer's Society: **www.alzheimers.org.uk**.

# Chapter Eleven
# No one is immortal

*'Die, my dear doctor? That's the last thing I shall do.'*

LORD PALMERSTON'S LAST WORDS

Preparing for the end of life isn't fun and it is something no-one wants to contemplate while they are healthy. But thinking about the issues involved and compiling information well beforehand can save someone's family huge amounts of angst. According to *Compassion in Dying*:

> ... seventy per cent of us want little or no medical intervention at the end of life; fifty-three per cent believe family can make healthcare decisions on behalf of a loved one; and only four per cent of us have made our treatment wishes known in an Advance Decision...
>
> (**www.compassionindying.org.uk**)

Making your wishes known and getting your affairs in order is not morbid: quite the reverse. It is prudent, sensible and unselfish. Being prepared will also allow more quality time with loved ones, particularly in those precious final days. It is helpful and will relieve family and care givers from a lot of strain and stress at a particularly difficult time. If possible everyone should attempt to get those tough discussions under way sooner rather than later. It is enormously helpful to have openly talked about end-of-life-related issues before there is an imminent need. Conversations will differ depending on when and with whom such things are being discussed. If you have reservations about airing such matters, commit them to paper instead. Maybe you are good at making lists, you have had your 'bucket list' prepared for years and are steadily working your way through it. If so, start writing down all your thoughts and wishes regarding end of life planning, but make sure you tell an appropriate person where this information is located.

## All you need to know about this chapter and what it contains

This chapter is vital reading for anyone undertaking pre-planning their end of life. Not everyone wants to think ahead, but there are a number of matters you should consider attending to as a first priority.

- First section is all about making your will, and how you can go about it. It also gives some pointers on the laws of intestacy and why making a will can save everyone pain and anguish.

- Inheritance tax is an issue for a growing number of people, but this was covered fully in Chapter 3 (Tax).

- Funeral planning is another important factor. You probably already know whether you want to be buried or cremated, but where do you want your funeral held?

- There is a section on dealing with a death, some information on the state benefits and tax, which might alleviate some of the unknowns and possible money worries.

- Read this chapter so that you feel you can take the initiative and set out your wishes now. Then you can get on with the rest of your life, knowing that when the time comes your loved ones will be aware of what you wanted and be spared making difficult decisions.

As a start, here are some good websites for advice on end of life planning:

- Compassion in Dying: **www.compassionindying.org.uk**;
- Dying Matters: **www.dyingmatters.org**;
- Final Fling: **www.finalfling.com**;
- Good Funeral Guide: **www.goodfuneralguide.co.uk**;
- Say It Once: **www.sayitonce.info**;
- Age UK: **www.ageuk.org.uk**.

Everyone deserves to have a 'good end of life'. If we've spent years trying to live well, why not make an attempt to die in the same way? When considering advance decisions, we need to get organized and communicate. As part of the plan people often explore their thoughts, feelings and preferences regarding some of the following issues:

- preferred place of care;
- advance decision to refuse treatment (ADRT);
- lasting power of attorney (LPA);
- wills;
- funeral arrangements;
- organ and tissue donation.

You can include in your advance care plan anything that is important to you. Talking openly to trusted friends, family, health care professionals or spiritual advisers can be helpful. It is essentially a matter of making sure everyone who needs to know does, and that your wishes are unambiguous and clearly recorded.

# Wills

Did you know that almost 60 per cent of the adult population of the UK currently has no will? Apparently, for over one in ten people in the UK, writing a will has never occurred to them. According to unbiased.co.uk, the South West is the most prepared region in the country, with more than half of the people surveyed saying they have already made a will. With people living longer, the need to protect money and assets to pass on to heirs is important.

Your will lets you decide what happens to your money, property and possessions after your death. Making a will can also ensure you don't pay more inheritance tax than you should. Having a will is especially important if you live with an unmarried partner, have remarried, or need to provide for someone with a disability. The importance of making a will cannot be overstressed. You can write your will yourself, but legal advice is thoroughly recommended, to make sure your will is interpreted in the way you wanted. Your will needs to be formally witnessed and signed to make it legally valid. If at any time you wish to update your will, this must be done officially, by means of a codicil, or if your circumstances have changed you should make a new will.

## *Laws of intestacy*

When a person dies without leaving a valid will, or the will has been lost, their property (the estate) must be shared out according to certain rules. These rules are quite archaic, and only married or civil partners (actually married at the time of death) and some other close relatives can inherit under the rules of intestacy. Your children might inherit, but not the amount you intended. An unmarried partner and stepchildren have no rights. Your husband, wife or civil partner does not automatically get the whole of your estate. Possessions, including your home, may have to be sold to split the proceeds between your heirs. If you have no partner or children, more distant relatives inherit. If there are no relatives, the state gets the lot.

## *Making a will*

It is never too early to make a will, but it is all too often left too late. There are several different types of wills:

- A *single will* relates to an individual.
- *Mirror wills* are designed for couples who have the same wishes.
- An *asset protection will* places the estate into trust for beneficiaries.
- A *discretionary trust will* allows trustees to decide what is best at the time of your death.

Research what kind of will is right for you, depending on your circumstances. Shop around to ensure you get the best deal. Make sure your will is stored where the relevant people can find it. Review it every few years, or sooner if your situation changes. If you get divorced, this doesn't automatically revoke but if you marry, this will automatically revoke an existing will. It is also important to update your will so that dependants (such as new grandchildren) are not excluded.

There are several ways of making a will: doing it yourself, asking a bank to help you, using a professional will-writing practitioner or a solicitor.

### Doing it yourself

If you have very simple circumstances, you can obtain 'template' will forms from stationers that can be completed and filled in at home. There are also online DIY wills, which can be searched for. You must be over 18, and have the mental capacity to make a will. Some useful information can be found at **www.moneysavingexpert.com/family/free-cheap-wills**.

## Banks

Some banks offer a will-writing service. If you do not have a family solicitor, you can ask if your bank will help. They can advise on wills and the administration of estates. They can introduce clients to a solicitor and keep a copy of the will – plus other important documents – in their safe, which avoids the risk of them being mislaid. If asking them to draw up your will for you, make sure that you can choose your own executor, as sometimes banks charge a lot for this service.

## Professional will-writing specialists

A will-writing service can be cheaper than using a solicitor, and more reliable than a DIY will. If considering this option make sure the will-writing service is accredited. There are online services where you visit a website and answer questions about your will. A will-writing service could be a good choice if you understand the basics of how wills work, you wish to pay less than a solicitor would charge and your estate is not complex. To find an accredited will-writing service, see:

- The Society of Will Writers: **www.willwriters.com**;
- The Institute of Professional Will Writers: **www.ipw.org.uk**.

## Solicitors

Asking a solicitor to draw up your will for you is usually the most expensive option. But if your estate is complex using a solicitor can save a lot of stress. Depending on where you live, a single will drawn up by a solicitor costs on average between £150 to £300. Joint wills for couples cost between £200 and £400. If your affairs are complex the cost will be higher. If you do not have a solicitor, ask friends for a recommendation, or ask at the Citizens Advice Bureau. The Law Society can also provide you with names and addresses – see: **www.lawsociety.org.uk**. Age UK Legal Services offers legal advice and support. This service is available free of charge to anyone of retirement age: **www.ageuk.org.uk**.

## Executors

An executor is the person you appoint in your will to be responsible for handling your estate and making sure your wishes are carried out after you die. It is usual to appoint more than one executor. It is important to choose your executors with care, since the job involves a lot of work and responsibility. The person must be over 18, have been informed of the decision and agreed to take on the role. Choosing a professional and impartial executor will incur charges, so bear this in mind if you appoint your solicitor, your accountant or your bank.

The following steps, if taken, will make your executor's job easier:

- List where important documents such as wills, bank accounts and share certificates are stored.
- Get regular valuations of your assets.
- Appoint more than one executor to share the workload.
- Ensure your will is up to date and safely stored.
- Be specific with your bequests – even for items of sentimental value.

(*Source*: *Saga* magazine January 2015 – Executor Decisions)

## Inheritance tax

This was dealt with in detail in Chapter 3 (Tax).

# Provision for dependent adult children

A particular concern for parents with a physically or mentally dependent son or daughter is what plans they can make to ensure his or her care continues when they are no longer in a position to manage. This is a complex area and there are no easy answers. Each case varies according to the severity of the disability or illness, the range of helpful voluntary or statutory facilities locally, and the extent to which they, as parents, can provide for their child's financial security in the long term. While social services may be able to advise, parents thinking ahead might do better to consult a specialist organization experienced in helping carers in this situation in order to explore the possible options available to them. Useful addresses are:

- Carers UK: **www.carersuk.org**;
- Carers Trust: **www.carers.org**.

Parents concerned about financial matters such as setting up a discretionary trust or making alternative provision in their will should consult their solicitor or accountant.

# Money and other worries – and how to minimize them

It is quite usual that people disregard forward planning until some important lifestyle change occurs, such as the death of a parent or sibling, or the birth of a first child. It is only then that they get a mortality jolt, and starting thinking, 'is it me next?' and other 'what ifs'. Anyone with a family should consider – and review from time to time – the following two things: life insurance and mortgage protection. Most banks and building societies urge homeowners to take out mortgage protection schemes. If you die, the loan is paid off automatically and the family home will not be repossessed. Banks also offer insurance to cover any personal or other loans. This could help a family to avoid being left with debts.

# Funeral plans

Taking the worry out of funeral costs is something everyone should consider because funerals are getting more expensive. According to funeral planner, Dignity, the average cost of a funeral has increased by about 60 per cent over the last seven years, with a typical cost being around £3,500. Pay now – die later, as it is known in the industry, is big business in the UK and is estimated to be worth over £500 million a year. Nearly ten per cent of funerals in the UK are now funded by pre-paid plans.

One of the key benefits of funeral plans is that they are guaranteed to cover the costs of the agreed funeral arrangements, regardless of any future rise in price. Pre-pay funeral plans can be bought in two main ways: from a funeral plan provider or from a local funeral director. Payment is flexible, most providers allow a one-off payment in advance, or the option to pay in instalments over 12 to 120 months. Before you take out a funeral plan, do check what's included. Cremation fees tend to be cheaper than burial fees, so if you opt for a cremation funeral plan that fully guarantees third-party costs, that is better cover than funeral plans for burials. Plan providers can register with the Funeral Planning Authority (FPA). You can find a list of registered plan providers at: **www.funeralplanningauthority.com.**

There are other ways to help offset funeral costs. One is by saving in an ISA for your funeral, or you could take out whole-of-life cover, or there is home burial – which is legal. You can be buried in your garden, but remember this could have an effect on the value of your property. If you or your partner are on low incomes or receive benefits and need help towards the cost of a funeral, there is a government subsidy available. Be aware that this may have to be repaid from any money tied up in the deceased's estate. See: **www.gov.uk** – Bereavement Benefits.

For information on funeral plans see the following websites:

- Age UK: **www.ageuk.org.uk;**
- Co-operative Funeral Care: **www.co-operativefuneralcare.co.uk;**
- Dignity: **www.dignityfunerals.co.uk;**
- Golden Charter: **www.goldencharter.co.uk;**
- Golden Leaves: **www.goldenleaves.com;**
- Perfect Choice Funeral Plans: **www.perfectchoicefunerals.com.**

## Dealing with a death

When someone dies there are many people to be informed, including many companies and organizations. You may find it helpful to make a list of all the people who need to be informed (either by letter or telephone) and work through it gradually over the coming days. Don't be afraid to ask family members and friends to help. This is an emotional time, but there are some important things that have to be done first, to comply with the law.

A medical certificate must be obtained immediately from a GP or hospital doctor. The certificate is free and should be given to you by a doctor. You will need this to register the death, which must be done within five days. You will then get the documents you need for the funeral. You can use the Tell Us Once service (**www.gov.uk/after-a-death/**

**organizations-you-need-to-contact-and-tell-us-once**) to report a death to most government organizations in one go. You do not need to deal with the will, money and property straight away.

Some useful websites which give detailed information and practical advice on what to do after a death, are:

- gov.uk: **www.gov.uk/after-a-death/organisations-you-need-to-contact-and-tell-us-once;**
- Age UK: **www.ageuk.org.uk;**
- Bereavement Advice Service: **www.bereavementadvice.org;**
- Money Advice Service: **www.moneyadviceservice.org.uk.**

Experiencing the loss of someone close through death is an inevitable part of life, but that does not make it any easier when we experience it, even when the death was expected. This can be even more difficult if circumstances mean that practical changes have to be made, such as moving house. Should this be the case, the bank manager should be notified as soon as possible, so that help can be given until the estate is settled. Adjusting to life without the person takes time, usually more than we realize. Receiving direct mail bearing the name of the deceased is often painful and unnecessary. To avoid this, contact The Bereavement Register: **www.thebereavementregister.org.uk** who will be able to help.

## State benefits and tax

There are some extra financial benefits for widowed people, most of which take the form of a cash payment: Bereavement Payment, Bereavement Allowance and Widowed Parent's Allowance. These have replaced the former widow's benefits, as all benefits are now payable on equal terms to men and women alike. To find out more information see website: **www.gov.uk** – Bereavement Benefits. You will be given a questionnaire (BD8) by the registrar when you register the death. It is important that you complete this, as it acts as a trigger to speed up payment of your benefits.

- *Bereavement Payment* is a tax-free lump sum of £2,000, paid as soon as people are widowed, provided that: the widowed person's spouse had paid sufficient NI contributions; the widowed person is under state retirement age; or, if over state retirement age, the widowed person's husband or wife had not been entitled to retirement pension.

- *Bereavement Allowance* is for those aged between 45 and state pension age who do not receive Widowed Parent's Allowance. It is payable for 52 weeks and, as with widow's pension before, there are various levels of payment: the full rate and age-related allowance. Receipt in all cases is dependent on sufficient NI contributions having been paid.

- *Full-rate Bereavement Allowance* is paid to widowed people between the ages of 55 and 59 inclusive. Age-related Bereavement Allowance is for younger widows or widowers who do not qualify for the full rate. Bereavement Allowance is normally paid automatically once you have sent off your completed form BB1, so if for any reason you do not receive it you should enquire at your social security office. In the event of your being ineligible, owing to insufficient NICs having been paid, you may still be entitled to receive Income Support, Housing Benefit or a grant or loan from the Social Fund. See website: **www.gov.uk** – Bereavement Benefits.

- *Widowed Parent's Allowance* is paid to widowed parents with at least one child for whom they receive Child Benefit. The allowance is usually paid automatically. If for some reason, although eligible, you do not receive the money, you should inform your social security office.

## Retirement pension

Once a widowed person reaches state retirement age, he or she should receive a state pension in the normal way. An important point to remember is that a widow or widower may be able to use the late spouse's NICs to boost the amount he or she receives. See leaflet RM1, Retirement – a guide to benefits for people who are retiring or have retired.

## Problems

Both pension payments and bereavement benefits are dependent on sufficient NICs having been paid. Your social security office will inform you if you are not eligible. If this should turn out to be the case, you may still be entitled to receive Income Support, Housing Benefit, Council Tax Benefit or a grant or loan from the Social Fund. If you are unsure of your position or have difficulties, ask at the Citizens Advice Bureau, which will at least be able to help you work out the sums and inform you of your rights. See website: **www.citizensadvice.org.uk**.

### Particular points to note

- Most widowed people's benefits are taxable. However, the £2,000 Bereavement Payment is tax-free, as are pensions paid to the widows or widowers of armed forces personnel. Widowed people will normally be able to inherit their spouse's additional pension rights, additionally, where applicable, all widowed people are entitled on retirement to half the graduated pension earned by their husband or wife.

- Women in receipt of widow's pension who remarry, or live with a man as his wife, lose their entitlement to the payment unless the cohabitation ends, in which case they can claim it again. If a woman is aged over 60, the fact that she is living with a man will not affect her entitlement to a retirement pension based on her late husband's contribution record. Widows and widowers of armed forces personnel whose deaths were a direct result of their service are now entitled to keep their armed forces attributable pension for life, regardless of whether they remarry or cohabit.

### Tax allowances

Widows and widowers receive the normal single person's tax allowance of £10,600 and, if in receipt of Married Couple's Allowance, are also entitled to any unused portion of the allowance in the year of their partner's death.

## Organizations that can help

People deal with bereavement in various ways. For some, money problems seem to dominate everything. For others, the hardest thing to bear is the loneliness of an empty house. For older people who have been part of a couple for decades, widowhood creates a great gulf where for a while there is no real sense of purpose. Many widowed men and women go through a spell of feeling enraged against their partner for dying. Talking to other people who know the difficulties from their own experience can be a tremendous help. The following organizations not only offer opportunities for companionship but also provide an advisory and support service:

- Cruse Bereavement Care: **www.cruse.org.uk**.
- The National Association of Widows: **www.widows.uk.net**.

Many professional and other groups offer a range of services for widows and widowers associated with them. These include:

- The Civil Service Retirement Fellowship: **www.csrf.org.uk**.
- The War Widows Association of Great Britain: **www.warwidows.org.uk**.
- Many local Age UK groups offer a counselling service. Trade unions are often particularly supportive, as are Rotary Clubs, all the armed forces organizations and most benevolent societies.

# Useful resources and contacts

## Benefits advice

Advice NI (Northern Ireland), tel: 088 988 2377, website: **www.adviceni.net**.
Age UK, tel: 0800 169 6565, website: **www.ageuk.org.uk**.
Citizens Advice Bureau, tel: 03444 111 444, website:
    **www.citizensadvice.org.uk**.
Citizens Advice Scotland, tel: 03454 04 05 06, website: **www.cas.org.uk**.
Entitled To – to identify what benefits you may be eligible for:
    **www.entitledto.co.uk**.
Government benefits adviser, website: **www.gov.uk/benefits-calculators**.
Money Advice Scotland, tel: 0141 572 0237, website:
    **www.moneyadvicescotland.org.uk**.
Turn2us – to identify potential sources of funding for those facing financial
    difficulty: **www.turn2us.org.uk**.

## Debt

Citizens Advice Bureau – free independent debt advice in England, Wales and
    Northern Ireland. Tel: 03444 111 444, website: **www.citizensadvice.org.uk**.
Citizens Advice Scotland, tel: 03454 04 05 06, website: **www.cas.org.uk**.
Debt Action NI tel: 0800 917 4607, website: **www.debtaction-ni.net**.
Money Advice Service – debt and borrowing. Tel: 0300 500 5000, website:
    **www.moneyadviceservice.org.uk**.
Money Advice Scotland, tel: 0141 572 0237, website:
    **www.moneyadvicescotland.org.uk**.
National Debtline, tel: 0808 808 4000, website: **www.nationaldebtline.co.uk**.
Step Change Debt Charity, tel: 0800 138 1111, website: **www.stepchange.org**.

## Disabilities

Age UK, tel: 0800 169 6565, website: **www.ageuk.org.uk**.
Wales: 08000 223 444; Northern Ireland: 0808 808 7575;
    Scotland: 0845 125 9732.

Action for Blind People – charity providing practical help and support. Tel: 0303 123 9999, website: **www.actionforblindpeople.org.uk**.

Action on Hearing Loss – provides advice and support for people who are deaf or hard of hearing. Tel: 0808 808 0123, website: **www.actiononhearingloss.org.uk**.

Disability Benefits Centre – helpline telephone numbers: **www.gov.uk/disability-benefits-helpline**.

Pension Credit, helpline: 0800 99 1234, website: **www.gov.uk/pension-credit**.

Winter Fuel Payment Helpline, tel: 08459 151515, website: **www.gov.uk/winter-fuel-payment**.

# Energy-saving advice and grants

National Energy Action (NEA) – the national charity working to eradicate fuel poverty. Tel: 0191 261 5677; Wales: 029 2064 4520; N Ireland: 028 9023 9909; website: **www.nea.org.uk**.

NEST (Welsh energy), tel: 0808 808 2244, website: **www.nestwales.org.uk**.

Greener Scotland, (Home Energy Scotland), tel: 0808 808 2282, website: **www.scotland.gov.uk**.

Warm Home Discount Scheme: **www.gov.uk/the-warm-home-discount-scheme**.

Warm Homes Scheme (Northern Ireland), tel: 0800 988 0559, website: **www.homeserve.com**.

UK Energy Efficiency Advice Centres, tel 0300 123 1234, website: **www.energysavingtrust.org.uk**.

# Funeral and inheritance tax planning

Bereavement Register, tel: 0800 082 1230, website: **www.thebereavementregister.com**.

Funeral Planning Authority Ltd, tel: 0845 601 9619, website: **www.funeralplanningauthority.com**.

HMRC Probate and Inheritance Tax Helpline, tel: 0300 123 1072, website: **www.gov.uk/inheritancetax/**.

## *For inheritance tax advice*

STEP – Society of Trust and Estate Practitioners, tel: 020 7340 0500, website: **www.step.org**.

## To register a death

General Register Office (England and Wales), website: **www.gro.gov.uk**;
Scotland: **www.nrsscotland.gov.uk**; Northern Ireland: **www.nidirect.gov.uk/general-register-office-for-northern-ireland**. To obtain a copy of the government booklet: 'What to do after a death', England and Wales, website: **www.gov.uk** – Death and bereavement; Scotland: **www.nrsscotland.gov.uk**; Northern Ireland: **www.nidirect.gov.uk**.

# Health and health care

NHS Low Income Scheme – provides full or partial help with health costs if you are on a low income. Tel: 0845 850 1166, website: **www.nhs.uk/NHSEngland/Healthcosts**.

Free prescriptions and other health benefits in the UK – booklet HC11 'Help with Health Costs' from your GP or pharmacies, or in PDF format, see website: **www.nidirect.gov.uk/help-with-health-costs/**. In Scotland, Northern Ireland and Wales prescriptions are free.

Prescription pre-payment certificates (England) orderline: 0300 330 1341, website: **www.gov.uk/get-a-pcc**.

NHS Health Scotland – promoting healthy living in Scotland.
Tel: 0800 22 44 88, website: **www.healthscotland.com**.

# Holidays

Apply for a European Health Insurance Card (EHIC) at a Post Office or tel: 0300 330 1350, or via website: **www.ehicdirect.com**

# House and home

For details about local domestic energy assessors, see EPC Register; website: **www.epcregister.com**.

Home Heat Helpline helps people to pay their heating bills and keep warm in winter. Tel: 0800 33 66 99, website: **www.homeheathelpline.org.uk**.

## To find an independent surveyor/valuer

Royal Institute of Chartered Surveyors, website: **www.rics.org/uk/**.

## For protection

The Property Ombudsman scheme provides a free fair independent service for settlement of unresolved disputes for consumers in the event of a complaint. See: **www.tpos.co.uk**.

## Help for the elderly

Action on Elder Abuse, tel: 0808 808 8141, website: **www.elderabuse.org.uk**.

Elderly Accommodation Counsel, tel: 0800 377 7070, website: **www.eac.org.uk**; or **www.firststopadvice.org.uk**; or **www.housingcare.org.uk**.

Independent Age, tel: 0800 319 6789, website: **www.independentage.org**.

NAPA – National Association for Providers of Activities for Older People offers stimulating activities for older people in care settings. Tel: 020 7078 9375, website: **www.napa-activities.co.uk**.

RoSPA – Royal Society for the Prevention of Accidents – promotes safety and prevention of accidents at work and in the home, and provides information on home safety. Tel: 0121 248 2000, website: **www.rospa.com**.

TPS – The Telephone Preference Service – register your phone number by calling their registration line: 0845 070 0707 or via their website: **www.tpsonline.org.uk**.

## Home improvement agencies

England – Foundations, tel: 0300 124 0315, website: **www.foundations.uk.com**.

Wales – Care and Repair Cymru, tel: 0300 111 3333, website: **www.careandrepair.org.uk**; Scotland – Care and Repair Scotland, tel: 0141 221 9879, website: **www.careandrepairscotland.co.uk**.

Northern Ireland – Fold Housing Care Support, tel: 028 9042 8314, website: **www.foldgroup.co.uk**.

## Help for tenants

Association of Retirement Housing Managers (ARHM), tel: 020 7463 0660, website: **www.arhm.org**.

Leasehold Advisory Service. England, tel: 0207 832 2500, Wales, tel: 02920 782 222, website: **www.lease-advice.org**.

Landmark Leasehold Advisory Services Ltd – providing legal services to residential leaseholders in England and Wales; see **www.landmarklease.com**.

Department for Communities and Local Government – for advice on leasehold legislation and policy, tel: 0303 444 0000, website: **www.gov.uk/ government/organisations/department-for-communities-and-local-government**.

# Independent financial advice

## *To find an independent financial adviser*

unbiased.co.uk, website: **www.unbiased.co.uk**.

Institute of Financial Planning, website: **www.financialplanning.org.uk**.

Personal Finance Society (PFS), website: **www.fthepfs.org**.

Financial Conduct Authority, tel: 0800 111 6768, website: **www.fca.org.uk**.

Financial Ombudsman Service, tel: 0300 123 9123 or 0800 0234 567, website:
**www.financial-ombudsman.org.uk**.

Financial Services Compensation Scheme, tel: 0800 678 1100, website:
**www.fscs.org.uk**.

MyLocalAdviser – for financial advisers in your area.
**www.mylocaladviser.co.uk**.

SOLLA – Society of Later Life Advisers, tel: 0845 303 2902; website:
**www.societyoflaterlifeadvisers.co.uk**.

## *To find a stockbroker*

See London Stock Exchange website: **www.londonstockexchange.com**, or
The Wealth Management Association (WMA) website: **www.thewma.co.uk**.

## *To find equity release providers*

Equity Release Council, tel: 0844 669 7085, website:
**www.equityreleasecouncil.com**.

## *To find a tax adviser*

Chartered Institute of Taxation, tel: 0844 579 6700, website: **www.tax.org.uk**.

# Insurance

Association of British Insurers – for advice and information on insurance.
Tel: 020 7600 3333, website: **www.abi.org.uk**.

Association of Medical Insurance Intermediaries (AMII), tel: 07971 231 869,
website: **www.amii.org.uk**.

Do you have sufficient buildings insurance? The ABI/BCIS Residential
Rebuilding Costs calculator – see website: **www.bcis.co.uk**.

To check a car's insurance group: **www.carpages.co.uk**; or CTC:
**www.checkthatcar.com**.

British Insurance Brokers' Association (BIBA) – to find an insurance broker. Tel: 0870 950 1790, website: **www.biba.org.uk**.

# Legal

## To find a solicitor

Law Society, tel: 0207 320 5650, website: **www.lawsociety.org.uk**.
Law Society of Scotland, tel: 0131 226 7411, website: **www.lawscot.org.uk**.
Law Society of Northern Ireland, tel: 028 9023 1614, website:
   **www.lawsoc-ni.org**.
Civil Legal Advice (CLA). Are you eligible for legal aid and free legal advice?
   Tel: 0345 345 4345. See website: **www.gov.uk/civil-legal-advice**.
Solicitors for Independent Financial Advice (SIFA), is the trade body for
   solicitor financial advisers, and now also includes accountancy IFAs as
   members. Tel: 01372 721 172, website: **www.sifa.co.uk**.
For complaints about a legal adviser, see Legal Ombudsman.
   Tel: 0300 555 0333, website: **www.legalombudsman.org.uk**.

## Making a will

Institute of Professional Will Writers, tel: 0345 257 2570, website:
   **www.ipw.org.uk**.
Society of Will Writers, tel: 01522 687 888, website: **www.willwriters.com**.

## Power of attorney

Office of the Public Guardian (England and Wales), tel: 0300 456 0300, website:
   **www.gov.uk/government/organisations/office-of-the-public-guardian**.
Office of the Public Guardian, Scotland, tel: 01324 678 300, website:
   **www.publicguardian-scotland.gov.uk**.
Office of Care and Protection, Northern Ireland, tel: 030 0200 7812, website:
   **www.courtsni.gov.uk**.

# Leisure

## Free digital TV channels

Freeview, advice line: 03456 505050, website: **www.freeview.co.uk**.
Freesat, tel: 0845 313 0051, website: **www.freesat.co.uk**.

### Free bus travel

England and Wales, your local council or website: **www.gov.uk/apply-for-elderly-person-bus-pass**; Scotland, your local council or website: **www.transportscotland.gov.uk/public-transport/concessionary-travel**; Northern Ireland, your local council or website: **www.nidirect.gov.uk/free-bus-travel-and-concessions**.

### Cheap rail and coach travel

Senior Railcard UK, tel: 0345 3000 250, website: **www.senior-railcard.co.uk**. Rail Europe Ltd, tel: 0844 848 5848, website: **www.uk.voyages-sncf.com**. National Express, tel: 0871 781 8181, website: **www.nationalexpress.com**.

## Money

Money Advice Service, tel: 0300 500 5000, website: **www.moneyadviceservice.org.uk**.
To trace lost savings: bank accounts, building society accounts and NS&I, see website: **www.mylostaccount.org.uk**.
To trace lost investments: Unclaimed Assets Register, tel: 0844 481 81 80, website: **www.uar.co.uk**.
Internet comparison sites:

- **www.comparethemarket.com**;
- **www.confused.com**;
- **www.gocompare.com**;
- **www.moneyfacts.co.uk**;
- **www.moneysupermarket.com**;
- **www.switch.which.co.uk**;
- **www.uswitch.com**.

## Pensions

State Pension Forecasting website: **www.gov.uk/state-pension-statement**.
The Pension Service queries on your State Pension, if you live in the UK, tel: 0345 606 0265. If you are within four months of your state pension age, tel: 0800 731 7898.

If you live abroad, The International Pension Centre, Pension Service, tel: 0191 218 7777, website: **www.gov.uk/international-pension-centre**.

To check your State Pension age, website: **www.gov.uk/calculate-state-pension**.

Pension Tracing Service, tel: 0845 6002 537, website: **www.gov.uk/find-lost-pension**.

Pensions Advisory Service – for any help understanding your pension rights, tel: 0300 123 1047, website: **www.pensionsadvisoryservice.org.uk**.

Pensions Ombudsman Service, tel: 020 7630 2200, website: **www.pensions-ombudsman.org.uk**.

Pension Protection Fund (PPF), tel: 0845 600 2541, website: **www.pensionprotectionfund.org.uk**.

Service Personnel and Veterans Agency Service – to claim a war widow or widower's pension, tel: 0808 1914 218, website: **www.gov.uk/government/organisations/veterans-uk**.

SOLLA – Society of Later Life Advisers, tel: 0845 303 2909, website: **www.societyoflaterlifeadvisers.co.uk**.

# Savings and investments

## To find a credit union

ABCUL – Association of British Credit Unions Ltd, tel: 0161 832 3694, website: **www.abcul.org**.

ACE Credit Union Services, tel: 02920 674 851, website: **www.acecus.org**.

Scottish League of Credit Unions, tel: 0141 774 5020, website: **www.scottishcu.org**.

UK Credit Unions, tel: 01706 214 322, website: **www.ukcu.coop**.

## To compare savings accounts

Money Advice Service, tel: 0300 500 5000, website: **www.moneyadviceservice.org.uk** – comparison tables.

## To find out about investment funds

Unit trusts and open-ended investment companies: The Investment Association, tel: 020 7831 0898, website: **www.theinvestmentassociation.org**.

Investment trusts: AIC – Association of Investment Companies, tel: 0207 282 5555, website: **www.theaic.co.uk**.

Life insurance funds: Association of British Insurers, tel: 0207 600 3333, website: **www.abi.org.uk**.

Ethical investments: Ethical Investment Research Service, tel: 0207 840 5700, website: **www.eiris.org**.

## To report suspected investment scams

If you spot a scam or have been scammed, report it and get help. Contact **Action Fraud**, the UK's national fraud and internet crime reporting centre on 0300 123 2040, or online at **www.actionfraud.police.uk** or the police in your area.

# Tax

## Free help with tax problems if your income is low

Tax Aid, for help in understanding UK tax, tel: 0345 120 3779, website: **www.taxaid.org.uk**.
Tax Help for Older People, tel: 0845 601 3321, or 01308 488 066, website: **www.taxvol.org.uk**.

## For tax help and advice

ATT – Association of Taxation Technicians, tel: 0207 340 0551, website: **www.att.org.uk**.
ACCA – Association of Chartered Certified Accountants, tel: 020 7059 5000, website: **www.acca.global.com**.
CIOT – Chartered Institute of Taxation, tel: 0844 579 6700, or 0207 340 0550, website: **www.tax.org.uk**.
ICAEW – Institute of Chartered Accountants in England and Wales, tel: 01908 248 250, website: **www.icaew.co.uk**.
CAI – Chartered Accountants Ireland, Chartered Accountants House, tel: 00353 1 637 7200, website: **www.charteredaccountants.ie**.
ICAS – Institute of Chartered Accountants of Scotland, tel: 0131 347 0100, website: **www.icas.ocom**.
HM Revenue and Customs for local enquiry centres, see website **www.hmrc.gov.uk**. For your local tax office, see your tax return, other tax correspondence or check with your employer or scheme paying you a pension.
Contact the Adjudicator's Office for information about referring a complaint. The adjudicator acts as a fair and unbiased referee looking into complaints about HMRC, including the Tax Credit Office, the

Valuation Office and the Office of the Public Guardian and the Insolvency Service. Tel: 0300 057 1111.
See website: **www.adjudicatorsoffice.gov.uk**.

If you have received an HMRC-related phishing/bogus e-mail, please forward it to the following e-mail address and then delete it: **phishing@hmrc.gsi.gov.uk**.

HMRC helplines:

- income tax helpline: 0300 200 3300;
- National Insurance enquiries: 0300 200 3500;
- capital gains tax: 0300 200 3300;
- self-assessment: 0300 200 3310;
- tax credit helpline: 0345 300 3900.

# Volunteering

To find out about how to volunteer across the UK:

- REACH: **www.reachskills.org.uk**;
- Volunteer Now (Northern Ireland): **www.volunteernow.co.uk**;
- Volunteer Scotland: **www.volunteerscotland.net**;
- Volunteering England: **www.volunteering.org.uk**;
- WCVA – Wales Council for Voluntary Action: **www.wcva.org.uk**.

Leading volunteering organizations:

- British Red Cross: **www.redcross.org.uk**;
- Citizens Advice Bureau: **www.citizensadvice.org.uk**;
- Lions Clubs UK: **www.lionsclubs.co/**;
- Royal Voluntary Service: **www.royalvoluntaryservice.org.uk**;
- Volunteering Matters: **www.volunteeringmatters.org.uk**.

Checks for volunteering:
DBS Disclosure Service, Helpline: 03000 200 190, website:
   **www.gov.uk/government/organisations/**
   **disclosure-and-barring-service**

# Work

## *To find out about rights at work*

ACAS, tel: 0300 123 1100, website: **www.acas.org.uk**.

Labour Relations Agency (N Ireland), tel: 028 9032 1442,
website: **www.lra.org.uk**.

Jobcentre Plus (Great Britain), tel: 0345 604 3719, new benefits claims only:
0800 055 6688, website: **www.gov.uk/contact-jobcentre-plus**.

Jobs and Benefits Office (Northern Ireland), tel: 0300 200 7822,
website: **www.nidirect.gov.uk/jobs-and-benefits-offices**.

National Careers Service (UK), tel: 0800 100 900,
website: **https://nationalcareersservice.direct.gov.uk**.

Skills Development Scotland, tel: 0800 917 8000,
website: **www.skillsdevelopmentscotland.co.uk**.

Careers Wales, tel: 0800 028 4844, website: **www.careerswales.com**.

REC – Recruitment and Employment Confederation, tel: 020 7009 2100,
website: **www.rec.uk.com**.

# To register a new business

HM Revenue and Customs (HMRC), newly self-employed helpline: 0300
200 3505, website: **www.hmrc.gov.uk/startingup/help-support**.

Companies House, tel: 0303 1234 500, website:
**www.companieshouse.gov.uk**.

HMRC Business Education and Support Team provides free training
events aimed at start-up businesses and on how to run a payroll:
**www.hmrc.gov.uk/startingup/help-support**.

# Organizations providing free or subsidized help

## *Government resources*

**www.gov.uk** contains the government's online resource for businesses.
Regional or country-specific support is also available at:

- Regional help – **www.nationalenterprisenetwork.org**;

- Northern Ireland – at **www.nibusinessinfo.co.uk**;

- Scotland – at **www.business.scotland.gov.uk;**
- Wales – at **www.business.wales.gov.uk.**

## Other resources

StartUp Britain – information about starting a business:
**www.startupbritain.org.**
PRIME (The Prince's Initiative for Mature Enterprise) is now incorporated with Business In the Community: **www.bitc.org.uk.**

# Index